अभिधम्मपिटके

पुग्गलपञ्ञत्तिपालि

(अंग्रेजी अनुवाद सहित)

सम्पादक

डॉ. ओम प्रकाश पाठक

एम्.ए.(पालि एवं बौद्ध अध्ययन), एम. फिल्., पी-एच.डी.

एवं

डॉ. वीणा गौड़

एम. ए.(संस्कृत, पालि), एम. फिल्., पी-एच.डी.

बौद्ध अध्ययन विभाग, दिल्ली विश्वविद्यालय,

दिल्ली

BOOK EASTERN EBL LINKERS

ईस्टर्न बुक लिन्कर्स

दिल्ली :: भारत

प्रकाशकः

ईस्टर्न बुक लिन्कर्स

5825, न्यू चन्द्रावल, जवाहर नगर

दिल्ली-110 007

प्रथम संस्करण : **2000**

ISBN : 81-86339-50-7

मुद्रक :

यूनिक प्रिंट मिडिया, दिल्ली-110 009

फोन : 725 2362

Abhidhammapiṭake

PUGGALAPAÑÑATTIPĀLI

[With English Translation]

EDITORS

Dr. Om Prakash Pathak

M.A. (Pāli & Buddhist Studies), M. Phil., Ph.D.

And

Dr. Veena Gaur

M.A. (Sanskrit & Pāli), M. Phil., Ph.D.

Department of Buddhist Studies

University of Delhi

Delhi

EASTERN BOOK LINKERS

DELHI : : INDIA

Published by :
Eastern Book Linkers
5825, New Chandrawal,
Jawahar Nagar,
Delhi–110 007

Price Rs. 650-

First Edition : 2000

ISBN : 81-86339-50-7

Printed by :
Unique Print Media, Delhi–110 009
Ph. 725 2362

DEDICATED TO

Late Mahāpaṇḍita Rahul Sānkrityāyaṅa who was the eminent scholar of various languages.

ये च बुद्धा अतीता च, ये च बुद्धा अनागता।
पच्चुप्पना च ये बुद्धा, अहं वन्दामि सब्बदा॥

ये च धम्मा अतीता च, ये च धम्मा अनागता।
पच्चुप्पन्ना च ये धम्मा, अहं वन्दामि सब्बदा॥

ये च सङ्घा अतीता च, ये च सङ्घा अनागता।
पच्चुप्पन्ना च ये सङ्घा, अहं वन्दामि सब्बदा॥

गन्थ-सूची

पठमो परिच्छेदो

मातिकानिद्देसो

दुतियो परिच्छेदो

ततियो परिच्छेदो

चतुत्थो परिच्छेदो

पञ्चमो परिच्छेदो

छट्ठो परिच्छेदो

सत्तमो परिच्छेदो

अट्ठमो परिच्छेदो

FOREWORD

Puggalapaññatti is a very important text of the Pali **Abhidhammapiṭaka** which lists and difines different human types. In the Buddhist teaching, the focus has always been on the mind **(citta)** and mental factors **(cetasika)** and a human being, according to Buddhism is a complex of these mental factors (nāma), apart from his or her physical form **(rūpa)**. A text fully devoted to the designation of different personalities is not only important from the religious and soteriological point of view but also for understanding of the different human beings and in knowing the wrong and the right, the unwholesome and the wholesome **(akusala and kusala)** traits in a personality.

I personally have liked this text very much from my initiation in Buddhist Studies in Nalanda in 1952 when under the benign guidance of Venerable Bhikkhu J.Kashyap, I opted for the Abhidhamma group in my Master's Degree in Pali. I loved to teach this text to my students in the Banaras Hindu University in the Department of Pali and Buddhist Studies. Recently there have been many studies on 'Personality' in the area of Business Management, Govt. Administration, Politics, Academic performance, etc. I feel a book like this has a great relevance and may be helpful in understanding personality traits, and Buddhist texts generally discuss these traits in details.

Earlier Dr. B.C. Law, the doyen of Buddhist Studies, translated this text from Pali (PTS, London, 1979) with the title "Designation of Human types". Dr. Om Prakash Pathak and Dr. Veena Gaur have now published the Pali text along with the English translation. This will help in knowing the original Pali terminology. Sometimes it is difficult to give an exact English rendering for Pali word (including the word **Puggala** Skt. **Pudgala**). Hence the text along with translation is always beneficial to a reader.

If we see the list of designated personalities in the **Puggalapaññatti,** we will simply be amazed at the diversity of human types included in this work, many of which we do meet in day-to-day life. Apart from 'Perfectly Enlightened One' (**Sammāsambuddha**) and 'Enlightened by Himself' (**Paccekasambuddha**, p. 40) and 'One capable of progress' and 'incapable of progress' (p.36), the angry (p.53), the vengeful (p.54), slanderer (p.55), quarrelsome (p.56), avaricious (p.57) and crafty (p.58)—list is very long have received attention in the **Puggalapaññatti.** The definitions of anger, envy, or explanation of moderation in food (p.76), a person of lovely disposition (p.126) are noteworthy to ponder over.

I heartily congratulate Dr. Pathak and his assistent Dr. Veena Gaur for working on this important treatise and bringing the text and translation together for the better understanding of Buddhist analysis of different human types.

I am sure the readers will be greatly benefited from this important work.

Buddha Purṇimā
Nagarjuna Nagar
14 May, 1996

N. H. SAMTANI
Hony. Director
Centre for Mahayana
Buddhist Studies,
Nagarjuna University (A.P.)

PREFACE

'Abhidhamma' is the name of the higher teaching of the Buddha. It expounds the quintessence of his most profound doctrine.[1] Here the term 'Abhi' is used to indicate the sense as excellent, deep, profound, subtle etc. Aṭṭhasālinī says: Atireka-visesatthadipako hi ettha 'abhi'-saddo.[2] 'Dhamma' is a multisignificant term which denotes a number of senses according to the various contexts. Teaching,[3] law,[4] nature,[5] intrinsic quality,[6] composite and non-composit things,[7] moral and immoral states,[8] the state of absence of some permanent essence,[9] action,[10] the reals[11] are its several meanings.

Abhidhamma exceeds and distinguished from the teaching of the Vinaya or discipline and Sutta or popular discourse, both in style and contents. To indicate such distinctions, the Vinaya[12] has been

1. Dhammātireka-dhammavisesa-aṭṭhena 'abhidhammo.' - Asl. 2.
2. Asl. 2.
3. Dhammaṁ deseti ādikalyāṇaṁ. -D.N. 1.55.
4. Esa dhammo sanantano. -Dhp. verse 5.
5. Bhedana-vidhvansana-dhammo. -D.N. 1.67.
6. Nahi dhammo ca...dhammo pāpeti suggatiṁ. -Tha. 290.
7. Sabbe dhammā anattā ti. -Dhp. verse 279.
8. Tasmiṁ kho pana samaye dhammā honti. -Dhs. 37.
9. Dhammesu dhammānupassī viharati. -D.N. 2.222.
10. Manopubbaṁgamā dhammā. -Dhp. verses 1-2.
11. Tattha vuttābhidhammatthā. -Abhs. 1.
12. Vividhavisesanayattā, vinayanato ceva kāyavācānaṁ; Vinayatthavidūhi ayaṁ, vinayo vinayo ti akkhāto. -Asl. 16-17.

explained with three attributes like, 'Āṇā-desanā' or teachings related to prescriptions to do this and not to do this; 'Yathāparādha-sāsana' or the regulations prescribing punishments according to transgressions; and 'Saṁvara-asaṁvara-kathā' or norms of putting restrains over psycho-physio-vocal deeds, indicating the situation where to put and where not to put. The Sutta[1] has also been described, similarly, with three attributes as, 'Vohāra-desanā' or its being the popular discourses; 'Yathānuloma-sāsana' or teaching given according to the temperament and the elevation of mind; and 'Diṭṭhiviniveṭhana-kathā' or the discourses related to removal of wrong views. Three attributes are also seen to highlight the nature of Abhidhamma[2] as, 'Paramattha-desanā' or the teachings related to ultimate truth; 'Yathādhamma-sāsana' or treatment of Dhammas as they really are; and 'Nāmarūpa-pariccheda-kathā' or the discourse related to minute analysis of mind and matter. A searching analysis of these nine attributes, given specially to the three types of teachings of the Buddha, the profundity of Abhidhamma may easily be glimpsed through.[3]

In this context, *'Puggala-Paññatti'* is the fourth book of the Abhidhamma. It is a very important book in Abhidhamma and it is a book of 'Psychology' or 'Manoviññāṇa.' The word Psychology has two component parts. One is 'Psyche' (Mana), another is 'Logy' (Viññāṇa). 'Psyche' means mind and 'Logy' is the name of science, knowledge, cognition etc.

---

1. Atthānaṁ sūcanato suvuttato, savanatotha sūdanato; Suttāṇā suttasabhāgato ca, suttaṁ suttaṁ ti akkhātaṁ. -Asl. 17.
2. Yaṁ ettha vuḍḍhimanto, salakkhaṇā pūjitā paricchinnā; Vuttādhikā ca dhammā, abhidhammo tena akkhāto. -Asl. 17.
3. Asl. 18.

Therefore 'Psychology' or 'Manoviññāṇa' means science of mind, the mental characteristics of a person, the study of mind and behaviour in relation to a particular field of knowledge, cognition of mind etc. This is the way to learn about the human mind, to observe what people do and what they say? A person can talk about his or her thoughts. Talk is a kind of behaviour which can be studied. There are many other kinds of behaviours that can be observed in order to learn about the human mind.

In Buddhist Philosophy, 'Psyche' (Mind or Mana) word is used in the sense of 'Nāma'. This comes under Citta (consciousness), Cetasika (Psychic factors) and Nibbāna (Salvation). The word 'Logy' (Viññāṇa) means knowledge or cognition. The word 'Psychology' means cognition of mind. That mind is used through the list of three kinds of actions (Physical, Vocal and Mental) of various persons. Here we should understand clearly that it is not at all related to the prevailing experimental psychology of modern era, which is usually the tradition. All these thinkings are centered towards the study of mind of various persons in the process of Abhidhamma.

This present edition is in Devanāgarī with English translation. Devanāgarī is based on the following versions of the text:

Nālandā edition— Sri Nava-Nālandā Mahāvihāra, 1960.

Burmese edition—Chaṭṭha-Saṅgāyana publication, 1956.

Siamese edition— Mahākūṭa Government Publication, 1926.

Sinhalese edition—Edited by Sri Piyatissatthera, 1954.

Sinhalese edition—Buddha-Jayantī Tripiṭaka series No. 47, with Sinhalese translation, 1976.

Roman edition— Edited by R. Morris, P.T.S., London, 1883.

For the benefit of the students and research scholars, I have been put the references to the page numbers of the Nālandā, Roman, Burmese and Sinhalese edition. An introduction has been given in the beginning of the text, and in the end of the text, the word index and similese index have been given. In this way this book is completed.

On this pious moment, I feel it my pious duty to express the deepest sense of gratitude to those teachers and friends who have helped me in various ways in giving a shape to this text. First of all, I am grateful to Late Prof. Bimala Charan Law whose translation has been used here. I express the deep sense of gratitude to my teacher Prof. Mahesh Tiwary, who helped and encouraged me every time. I also owe the debt of gratitude to Rev. Dr. Bhikshu Satyapal, Delhi University for his help and suggestions. Prof. Angraj Chaudhary and Prof. N. H. Samtani always helped me. I am grateful to them.

Dr. Ramanath Pandey, Dr. Veena Gaur and Shri Mayank Kumar, Delhi University, have spared their valuable time, for correcting the proofs and helped in preparing the index and expediting the printing work of the text. My sincerest thanks go to them for their ungrudging help. I can not forget to my Kalyāṇa-mitra Dr. Dhananjay Chavan, who has helped me in various ways. I offer my thanks to him.

The Unique Print Media and proprietor of Eastern Book Linkers, Delhi, have given me the full co-operation in completing the work in time. I thanks to its authorities.

In the end, I sincerely hope that this book will provide immense benefit to students as well as research scholars.

Bhavatu Sabba Maṅgalaṃ

Buddha Tri-ratna Mission
New Delhi

Om Prakash Pathak

INTRODUCTION

The *'Puggala-Paññatti'* is a book of immense importance for knowing the human types. It is the fourth book of the Abhidhamma-Piṭaka and is different in some aspects from the other books of the Abhidhamma-Piṭaka, both in language and style. It is entirely devoted to giving description of the human types from several standpoints and proceeds in the form of questions and answers. The book is introduced with the establishment of six Mātikās enumerating six kinds of description, such as the description of aggregates, description of bases, description of elements, description of truths, description of faculties and description of the human types. The first five Mātikās have simply been introduced here and the last one i.e. description of the human types has been thoroughly explained and illustrated in this text. In the treatment of the subject, first a table of contents of the whole work is given, and then follows the detail of the whole work.

The ***'Puggala-Paññatti'*** is a book of mixed character. It contains the characteristics of both the Abhidhamma-Piṭaka and Sutta-Piṭaka. It has the six Mātikās in the beginning of the text which is one of the characteristics of the Abhidhamma-Piṭaka. But it is closely allied to the Sutta-Piṭaka so far as form and contents are concerned. The language used here is conventional and the style is very akin to the Sutta-Piṭaka. It has followed the method of the Aṅguttara-Nikāya in grouping the classifications of the persons in an ascending numerical order from one to ten. There are passages in this text which read exactly like Suttas in one of the Nikāya.[1] Most of its contents have literal parallels in the Aṅguttara-Nikāya[2] and the Saṅgīti-Sutta of the Dīgha-Nikāya.[3]

The *'Puggala-Paññatti'* begins with the statement of six kinds of descriptions and gives a simple introduction to each of them. Then it entirely leaves out the first five (Khandha-Paññatti, Āyatana-Paññatti, Dhātu-Paññatti, Sacca-Paññatti, Indriya-Paññatti) and devotes itself to Puggala-Paññatti alone. Why is it so? Because the Buddha has thoroughly discussed them in Vibhaṅga. The description of persons has not been discussed there and for this reason, it has been treated here thoroughly.[4] The Puggala-Paññatti Mūla-Ṭikā also endorses this view.[5]

The *'Puggala-Paññatti'* has two component parts—Puggala and Paññatti. The word 'Puggala' means here an individual, a person, a being, a man, a human. It is generally understood by it the soul or some permanent principle in later Abhidhammika texts. The Milinda-Pañho[6] clearly mentions that there is no

1. D. N. 1.55-74.
2. A. N. 1.22-27.
3. D. N. 3.166-209.
4. Sammāsambuddhena hi tile visārayamānena viya, vāke hīrayamānena viya ca, heṭṭhā Vibhaṅgappakaraṇe imāsaṁ pañcannaṁ paññattīnaṁ vatthubhūtā khandhādayo nippadesena kathitā ti tena idha ekadeseneva kathesi. Chaṭṭhā Puggala-Paññatti heṭṭhā akathitā va, idhāpi uddesavāre ekadeseneva kathitā; tasmā taṁ vitthārato kathetukāmo ...pe... ekekato paṭṭhāya yāva dasakā mātikaṁ ṭhapesi. -P.P.A. 1.42.
5. Dhammasaṅgahādīsu vibhattā sabhāvapaññatti sabbā pi saṅgahitā hoti. Puggala-Paññatti pana asabhāvapaññatti. Tāya ca samayavimuttādippabhedāya ...pe... sabbā asabhāvapaññatti saṅgahitā hoti. -Pug. MuṬ. 149.
6. Miln. 23.

Puggala at all in the real sense. It is only a convention, a mere name that one gives for serving some practical purpose. In the Kathāvatthu, there is as Puggalavādins, who believe in the existence of Puggala, neither identical nor different from the five aggregates. There is a logical discussion on this problem in the first chapter of the Kathāvatthu.[1] However, the Puggala of the Puggala-Paññatti is only an apparent truth or Sammutisacca as opposed to real truth or Paramatthasacca. It indicates the person of the common life.

The word 'Paññatti' means notion, designation etc. It means what the mind both conceives and renders articulate.[2] It is stated that Paññatti is twofold according as it is known (Paññāpiyatīti) or as it makes known (Paññāpetīti).[3] There are ideas such as 'land, mountain' and the like, designated accordingly and derived from some mode of physical changes in nature. There are ideas as 'house, chariot, cart' and the like named accordingly and derived from various modes of construction of materials.

"In the highest sense we do not find these distinctions to exist, but nevertheless as modes of shadowing forth the meaning of things, they become objects of thought genesis as our ideas. And the idea is referred to, derived from, or determined by, this or that thing, and is called idea of thing because it is conceived and reckoned, named, currently expressed, or made known. This idea of thing is designated 'Atthapaññatti' because it is made known by term, word or sign."[4]

1. Kvu. 1-71.
2. Expositor by Maung Tin and Mrs. Rhys Davids, 2.499.
3. Compendium of Philosophy, p. 4.
4. Ibid 199.

According to the commentary, 'Paññatti' means Paññāpanā, Dassanā, Pakāsanā etc.[1] which means preaching, pointing out, explaining etc. Puggala-Paññatti means preaching, pointing out, showing, expositions, establishing or deposition of persons.[2] The commentary has also given a list of varieties of such Paññatti and explained them in proper places.[3] In short, it means the designation of types of persons.

The Puggala-Paññatti contains ten chapters. Each chapter deals with a number of persons from different angles. The classification of persons have been made in an ascending numerical order, from one to ten. The first chapter deals with one type of persons i.e. single individuals, the second chapter deals with pairs, the third chapter deals with groups of three, the fourth chapter deals with groups of four, the fifth chapter deals with groups of five and so forth. This makes ten fold classifications of persons. It takes into consideration their ethical behaviour, mental attitude, like latent factors, belief and other defiling and purifying factors connected with the worldly and spiritual life. The following table will give exact figure of the persons treated here in chapter.

1. Paññāpanā dassanā pakāsanā ṭhapanā nikkhipanā paññatti nāma. -P.P.A. 1.37.
2. Puggalānaṁ puggalā ti paññāpanā dassanā pakāsanā ṭhapanā nikkhipanā puggalapaññatti nāma. -P.P.A. 1.38.
3. Cha paññattiyo: vijjamānapaññatti, avijjamānapaññatti, vijjamānena avijjamānapaññatti, avijjamānena avijjamānapaññatti, vijjamānena vijjamānapaññatti, avijjamānena avijjamānapaññatti. -Ibid.

   Cha paññattiyo: upādāpaññatti, upanidhāpaññatti, samodhānapaññatti, upanikkhittapaññatti, tajjāpaññatti, santatipaññattī ti. -Ibid 1.39.

   Cha Paññattiyo: kiccapaññatti, saṇṭhānapaññatti, liṅgapaññatti, bhūmipaññatti, paccattapaññatti, asaṅkhatapaññattī ti. -Ibid 1.40.

Chapters	Groups of persons	Number of persons in each group	Total number of persons
1	54	1	54
2	26	2	52
3	17	3	51
4	29	4	116
5	14	5	70
6	1	6	6
7	2	7	14
8	1	8	8
9	1	9	9
10	1	10	10
	147		390

In the Puggala-Paññatti, there are three hundred and ninety types of persons. They are related to Kāmāvacaraloka, Rūpāvacaraloka, Arūpāvacaraloka and Lokuttaraloka. I will discuss a few of them here.

PUTHUJJANA PUGGALA

Puthujjana has two component parts : Puthu and Jana. 'Puthu' means common, average, ordinary, worldling etc. and 'Jana' is the name of person, man, being, individual etc. 'Puthujjana' means an ordinary man or average person. The text says that the person whose three fetters have not been put away and who is not proceeding to put these away, such a person is said to be a worldling. The commentary says that the three fetters are Sakkāyadiṭṭhi or self illusion, Vicikicchā or scepticism and Sīlabbataparāmāsa or attachment to rites and rituals. These are destroyed in the Phala-khaṇa (moment of fruit); in the Magga-khaṇa (moment of path) one endeavours for their destruction. One who neither exerts during the moment of path (Magga-khaṇa) nor destroys them during the moment of fruit (Phala-khaṇa), is a worldling.[1]

Puthujjana[2] is of two types— Andha Puthujjana and Kalyāṇa Puthujjana. 'Andha Puthujjana' means who professes Buddhism, may be either a 'blind worldling' who has neither knowledge of, nor interest in the fundamental teaching. 'Kalyāṇa Puthujjana' means a person who is a 'noble worldling' who has such knowledge and earnestly strives to understand and practise the teaching.[3]

ANARIYA PUGGALA

The word Anariya has two parts— Ana and Ariya. 'Ana' indicates the negative sense and 'Ariya' means noble. It means a person who is not noble or not Ariya. The eight types of noble persons are the Ariyas and the remaining persons are not Ariyas.[4] The eight types of noble persons are Sotāpatti magga sampayutta puggala, Sotāpatti phala sampayutta puggala, Sakadāgāmī magga sampayutta puggala, Sakadāgāmī phala sampayutta puggala, Anāgāmī magga sampayutta puggala, Anāgāmī phala sampayutta puggala, Arahata magga sampayutta puggala and Arahata phala sampayutta puggala. The remaining persons are Kāmāvacara Citta sampayutta, Rūpāvacara

1. Tīṇi saṁyojanānīti diṭṭhisaṁyojana-sīlabbataparāmāsa-saṁyojana-vicikicchāsaṁyojanāni. Etāni hi phalakkhaṇe pahīnāni nāma honti. Maggakkhaṇasmiṁ hi tesaṁ pahānāya paṭipanno nāma hoti. -P.P.A. 1.49.
2. M.N.A. 1.27-28.
3. "Duve puthujjanā vuttā, buddhenādiccabandhunā; Andho puthujjano eko, kalyāṇeko puthujjano" ti. D.N.A. 1.75; M.N.A. 1.28.
4. Pug. 38.

Citta sampayuttta and Arūpāvacara Citta sampayutta. These remaining persons are the Anariya puggala or not noble person.

Kāma and Avacara are the two words of Kāmāvacara. 'Kāma' means desire. It is six fold, namely— desire for visible objects, audible objects, odorous objects, sapid objects, tangible objects and ideational objects. 'Avacara' means that which moves. 'Citta' is the consciousness. Thus the consciousness which moves in the world of desires is Kāmāvacara Citta.[1] It is fickle, restless and unsteady.[2] It always roams from one object to another and creates attachment with them. The more it roams, the greater number of attachments it creats. The greater becomes the number of attachments, the bigger becomes the degree of suffering. In such a net work of desire, one becomes awfully surrounded with suffering. It is the nature of Kāmāvacara Citta.

Rūpāvacara has two component parts— Rūpa and Avacara. The literal meaning of the word 'Rūpa' is form. Technically, it refers to an object which has form and colour (Rūpālambana). It is a gross type of object selected for developing concentration at initial stage. In this sense, the term 'Avacara' means that which gets concentration. Thus , a consciousness which develops concentration on an object associated with form and colour, is called Rūpāvacara Citta. Such consciousness , before developing concentration, moves here and there on different objects and does not remain concentrated on any one of them even for a short period. There are causes of its flittering nature. They are five factors responsible for its taking away from one object to another. They are the 'Nīvaraṇas' or hindrances. They should be rightly understood and

1. 'Kāme avacaratīti kāmāvacaraṁ'. -Asl. 42,52.
2. 'Phandanaṁ capalaṁ cittaṁ.' -Dhp. verse 33.

properly controlled. It should also be understood that there are five factors helpful in developing concentration. They are the 'Jhānaṅgas'. The mind gets concentration on arising of these Jhānaṅgas. They should also be rightly understood and properly nourished.

First of all, I will discuss the Nīvaraṇas or hindrances. They are five in number, i.e. Kāmacchanda, Vyāpāda, Thīnamiddha, Uddhacca-kukucca and Vicikicchā. 'Kāmacchanda' is a strong desire for enjoying the pleasure connected with the objects of senses. It is a strong urge for sensual pleasure. 'Vyāpāda' means ill-will, antipathy or strong desire to harm others. It is a forceful leaning for creating disturbance. 'Thīnamiddha' is the name of sloth and torpor.[1] 'Thīna' means laziness, specially connected with the consciousness. 'Middha' is also the name of laziness connected with psychic factors. Since the consciousness and psychic factors function together as an unitary whole, therefore, it is generally understood that 'Thīnamiddha' is the name of laziness connected with consciousness alone. 'Uddhaccakukucca' means worry and flurry.[2] It is rather a factor which takes the mind away from the object. Here also one should understand that 'Uddhacca' is the bewilderment of the consciousness. 'Kukucca' means brooding over what has been done and what has not been done. They in combination serve as the distracting factors. 'Vicikicchā' means doubt about the Buddha, Dhamma and Saṅgha.[3]

Here the Jhānaṅgas are also five in number, i.e. Vitakka, Vicāra, Pīti, Sukha and Ekaggatā. 'Vitakka' is the initial application of mind on the object. The mind, which is of fleeting nature, is trained to lean

1. Dhs. 259.
2. Abhs. 27.
3. Dhs. 259.

towards the object. Such leaning towards the object is Vitakka. 'Vicāra' means sustaining the mind on the object. Its function is to keep the mind on the object and make it stayed on it. It is the sustained application of mind on the object. 'Pīti' is the name of the thrill of subtle pleasant sensation, appearing from within. It is a type of inner joy one receives in anticipation of the realization of the object. 'Sukha' is composure. It is the saturation of mind and body with inner pleasure. 'Ekaggatā' is the name of one pointedness. With the appearance of these five constituents of concentration, the five hindrances are suppressed and the concentration starts developing.

Here it should be understood that all the hindrances are not suppressed by all constituents of concentration. Suppression is individual but its expression is collective. The desire for sensual pleasure or Kāmacchanda is suppressed by Ekaggatā or one-pointedness; the desire to harm others or Vyāpāda is suppressed by Pīti or the thrill of pleasant sensation; sloth and torpor or Thīnamiddha is suppressed by Vitakka or initial application of mind on the object; worry and flurry or Uddhaccakukucca is suppressed by Sukha or composure and doubt or Vicikicchā is suppressed by Vicāra or sustained application of mind on the object.[1] In this way with the suppression of

---

1. "Ekasmiṁ visaye yeva, samādhānena cetaso;
Samādhi kāmacchandassa, paṭipakkhoti vuccati.
Pāmojjabhāvato ceva, sītalattasabhāvato;
Vyāpādassa tato pīti, paṭipakkhāti bhāsitā.
Savipphārikabhāvena, nekkhammādippavattito;
Vitakko thīnamiddhassa, paṭipakkhoti vaṇṇito.
Avupasantabhāvassa, sayañcevātisantato;
Sukhaṁ uddhaccakukuccadvayassa paṭipakkhakaṁ.
Matiyā anurūpattā, anumajjanalakkhaṇo;
Vicāro vicikicchāya, paṭipakkhoti dīpito." -Abhv. 141.

five hindrances and appearance of five constituents of Jhāna, there begins the one-pointedness on the object with form or Rūpālambana.

It is the fact that with the practice of the five stages of Rūpa-jhāna, the mind becomes serene, calm, concentrated, subtle and pliable, but there is still scope for making it more subtle. A consciousness immensely penetrative alone may easily proceed for realization of right understanding. Therefore, the person knowing the level of mind at Rūpāvacara stage, starts right effort for having Arūpāvacara-citta, which is relatively more subtle, calm and tranquil.

The word Arūpāvacara has three component parts— A, Rūpa and Avacara. 'A' is a prefix indicating the sense of negation. 'Rūpa' means an object which has form and colour. 'Avacara' refers to that which move, gets concentration. Therefore, Arūpāvacara Citta is a type of consciousness which attains concentration on an object which is formless. The object with form is gross and the object having no form is subtle. Thus taking the formless object, one makes right effort, for developing concentration on it. In course of such continuous effort, there comes a moment, when the mind gets concentration on the object. Thus the consciousness through which concentration is achieved on such formless object is called 'Arūpāvacara-citta'. There are four stages of Arūpāvacara-citta. They are the Ākāsānañcāyatana-citta, Viññāṇañcāyatana-citta, Ākiñcaññāyatana-citta and Nevasaññānāsaññāyatana-citta. Ākāsānañcāyatana-citta means the consciousness dwelling upon the infinity of space. The Jhāna consciousness dwelling upon the infinity of consciousness known as Viññāṇañcāyatana-citta. Ākiñcaññāyatana-citta is a consciousness dwelling upon nothingness and Nevasaññānāsaññāyatana-citta means a consciousness dwelling upon there is neither perception nor there is not.

ARIYA PUGGALA

Ariya means noble, elect. Ariya puggala means noble ones, noble persons. The eight type of noble persons are the Ariya. They are Sotāpatti magga or the one realizing the path of stream-winning, Sotāpatti phala or the one realizing the fruition of stream-winning, Sakadāgāmī magga or the one realizing the path of once-return, Sakadāgāmī phala or the one realizing the fruition of once-return, Anāgāmī magga or the one realizing the path of non-return, Anāgāmī phala or the one realizing the fruition of non-return, Arahata magga or the one realizing the path of Arahantship, Arahata phala or the one realizing the fruition of Arahantship. These stages are determind on the basis of destruction of the fetters or Saṁyojanas, the last residuals of the pollution to bind one to the process of repeated existence. The noble person understands their potentiality and exerts for their destruction. The fetters are the Sakkāyadiṭṭhi, Vicikicchā, Sīlabbataparāmāsa, Kāmarāga, Paṭigha, Rūparāga, Arūparāga, Māna, Uddhacca and Avijjā.

Sakkāyadiṭṭhi is a wrong view related to the belief of existence of a permanent soul. It leads one to think that there is a permanent essence in each of the five aggregates.

Vicikicchā means doubt. It is the doubt related to the Buddha, Dhamma, Saṅgha and also in past existence, future existence, both the past and future forms of existence and the law of dependent origination.

Sīlabbataparāmāsa is a type of belief of getting purification by observing some rites and rituals. It is also a wrong notion that one can get the state of purity of consciousness simply by following some vows or keeping fast on a particular day or taking bath in a particular river on a definite day etc.

Kāmarāga means taking delight in sensual pleasure. The word Kāma stands for five Kāmarāga or the five types of pleasure connected with the objects by the senses. There are six senses: eye, ear, nose, tongue, body and mind. And there are six objects: visible object, audible object, odorous object, sapid object, tangible object and ideational object. Each sense-organ has a desire to relish the pleasure related to its object. Such desire or the delightful urge is known as Kāmarāga.

Paṭigha means ill-will, hatred, antipathy or the desire to harm others. The desire of killing, injuring, destroying or doing any type of harm to any kind of living being is inspired by it.

Rūparāga is a feeling of delight in having existence in the Rūpa-Brahmaloka. It is a delightful desire for becoming a divine being in the Rūpaloka and enjoying pleasure available therein.

Arūparāga refers to a delightful desire of having existences in Arūpa-Brahmaloka. It is a name of a strong desire saturated with delight for having birth in the divine kingdom of the Arūpa-Brahmās. Remembering the such pleasure of this type of divine kingdom, one possesses a delightful urge to be there and share the pleasurable experiences.

Māna means conceit. It is the name of Ahaṁkāra and Mamakāra. It gives rise to ego and wrongly manifests as 'I am superior, I am equal, I am inferior' etc. In all such expressions, the ego, lifted with false pride, function as a dominant force.

Uddhacca means distraction of mind. It is an immoral force, the function of which is to take the mind away from the object. It also appears as a state of bewilderness, due to which the mind roams here and there, without any sequence. Causing aimless roaming is its main function.

Avijjā is darkness of ignorance. Technically, it is the ignorance of the four noble truths, past existence, present existence, both the past and present existence and the law of dependent origination.

The first five fetters are technically named as Orambhāgiya-Saṁyojana or lower fetters and another five fetters are called Uddhambhāgiya-Saṁyojana or upper fetters. These are the ten fetters which keep the being bound with the process of repeated existence.

PAṬIPANNAKA PUGGALA

'Paṭipannaka' means path attainer, path walker or one who has entered upon the path. 'Paṭipannaka' is he who has reached one of the four supramundane path. The text says that the four persons who possess the path are path attainer. That is the Sotāpatti magga, Sakadāgāmī magga, Anāgāmī magga and Arahata magga.

PHALE ṬHITO PUGGALA

A person who established in the fruition is called Phale Ṭhito Puggala. The four persons are established in the fruition, i.e. Sotāpatti phala, Sakadāgāmī phala, Anāgāmī phala and Arahata phala.

SEKKHA PUGGALA

Sekkha means learner. A person who is learner, is called Sekkha Puggala. The four persons who possess the path and the three persons who possess the fruition are learners.[1] It means seven persons are learners.

1. Cattāro maggasamaṅgino tayo phalasamaṅgino puggalā sekkhā. -Pug. 39.

They are Sotāpatti magga, Sotāpatti phala, Sakadāgāmī magga, Sakadāgāmī phala, Anāgāmī magga, Anāgāmī phala and Arahata magga.

ASEKKHA PUGGALA

Asekkha has two component parts— A and Sekkha. 'A' is prefix, indicative of the sense of negation. 'Sekkha' means learner, belonging to training, still to learn. Thus the word Asekkha means not requiring to be trained, not requiring to be perfect. One who has learned each and every thing, is called Asekkha.[1] He has reached the perfection in higher moral training, higher mind training and higher wisdom training and needs no longer to train himself therein.

NEVASEKKHANĀSEKKHA PUGGALA

A person who is neither learner nor non-learner, is called Nevasekkhanāsekkha Puggala. It means this person belong to the Lokiya-loka or mundane world, i.e. Kāmāvacara-citta sampayutta puggala, Rūpāvacara-citta sampayutta puggala and Arūpāvacara-citta sampayutta puggala.

BHAYŪPARATA PUGGALA

Bhaya and Uparata are the two words of Bhayūparata. 'Bhaya' is the name of fear. 'Uparata' means restrain. 'Bhayūparata' means restrained by fear. The text says that the seven kinds of learners are restrained by fear and those average persons who observe the precepts. According to the commentary, seven learners and average men are restrained from sin through fear. Therefore, such a person is said to be a person who is free from fear or Bhayūparata.

1. Arahā asekkho. -Pug. 39.

ABHAYŪPARATA PUGGALA

Abhayūparata has three component parts—A, Bhaya and Uparata. 'A' is prefix which denotes the negative sense; 'Bhaya' is the name of fear and 'Uparata' means restrain. Thus the literal meaning of the term Abhayūparata is not restrained by fear. It means whose sins are extinct. The commentary says that Arahants have completely uprooted their fear, therefore, they are called Abhayūparata Puggala.

SAMASĪSĪ PUGGALA

Sama and Sīsī are the two parts. 'Sama' means equal and 'Sīsī' means headed. Therefore Samasīsī means equal-headed. It means a person who attains two ends simultaneously, one is the extinction of cankers and another is the end of life. It is said that "such is the case with a monk who dwells in the contemplation of impermanency of all forms of existence, keeping before his eyes their impermanency, perceiving their impermanency, perseveringly, steadfastly, undisturbed, of firm mind, wisely absorbed; and in whom at one and the same time the extinction of cankers and the end of life take place."

PARIHĀNADHAMMA PUGGALA

'Parihāna' means diminution, decrease, wasting away, decay, decline. Parihānadhamma means liable to decline or of fallible nature. It means a person who obtains the attainments accompanied by an idea of form (Rūpasahagata) or by an idea of formlessness (Arūpasahagata); but he does not reach them according to his wish, and not without trouble and exertion; and not according to his wish with regard to place, object and duration, does he enter them, or rise therefrom. Therefore it is well possible that such a monk, through negligence, may loose these attainments.

Such a person is said to be of fallible nature. And Aparihānadhamma Puggala is just opposite of the Parihānadhamma Puggala.

SAMAYAVIMUTTA PUGGALA

A person who is emancipated at times. It means this person goes on experiencing the eight stages of emancipation or Aṭṭha Vimokkha from time to time, and having seen them through insight, some of sinful tendencies (Āsavas) are completely destroyed. Here Vimokkha means emancipation, liberation, deliverance. There are eight types of liberations. What are they? They are:[1]

1. *Rūpī* or whilst remaining in the fine-material sphere, one perceives corporeal forms, this is the first liberation.

2. *Arūpasaññī* or not perceiving corporeal forms on one's own person, one perceives corporeal forms externally, this is the second liberation.

3. *Subha* or by thinking of the beautiful, one is filled with confidence, this is the third liberation.

4. *Ākāsānañcāyatana* or through the total overcoming of the corporeality-perceptions, the vanishing of the reflex-perceptions and the non-attention to the multiformity-perceptions, with the idea 'unbounded is space', one reaches the 'sphere of unbounded space' and abides therein, this is the fourth liberation.

5. *Viññāṇañcāyatana* or through the total overcoming of the sphere of unbounded space, and with the idea 'unbounded is consciousness', one reaches the 'sphere of unbounded consciousness' and abides therein, this is the fifth liberation.

---

1. D.N. 3.202; A.N. 3.394-395.

6. *Ākiñcaññāyatana* or through the total overcoming of the sphere of unbounded consciousness, and with the idea 'nothing is there', one reaches the 'sphere of nothingness' and abides therein, this is the sixth liberation.

7. *Nevasaññānāsaññāyatana* or through the total overcoming of the sphere of nothingness, one reaches the 'sphere of neither-perception-nor-nonperception' and abides therein, this is the seventh liberation.

8. *Saññāvedayitanirodha-samāpatti* or through the total overcoming of the sphere of neither-perception-nor-nonperception, one reaches the 'extinction of perception and feeling', this is the eighth liberation.

These are the eight types of liberation. And Rūpī, Arūpasaññī and Subha are called Abhibhāyatana; Ākāsānañcāyatana, Viññāṇañcāyatana, Ākiñcaññāyatana and Nevasaññānāsaññāyatana are called Jhāna.

The commentary says that 'Samayavimutta' applies to a 'stream-attainer' (Sotāpanna), 'once-returner' (Sakadāgāmī) and 'never-returner' (Anāgāmī). Asamayavimutta applies to Arahants who do not practise Jhāna (Sukkhavipassaka-khīṇāsava or dry-visioned saints).[1]

KUPPADHAMMA PUGGALA

This term is applied to an ordinary person who has attained eight attainments (Aṭṭha Samāpattis). It is also applied to a 'stream-attainer' and to a 'once-returner'.[2] It means a person who is unsteady or not firmly established in the path. It is so called because in his case the mental conditions which are antagonistic to Samādhi (concentration) and Vipassanā

1. P.P.A. 1.44-45.
2. P.P.A. 1.46.

(insight) have not been completely stopped nor well-washed off, and it is for this reason that their attainment perishes and falls away.

'Akuppadhamma' is applied to an 'Anāgāmī' or 'never-returner' who has attained eight attainments (Aṭṭha Samāpattis) and to a Khīṇāsava. It means a person who does not go astray. He is steady or firmly established in the path. Hindrances of Samādhi (concentration) and Vipassanā (insight) in such a person are completely destroyed. His attainment is not broken or destroyed by useless talks, or by any other unsuitable act committed through negligence.[1]

Now question arises that what is the difference between Kuppadhamma Puggala and Akuppadhamma Puggala? Kuppadhamma Puggala does not gain them at his wish, not without toil and exertion; and not at his wish as regards place, object and duration, does he enter them or arise from them. Thus it is well possible that in case of such a person, through negligence, the attainments will become perturbed. But Akuppadhamma Puggala gains them at his wish, without toil and exertion; and according to his wish, as regards place, object and duration, enters them or arises from them, then it is impossible that in such a person the attainments may become shaken through negligence.

GOTRABHŪ PUGGALA

The term Gotrabhū comes from the word Gotra. 'Gotra' means 'lineage' and 'Bhū' means 'born of'. Here the word lineage refers to the lineage of Ariyas. 'Evolving the lineage' "is the name for the stage when, in a moment of spiritual regeneration, the kinship to Kāmaloka is rejected for the communion of

1. P.P.A. 1.47.

the Ariyas, i.e. all who have taken Nibbāna as their quest."[1]

"The evolution of 'adoption or Gotrabhu', which follows 'the adaptation' (Anuloma) already described, cuts off the heritage of the ordinary average person or Puthujjana and evolves the lineage of the Transcendental (Supramundane). It is followed by a single moment of Path-consciousness, by which the first of the Four Noble Truths is clearly discerned." "In the three Higher Paths, adoption (Gotrabhū) receives the special name of the moment of purification (Vodāna), each of the three Higher Paths being possible only to a being who has attained the next lower."[2] According to the commentary, Gotrabhū is applied to a person who has reached the family, circle, or designation of Ariyas by surpassing the family, circle, or designation of ordinary persons through the knowledge acquired by meditation on Nirvāṇa (summumbonum).[3]

Here there is a change in the lineage of the man (Gotrabhū). The career as a 'worldly man' (Puthujjana) ends and that of a 'noble man' (Ariya) begins. He is no longer then in the lineage of the 'worldly man' but he is the one, stepped in the lineage of the Ariya-Puggala. He has then the arising of a Gotrabhū-consciousness.[4]

The text Abhidhammāvatāra describes 'Gotra' as Nibbāna.[5] It means that Nibbāna, then, becomes the

1. Compendium of Philosophy, p. 129.
2. Compendium of Philosophy, p.68.
3. P.P.A. 1.49.
4. Abhv. 185.
5. Puthujjaniyagottaṁ vā, abhibhuyya pavattito;
Gottaṁ vuccati nibbānaṁ, tato bhavati gotrabhū.
Abhv. 185.

object of his consciousness. Prior to this, he had various objects of mundane sphere. Here, he has Nibbāna as the object. He is, then, in the lineage of such persons who have Nibbāna as their objects. It is having the supra-mundane object and also entering into the supra-mundane sphere. The person finds himself in the state of Gotrabhū. Thus, in the technical sense, the term Gotrabhū means entrance of the person in supra-mundane sphere where the beings have Nibbāna as their objects. He is included in their lineage.

ABHABBĀGAMANA PUGGALA

Abhabbāgamana means 'incapable of progressing'. Those beings who are obstructed by their evil action, by their defilements, by the result of their evil actions, or who are devoid of faith, energy and knowledge, and unable to enter the right path and reach perfection in wholesome things, all those are said to be incapable of progressing. According to the commentary the 'evil actions' denote the five heinous deeds with immediate result (Ānantarika-kamma), whilst the 'defilements' refer to the 'evil views with fix destiny' (Niyata-micchādiṭṭhi).[1] The five heinous 'actions with immediate destiny' are— parricide, matricide, killing an Arahata, wounding a Buddha, creating schism in the monks order. 'Evil views with fixed destiny' are— the views of uncausedness of existence (Ahetuka-diṭṭhi), of the inefficacy of action (Akiriya-diṭṭhi), and nihilism (Natthika-diṭṭhi). Bhabbāgamana Puggala is just opposite of this person.

NIYATA PUGGALA

A 'person with a fixed destiny' (Niyata), may be either one who has committed one of the five 'heinous deeds with immediate result' or one who follows 'wrong

1. P.P.A. 1.50.

views with fixed destiny', or one who has reached one of the four stages of Ariya Puggala. Those persons in whom the three fetters have vanished, they all have entered the stream, have for ever escaped the states of woe; fixed is their destiny (Niyata), assured their final enlightenment. The remaining persons are with undetermined destiny (Aniyata).

TEVIJJA PUGGALA

Tevijja means 'one endowed with three fold higher knowledge', or a person who is a master of three fold lore. In Vedic tradition, Tevijja means 'one endowed with three Vedas'. But means in Buddhism one who has realised three kinds of knowledge, to wit: remembrance of former rebirths (Pubbenivāsañāṇa), the divine eye (Dibbacakkhuñāṇa), extinction of all cankers (Āsavakkhayañāṇa).

The text[1] explains in the following ways—

1. ***Pubbenivāsañāṇa:*** It is said that "the person remembers manifold former rebirth, such as one birth, two birth, three, four and five births or hundred births; remembers many formations and dissolutions of world—'There I was, such name I had and vanishing from there I entered somewhere else into existence and vanishing from there I again reappeared here.' Thus he remembers, always together with the marks and peculiarities, many a former existence."

2. ***Dibbacakkhuñāṇa:*** "With the divine eye, the pure one, he sees beings vanishing and reappearing, low and noble ones, beautiful and ugly ones, sees how beings are reappearing according to their deeds—'These beings, indeed, followed evil ways in bodily actions, words and thoughts, insulted the noble ones, held evil views, and according to their evil views they acted. At

1. D.N. 1.71-74.

the dissolution of their body, after death, they have appeared in lower worlds, in painful states of existence, in the world of suffering, in hell.' Those other beings, however, are endowed with good action have appeared in a happy state of existence, in a heavenly world."

3. ***Āsavakkhayañāṇa:*** "Through the extinction of all cankers even in this very life he enters into the possession of deliverance of mind, deliverance through wisdom, after having himself understood and realized it."

According to the Aṭṭhakathā, a person who has first obtained knowledge of previous births (Pubbenivāsañāṇa) and knowledge of deva-sight (Dibbacakkhuñāṇa) and then knowledge of Arahantship (Arahantaphalañāṇa), is called a Tevijja. A person attaining Arahantship first and then the other two is also called Tevijja.[1] Vijjā has been translated there as 'wisdom'.[2]

CHALABHIÑÑA PUGGALA

A person who is a possessor of the six supernormal knowledges is called 'Chalabhiñña Puggala.' The person gains supernormal knowledge in the process of attainment of different stages of Rūpa-Samādhi and Arūpa-Samādhi. The consciousness becomes immensely pure and is in possession of ecstatic qualities.[3] It becomes controlled (Danta), one pointed (Samāhita), pure (Parisuddha), free from pollutions (Pariyodāta), mild (Mudu), steadfast (Ṭhita) and pliable

1. P.P.A. 1.54.
2. Psalms of the Brethren, p. 29.
3. Dante samāhite suddhe, pariyodāte anaṅgaṇe;
Anupakkilese mudubhūte, kammaniye ṭhite cale.
-Abhv. 154.

(Kammaniya). Supernormal knowledge is achieved with such consciousness.

According to the Abhidhammāvatāra, the supernormal knowledge is of five types,[1] but according to the Puggalapaññatti Aṭṭhakathā, the supernormal knowledge is of six types.[2] They are, Iddhividha or various sorts of magical power, Dibbasota or divine ear, Dibbacakkhu or divine eye, Paracetoñāṇa or power of knowing another's thought, Pubbenivāsañāṇa or power of remembering previous births and Āsavakkhayañāṇa or knowledge of destruction of sinful tendencies.

The first Abhiññā is the practice of miraculous acts. He becomes many from one and one from many. He walks on water just like on earth. He deeps down into to the earth just like water. He moves in the air just like the birds. He touches the powerful moon and sun with his hands. He makes his body so light and performs various types of wonderful performances with it.

The second Abhiññā is the divine ear. With one's divine ear, he may hear the sound, both human and divine, with minute details. It does not mean that he hears all the various types of sound at the same moment. He makes resolution about the area and types of sound and directs his mind accordingly. As per his wish and recollection, the desired sound or types of sound are heared by him.

The third Abhiññā is the divine eye. With the possession of the divine eye, the person (Yogāvacara) may see the things of far and near without any obstruction. He may also see the beings going to

1. Dibbāni cakkhusotāni, iddhi cittavijānanaṁ;
Pubbenivāsañāṇaṁ ti, pañcābhiññā imā siyuṁ.
-Abhv. 154.
2. P.P.A. 1.54.

different states of existence due to the resultant force of their moral and immoral deeds. Thus 'the possession of the divine eye' and 'the knowledge of dying and coming into existence of different beings' are stated to be the one. Here in the process of diverting his eye for seeing all such visible things, the spatio-temporal barrier is removed for him.

The fourth Abhiññā is the power of knowing another's thought or consciousness. He directs his mind and becomes able to know the various types of consciousness, beginning from the consciousness of sensual sphere or Kāmāvacara to the supramundane sphere or Lokuttara. The details of the nature of consciousness as associated with attachment (Sarāgacitta) or free from attachment (Vitarāgacitta), consciousness with antipathy (Sadosacitta) or consciousness free from antipathy (Vitadosacitta), consciousness with ignorance (Samohacitta) or consciousness free from ignorance (Vītamohacitta) are crystal clear to him. He also knows the types of consciousness arising and ceasing in others. The author remarks: "Kāmāvacaracittaṁ ca, rūpārūpesu mānasaṁ; sabbameva vijānāti, sarāgādippabhedakaṁ."[1]

The fifth Abhiññā is the knowledge of the previous births. He makes resolution and directs his mind to know the states of previous existence. As he knows the details of the present state of existence, similarly he knows the previous ones. The span of life, food taken, pleasure and pain experienced, form and colour possessed etc. are known to him with minute details.

The sixth Abhiññā is the knowledge of destruction of sinful tendencies or the extinction of all cankers. Through the extinction of all cankers even in this very life he enters into the possession of deliverance of

---

1. Abhv. 156.

mind, deliverance through wisdom, after having himself understood and realized it.

DIṬṬHIPPATTA PUGGALA

A person who thoroughly knows that this is the suffering, this is the cause of suffering, this is the cessation of suffering and this is the path leading to the cessation of suffering, is said to be one who has won vision.

The suffering is inherent in the very nature of things. Birth is suffering, old age is suffering. Disease, death, association with unpleasant and separation from lovable is suffering. Not getting what one desires, is also suffering. Thus suffering is the fact, the truth of life. The Buddha admits that there are different forms of happiness but they are all impermanent, full of suffering and subject to change. We have our own experience that even the best enjoyments of life are transitory, fleeting, and never lead to satisfaction. Therefore the Buddha is realistic and objective when he says: "Everything is suffering."

According to the Buddha the cause of suffering is not due to arbitrary will of unknown powers. The cause of suffering is our craving, which, as the texts explain, lead to rebirth again and again and is accompanied by lust and pleasure seeking pleasure now here now there.

The craving is never satisfied and manifests in various ways. The craving includes not only hankering after sense pleasures, power, wealth, position but also attachment to wrong ideas, views, opinions, theories and beliefs. All the trouble, according to the Buddha arises out of selfish desires which are never satisfied.

The Buddha does not teach only suffering but shows the path towards the cessation of suffering also. Now, to eliminate suffering, one must eliminate its cause desire, craving, thirst, whatever you call it. And briefly speaking is nothing but extinction of craving. The state of desirelessness, of absence of craving is Nibbāna, here and now. It is difficult to define Nibbāna, the most important term and also the final aim in Buddhism.

The Buddha has shown us the path leading to the cessation of suffering. It is the eightfold path, viz. right understanding, right thought, right speech, right action, right livelihood, right effort, right mindfulness and right concentration.

SOTĀPANNA PUGGALA

The person's first effort is directed towards the distruction of the first three fetters—Sakkāyadiṭṭhi, Vicikīcchā and Sīlabbataparāmāsa.[1] These fetters are the embodiments of ignorance and give rise to wrong belief. Sakkāyadiṭṭhi generates the notion of the existence of the permanent soul and puts a check on the possibility of any change whatsoever. The hope of coming out from the state of bondage to freedom, from suffering to happiness is marred until this fetter, Sakkāyadiṭṭhi, is not destroyed. Vicikicchā, which means doubt, is the onesided springing of ignorance that mars the authenticity, validity and pliability of right understanding, and its power to ameliorate activities. The Sīlabbataparāmāsa imprisons the mind and makes it a prisoner of superstitious belief in getting purification through rites and rituals. It creates confusion between means and ends and makes one lose himself in the thickets of means. These three fetters symbolise the atomic layers of ignorance. The person makes right efforts for this end. In due course, he is able to destroy them and thereby becomes Sotāpanna

1. Pug. 50.

or the stream-attainer. Here 'Sota' means a path or stream and 'Āpanna' means to set in. Thus a Sotāpanna is one who is set in on the path leading to Nibbāna. It is expressed by two more expressions Dhammacakkhu-udapādi and Dassana. In earlier texts, it often appears as "Dhammacakkhu-udapādi", there appeared the divine eyes. The term "Dassana" indicates the sense of vision. Here at this stage, the person has the vision of Nibbāna. He has not realized it but only has an inner vision. It is just like standing on the road leading to the royal palace and having the vision of the king moving on the terrace of the palace. As this vision generates hope in the man of meeting the king, so also the person, having the Sotāpanna stage, finds within himself the soothing rays of hope of realization of Nibbāna.

A Sotāpanna takes two steps at this stage. At the first step, he cuts the three fetters and at the other he realizes that they have been destroyed. The former is called Sotāpatti-magga and the latter, the Sotāpatti-phala. Thus the total destruction together with its understanding makes a person Sotāpanna. In this context, it is said that if such a person does not realize Nibbāna in this life, he will come here for seven times more as a maximum limit to attain the same. He may attain it before this temporal limit but never exceeds the limit of seven times— "Na aṭṭhaṁ bhavaṁ ādiyanti."

There are three classes of Sotāpanna or stream-attainer.[1] They are Sattakkhattuparama, Kolaṅkola and Ekabījī. Sattakkhattuparama applies to the stream-attainer who obtains Arahatship at the seventh birth.[2] Kolaṅkola means the one passing from one noble family to another. After the realization of the fruition of Sotāpatti, one is not reborn in a low family. He is

1. Pug. 44-46.
2. P.P.A. 1.60-61.

reborn amongst devas and men six time only.[1] Ekabījī is applicable to a stream-attainer who is reborn once only. In the determination of the single-seeded, the seed of Khandha, or group, has been spoken of. The stream-attainer who has only one seed of the Khandhas and who has to assume one body only is called Ekabījī.[2]

SAKADĀGĀMĪ PUGGALA

The term Sakadāgāmī has two component parts, namely Sakiṁ and Āgāmī. 'Sakiṁ' means once, one time. 'Āgāmī' means comer or returner. It literally means once-returner.[3] The person, after the destruction of the first three fetters, makes the second effort for further uprooting of fetters. He finds that the immediately succeeding fetters are the Kāmarāga and Paṭigha. These two fetters are very strong and not destroyable at one stroke. Therefore he makes right efforts to cut down their strings and make them weak. After due practice and continuous endeavour, there comes a moment when they become weak. It is after their weakening, he becomes a Sakadāgāmī. There are also two moments in it. The moment in which he makes them weak is called the stage of Sakadāgāmī-magga and the moment in which he realizes that they have been destroyed is the Sakadāgāmī-phala. The two together make the stage of Sakadāgāmī.

It is said that the man set in the path is bound to realize Nibbāna. In case he does not do so in this life, he will have to come once more for its realization here on this earth. He will come once more and not

---

1. P.P.A. 1.61.
2. Ekabījīniddese: Khandhabījaṁ nāma kathitaṁ. Yassa hi Sotāpannassa ekaṁeva khandhabījaṁ atthi, ekaṁ attabhāvagahaṇaṁ, so ekabījī nāma. -P.P.A. 1.61-62.
3. Yassa puggalassa kāmarāgabyāpādā tanubhūtā, ayaṁ vuccati puggalo "Sakadāgāmī." -Pug. 51.

two or more. The reason behind it is that the vital force of becoming is the Kāmarāga which has not totally been uprooted; it has been weakened only. Therefore, due to its residual force of enjoying the sensual pleasure, there remains the possibility of his coming once more.

ANĀGĀMĪ PUGGALA

The term 'Ana' is a prefix denoting the sense of negation, 'Āgāmī' means comer or returner. It means he does not come to this world again. He is a never-returner. The person whose ạttachment to sensual pleasures and malevolence has been entirely put away is said to be a never-returner.[1]

The person, in course of his right efforts, makes the endeavour for uprooting the weakened fetters. He, with his spiritual power, puts them to end and he becomes a Anāgāmī. Here also there are two moments. In the former, he uproots them and finds himself in the Anāgāmī-magga stage and in the latter moment, he becomes aware of their destruction and enters into Anāgāmī-phala stage. The two combined indicate the stage of Anāgāmī. Anāgāmī is the indication of a person who has no further coming to this world. In general case, he realizes Nibbāna here in the present state of existence. In case, he does not realize it so, he is not born again here. He is born in the divine kingdom, preferably in the Suddhāvāsa-loka and therefrom gets liberation.

ARAHATA PUGGALA

The person attains it after the total destruction of the five fetters: Rūparāga, Arūparāga, Māna, Uddhacca and Avijjā. The person fully understands

1. Pug. 51.

and sees them and makes final efforts for their destruction. He exerts and makes endeavours and there comes the moment when they are totally destroyed. Here also there are two moments. There is the moment when, he cuts these five fetters is called the stage of Arahata-magga. There is another moment, when he realizes that they have been destroyed is the Arahata-phala. In this way, after total destruction of the remaining five fetters, he becomes an Arahata, a person immensely pure, free from pollution and capable to put to end the process of repeated existences.

The Arahata is an ideal person in Buddhist tradition. Attainment of the stage of the Arhathood is the summum-bonum of life. One abandons the household life, takes the life of a recluse and direct his entire activities towards it. After its attainment he becomes free from the chain of becoming and experiences eternal bliss. He is the Jivana-mukta. He lives here on this earth till the karmic forces continue to maintain his body. Neither he has craving for its continuity nor desire for its destruction. He simply lives quite detachedly just like the lotus in the pond. When, he moves in the society, collects his requisites from it, but developes no attachment to anything. He is in possession of a consciousness free from all attachments known as Kiriyā-citta.

Buddhaghosa has explained the concept of an Arahata in many ways and with several attributes. He enumerates firstly the five reasons and says that— "he is an Arahata (1) because of remoteness from immoral states, (2) killing of the enemies of defilements, (3) destroying of the spokes of the wheels of the process of repeated existence, (4) becoming worthy of his requisites and (5) because of the absence of the secret of evil doings."

"Ārakattā hatattā ca, kilesārīna so muni;

Hatasaṁsāracakkāro, paccayādīna cāraho;

Na raho karoti pāpāni, Arahaṁ tena vuccatī" ti.[1]

In this way an Arahata, pure in his physical actions, pure in his vocal actions and pure in his mental actions, dwells among the people, doing all possible moral deeds for their threefold benefits, experiencing the joy of ambrosial bliss, making this world of human beings as the best place of living.

"Gāme vā yadi vāraññe, ninne vā yadi vā thale;

Yattha arahanto viharanti, taṁ bhūmirāmaṇeyyakaṁ."[2]

PARINIBBĀYĪ PUGGALA

A person who cuts the five lower fetters, is said to be Parinibbāyī Puggala. Parinibbāyī persons are the five types. They are Antarāparinibbāyī Puggala, Upahaccaparinibbāyī Puggala, Asaṅkhāraparinibbāyī Puggala, Sasaṅkhāraparinibbāyī Puggala and Uddhaṁsota Akaniṭṭhagāmī Puggala. They all are Anāgāmī. It means Anāgāmi is the five types or we can say that there are five classes of Anāgāmi or never-returner.[3] A person who obtains Nirvāṇa before reaching the middle of the term of life is called 'Antarāparinibbāyī Puggala.'[4] 'Antarāparinibbāyī' is an Anāgāmi, who having been reborn in the Suddhāvāsa heavens, dies and attains Parinibbāna before half the term of his life as a Suddhāvāsa is completed.[5] 'Upahaccaparinibbāyī' applies to a person who obtains Parinibbāna after passing the middle of the term of life, but does not reach the end.[6] A person who attains

1. Vism. 1.420.
2. Dhp. verse 98.
3. Pug. 47-50.
4. P.P.A. 1.63.
5. D.P.L. 344.
6. P.P.A. 1.64.

complete passing away of mental impurities (Kilesaparinibbāna) is said to be 'Asaṅkhāraparinibbāyī Puggala.'[1] 'Sasaṅkhāraparinibbāyī' applies to a person who obtains the foregoing with instigation, with trouble and with exertion.[2] A person goes to the highest Brahmaloka passing through four intermediate Brahma Worlds, viz., Aviha, Atappa, Sudassa and Sudassī. He goes one by one. After vanishing from the heaven of the Aviha-Gods, he appears in the heaven of the unworried (Atappa) Gods. After vanishing from there he appears in the heaven of the clearly-visible (Sudassa) Gods, from there in the heaven of the clear-visioned (Sudassī) Gods, from there in the heaven of the highest (Akaniṭṭha) Gods. There he attains the holy path for the overcoming of the higher fetters. Such a person is called 'Uddhaṁsota Akaniṭṭhagāmī.[3]

PACCEKASAMBUDDHA PUGGALA

'Paccekasambuddha' means one Enlightened by himself, i.e. one who has attained to supreme and perfect insight, but dies without proclaiming the truth to the world.[4] A Paccekasambuddha, that is, one who has attained like a Buddha by his unaided powers the knowledge necessary to Nirvāṇa, but does not preach it to men.[5] Kern says that "Paccekasambuddha is a being who has attained, like a Buddha, by his unaided powers the knowledge necessary to Nirvāṇa, but does not preach it. He is not omniscient, and is in all respects inferior to a Supreme Buddha. It is a law of nature that he can not live at the same time with a Buddha."[6]

1. P.P.A. 1.64.
2. Ibid.
3. P.P.A. 1.64-68.
4. P.E.D. 385.
5. D.P.L. 309.
6. Manual of Indian Buddhism by H. Kern, p. 61-62.

And the text says that a person who himself thoroughly understands the truths in regard to doctrines unheard of before, but attains neither omniscience nor mastery over the fruitions thereof: this sort of person is said to be one Enlightened for himself.[1] This is a term for an Arahata who has realized Nibbāna without having heard the Buddha's doctrine from others. He comprehends the four Noble Truths individually, independent of any teacher, by his own effort. He has, however, not the capacity to proclaim the teaching effectively to others, and therefore does not become a 'Teacher of Gods and Men, a Perfect or Universal Buddha or Sammāsambuddha.' Paccekasambuddhas are described as frugal of speech, cherishing solitude. According to the tradition, they do not arise while the Teaching of a Perfect Buddha is known; but for achieving their rank after many aeons of effort, they have to utter an aspiration before a Perfect Buddha.

VALĀHAKŪPAMĀ PUGGALA

Valāhakūpamā means compared to the cloud. It means there are the four types of person comparable to the four types of clouds. What are the four kinds of clouds? They are: that which thunders but does not rain, that which rain but does not thunders, that which both thunders and rains, and that which neither thunders nor rains. Thus are to be found in this world four types of persons who are comparable to these four kinds of clouds. What are they?

One who speaks much but does not act accordingly, is a person like the cloud that thunders but does not rain. The commentary adds here that only thundering of the cloud and not raining is dangerous. The farmers marking the cloud thundering, think that there shall be good rain and thinking so,

1. Pug. 40.

they take seeds from the granary, and sow them in fields. In absense of rain, the seeds are destroyed. As a result of that there is famine in the country.[1]

One who acts but does not speak, thus a person is like the cloud that rains but does not thunders. The commentary adds that raining without thundering is also dangerous. Not hearing the roaring of clouds, people presume to have no rain that year. Thinking so, they cultivate only those pieces of land which are low. After sometimes, when it rains, the low lands turn into ocean and there is no crop at all. This also results into bringing famine in the country.[2]

One who speaks and also acts accordingly, is a person like the cloud that thunders and rains as well. The commentary says that this type of thundering and raining is good. It brings good crop and happiness to the farmers.[3]

One who neither speaks nor acts, is a person like the cloud that neither thunders nor rains. The commentary says that neither thundering nor raining is totally bad.[4]

Om Prakash Pathak

1. P.P.A. 1.94.
2. P.P.A. 1.94.
3. Gajjitvā vassanabhāvo pana bhaddako. Tathā hi subhikkhaṁ hoti. -P.P.A. 1.94.
4. No gajjitvā no vassanabhāvo ekantapāpako. -Ibid.

ABBREVIATIONS

A.	Aṭṭhakathā	Nālandā Edition
A.N.	Aṅguttara-Nikāya	Nālandā Edition
Asl.	Aṭṭhasālinī	Bombay Edition
Abhs.	Abhidhammattha-saṅgaho	Mahābodhi Society Vārāṇasī
Abhv.	Abhidhammāvatāro	Pāli Pariveṇa, Delhi
Kvu.	Kathāvatthu	Nālandā Edition
D.P.L.	Dictionary of the Pāli Language	R.C. Childers
Tha.	Theragāthā	Nālandā Edition
D.N.	Dīgha-Nikāya	Nālandā Edition
Dhp.	Dhammapada	Nālandā Edition
Dhs.	Dhammasaṅgaṇi	Nālandā Edition
P.P.A.	Pañcappakaraṇa Aṭṭhakathā	Nālandā Edition
P.E.D.	Pāli English Dictionary	Rhys Davids
Pug.	Puggala-Paññatti	Present Edition
Pug.MūṬ.	Puggala-Paññatti Mūla-Ṭīkā	Nālandā Edition
M.N.	Majjhima-Nikāya	Nālandā Edition
Miln.	Milindapañho	Bombay Edition
Vism.	Visuddhimagga	Vārāṇasī Edition
S.N.	Saṁyutta-Nikāya	Nālandā Edition

IN THE FOOT-NOTES

ना॰	नालन्दा संस्करण	Nālandā Edition
म॰	बर्मी संस्करण	Burmese Edition
रो॰	रोमन संस्करण	Roman Edition
सी॰	सिंहली संस्करण	Sinhalese Edition
स्या॰	स्यामी संस्करण	Syamese Edition

IN THE PĀLI TEXT

B.	Burmese Edition
N.	Nālandā Edition
R.	Roman Edition
S.	Sinhalese Edition

॥ नमो तस्स भगवतो अरहतो सम्मासम्बुद्धस्स ॥

पुग्गलपञ्ञत्तिपालि[१]

मातिकाउद्देसो

Homage to Him, the Blessed One, the Conqueror, the Perfectly Enlightened One.

DESIGNATION OF HUMAN TYPES

Table of Matrices

छ पञ्ञत्तियो

१. [N.3; R.1; B.101; S.240] छ पञ्ञत्तियो—खन्धपञ्ञत्ति, आयतनपञ्ञत्ति, धातुपञ्ञत्ति, सच्चपञ्ञत्ति, इन्द्रियपञ्ञत्ति, पुग्गलपञ्ञत्तीति ।

The six designations

1. The six designations are— The notion of the aggregates, the notion of the bases, the notion of the elements, the notion of the truths, the notion of the faculties and the notion of the human types.

१. खन्धानं खन्धपञ्ञत्ति

२. कित्तावता खन्धानं खन्धपञ्ञत्ति ? यावता पञ्चक्खन्धा—रूपक्खन्धो, वेदनाक्खन्धो, सञ्ञाक्खन्धो, सङ्खारक्खन्धो, विञ्ञाणक्खन्धो; एत्तावता खन्धानं खन्धपञ्ञत्ति ।

---

१. पुग्गलपञ्ञत्तिप्पकरणं – सी०; पुग्गलपञ्ञत्ति – स्या०, रो० ।

1. The designation of the aggregate of the aggregates

2. In what ways is there a designation of the aggregates? So far as there are five aggregates viz.— Material aggregate, sensation aggregate, perception aggregate, mental formation aggregate, consciousness aggregate. In these ways is there a designation of the aggregates.

२. आयतनानं आयतनपञ्ञत्ति

३. कित्तावता आयतनानं आयतनपञ्ञत्ति ? यावता द्वादसायतनानि— चक्खायतनं[१], रूपायतनं, सोतायतनं, सद्दायतनं, घानायतनं, गन्धायतनं, जिव्हायतनं, रसायतनं, कायायतनं, फोट्ठब्बायतनं, मनायतनं, धम्मायतनं; एत्तावता आयतनानं आयतनपञ्ञत्ति ।

2. The designation of the base of the bases

3. In what ways is there a designation of the bases? So far as there are twelve bases viz.— Eye base, visible object base, ear base, sound base, nose base, odour base, tongue base, taste base, body base, tangible object base, mind base, cognizable base. In these ways is there a designation of the bases.

३. धातूनं धातुपञ्ञत्ति

४. कित्तावता धातूनं धातुपञ्ञत्ति ? यावता अट्ठारस धातुयो— चक्खुधातु, रूपधातु, चक्खुविञ्ञाणधातु, सोतधातु, सद्दधातु, सोतविञ्ञाणधातु, घानधातु, गन्धधातु, घानविञ्ञाणधातु, जिव्हाधातु, रसधातु, जिव्हाविञ्ञाणधातु, कायधातु, फोट्ठब्बधातु, कायविञ्ञाणधातु, मनोधातु, धम्मधातु, मनोविञ्ञाणधातु; एत्तावता धातूनं धातुपञ्ञत्ति ।

3. The designation of the element of the elements

4. In what ways is there a designation of the elements? So far as there are eighteen elements viz.—

---

१. चक्खायतनं — स्या०, एवमुपरि पि ।

Eye element, visible object element, eye consciousness element, ear element, sound element, ear consciousness element, nose element, odour element, nose consciousness element, tongue element, taste element, tongue consciousness element, body element, tangible object element, body consciousness element, mind element, cognizable element, mind consciousness element. In these ways is there a designation of the elements.

४. सच्चानं सच्चपञ्ञत्ति

५. [N.4; R.2; B.102;] कित्तावता सच्चानं सच्चपञ्ञत्ति ? यावता चत्तारि सच्चानि— दुक्खसच्चं, समुदयसच्चं, निरोधसच्चं, मग्गसच्चं; एत्तावता सच्चानं सच्चपञ्ञत्ति ।

4. The designation of the truth of the truths

5. In what ways is there a designation of the truths? So far as there are four truths viz.— The truth of suffering, the truth of its origin, the truth of cessation, the truth of the path. In these ways is there a designation of the truths.

५. इन्द्रियानं इन्द्रियपञ्ञत्ति

६. [S.242] कित्तावता इन्द्रियानं इन्द्रियपञ्ञत्ति ? यावता बावीसतिन्द्रियानि— चक्खुन्द्रियं, सोतिन्द्रियं, घानिन्द्रियं, जिव्हिन्द्रियं, कायिन्द्रियं, मनिन्द्रियं, इत्थिन्द्रियं, पुरिसिन्द्रियं, जीवितिन्द्रियं, सुखिन्द्रियं, दुक्खिन्द्रियं, सोमनस्सिन्द्रियं, दोमनस्सिन्द्रियं, उपेक्खिन्द्रियं, सद्धिन्द्रियं, विरियिन्द्रियं[१] सतिन्द्रियं, समाधिन्द्रियं, पञ्ञिन्द्रियं, अनञ्ञातञ्ञस्सामीतिन्द्रियं[२], अञ्ञिन्द्रियं, अञ्ञाताविन्द्रियं; एत्तावता इन्द्रियानं इन्द्रियपञ्ञत्ति ।

---

१. वीरियिन्द्रियं — म०, एवमुपरि पि ।

२. अनञ्ञातञ्ञस्सामितिन्द्रियं — सी०; अनञ्ञतञ्ञस्सामीतिन्द्रियं — स्या० ।

5. The designation of the faculty of the faculties

6. In what ways is there a designation of the faculties? So far as there are twenty two faculties viz.— Eye faculty, ear faculty, nose faculty, tongue faculty, body faculty, mind faculty, famininity faculty, masculinity faculty, vitality faculty, pleasure faculty, pain faculty, gladness faculty, sadness faculty, indifference faculty, faith faculty, energy faculty, mindfulness faculty, concentration faculty, wisdom faculty, will-to-know-what-is-unknown faculty, the faculty of highest knowledge, the faculty of having come to know the unknown. In these ways is there a designation of the faculties.

६. पुग्गलानं पुग्गलपञ्ञत्ति

७. कित्तावता पुग्गलानं पुग्गलपञ्ञत्ति ?

6. The designation of the human type of the human types

7. In what ways is there a designation of the human types?

पुग्गलपञ्ञत्तिमातिका

Matrices of Designation of Human Types

(१) एको पुग्गलो

Grouping of Human Types by One

(१) समयविमुत्तो	One emancipated at times.
(२) असमयविमुत्तो	One emancipated not at times.
(३) कुप्पधम्मो	One of perturbable nature.
(४) अकुप्पधम्मो	One of imperturbable nature.
(५) परिहानधम्मो	One fallible nature.
(६) अपरिहानधम्मो	One infallible nature.

(७) चेतनाभब्बो	One competent in will.
(८) अनुरक्खणाभब्बो[१]	One competent in watchfullness.
(९) पुथुज्जनो	An average person.
(१०) गोत्रभू	One of the noble family.
(११) भयूपरतो	One restrained through fear.
(१२) [N.5] अभयूपरतो	One unrestrained through fear.
(१३) अभब्बागमनो	One incapable of progress.
(१४) भब्बागमनो	One capable of progress.
(१५) नियतो	One with determined destiny.
(१६) अनियतो	One with undetermined destiny.
(१७) [B.103] पटिपन्नको	The path-attainer.
(१८) फले[२] ठितो[२]	One established in the fruition.
(१९) समसीसी	The equal-headed.
(२०) ठितकप्पी	The aeon-arrester.
(२१) अरियो	Noble.
(२२) अनरियो	Not noble.
(२३) सेक्खो[३]	The learner.
(२४) असेक्खो	The non-learner.
(२५) नेवसेक्खनासेक्खो[४]	Neither a learner nor a non-learner.
(२६) तेविज्जो	One with threefold lore.
(२७) छळभिञ्ञो	One with six superknowledges.

१. अनुरक्खनाभब्बो — सी०, स्या० ।

२-२. फलेट्ठितो — स्या० ।

३. सेखो — स्या०, एवमुपरि पि ।

४. नेवसेक्खा नासेक्खो– सी० ; नेवसेखोनासेखो– स्या० ; नेवसेक्खो नासेक्खो — रो० ।

(२८) [R.3] सम्मासम्बुद्धो The Perfectly Enlightened One.

(२९) पच्चेकसम्बुद्धो[1] The One Enlightened for himself.

(३०) उभतोभागविमुत्तो One emancipated in both ways.

(३१) पञ्ञाविमुत्तो One emancipated by way of insight.

(३२) कायसक्खी The eye-witness.

(३३) दिट्ठिप्पत्तो[2] One who has won vision.

(३४) सद्धाविमुत्तो One emancipated by faith.

(३५) धम्मानुसारी One conforming to the Law.

(३६) सद्धानुसारी One conforming by faith.

(३७) सत्तक्खत्तुपरमो[3] One undergoes rebirth seven times.

(३८) कोलङ्कोलो One transmigrating through family to family.

(३९) [N.6] एकबीजी The single-seeded.

(४०) [B.104] सकदागामी The once-returner.

(४१) अनागामी The never-returner.

(४२) अन्तरापरिनिब्बायी[4] One who attains nirvāṇa before reaching the middle of the term of life in the Brahma World.

(४३) उपहच्चपरिनिब्बायी The term-curtailing passer-away.

(४४) असङ्खारपरिनिब्बायी The automatic passer-away.

(४५) ससङ्खारपरिनिब्बायी The passer-away after strenuous exertions.

---

१. पच्चेकबुद्धो—सी० ।

२. दिट्ठिपत्तो — रो० ।

३. सत्तक्खत्तुंपरमो — स्या०, रो० ।

४. अन्तरापरिनिब्बायि — सी०, एवमुपरि पि ।

(४६) उद्धंसोतो अकनिट्ठगामी	The stream-ascending Akaniṭṭha traveller.
(४७) [S.244] सोतापन्नो	The stream-attainer.
(४८) सोतापत्तिफलसच्छि-किरियाय पटिपन्नो	The stream-attainer walking in the realisation of the fruition stage.
(४९) सकदागामी	The once-returner.
(५०) सकदागामिफल-सच्छिकिरियाय पटिपन्नो	The once-returner walking in the realisation of the fruition stage.
(५१) अनागामी	The never-returner.
(५२) अनागामिफलसच्छि-किरियाय पटिपन्नो	The never-returner walking in the realisation of the fruition stage.
(५३) अरहा	The Arahant.
(५४) अरहत्तफलसच्छि-किरियाय[1] पटिपन्नो	The Arahant walking in the realisation of the fruition stage.

(२) द्वे[2] पुग्गला[2]

Grouping of Human Types by Two

(१) क. कोधनो च	The angry and
ख. उपनाही च	The vengeful.
(२) क. मक्खी च	The slanderer and
ख. पळासी[3] च	The quarrelsome.
(३) क. इस्सुकी च	The envious and

१. अरहत्ताय — रो० ।

२-२. स्या० पोत्थके नत्थि ।

३. पलासी — स्या० ।

	ख. मच्छरी च	The avaricious.
(४)	क. सठो च	The crafty and
	ख. मायावी च	The deceitful.
(५)	क. [B.105] अहिरिको च	The shameless and
	ख. अनोत्तप्पी च	The impudent.
(६)	क. [N.7] दुब्बचो च	The disobedient and
	ख. पापमित्तो च	The associate of the wicked.
(७)	क. [R.4] इन्द्रियेसु अगुत्तद्वारो च	One unguarded as to the sense-doors and.
	ख. भोजने अमत्तञ्ञू च	One immoderate as to food.
(८)	क. मुट्ठस्सति च	The forgetful and
	ख. असम्पजानो च	The unmindful.
(९)	क. सीलविपन्नो च	The infringer of moral law and
	ख. दिट्ठिविपन्नो च	The upholder of wrong views.
(१०)	क. अज्झत्तसंयोजनो[१] च	One with internal fetters and
	ख. बहिद्धासंयोजनो च	One with external fetters.
(११)	क. अक्कोधनो च	Without anger and
	ख. अनुपनाही च	The unrevengeful.
(१२)	क. अमक्खी च	The not a slanderer and
	ख. अपळासी च	The not quarrelsome.
(१३)	क. अनिस्सुकी च	The unenvious and
	ख. अमच्छरी च	The unavaricious.
(१४)	क. असठो च	The not crafty and
	ख. अमायावी च	The undeceiving.

१. अज्झत्तसञ्ञोजनो — सी०, स्या०, रो०, एवमुपरि पि ।

(१५) क. हिरिमा[१] च	The scrupulous and
ख. ओत्तप्पी च	The discreet.
(१६) क. सुवचो च	The obedient and
ख. कल्याणमित्तो च	The associate of the good.
(१७) क. इन्द्रियेसु गुत्तद्वारो च	One guarded as to the sense-doors and
ख. भोजने मत्तञ्ञू च	One moderate as to food.
(१८) क. उपट्ठितस्सति[२] च	The alert and
ख. सम्पजानो च	The understand.
(१९) क. [N.8] सील-सम्पन्नो च	The observer of the moral law and
ख. दिट्ठिसम्पन्नो च	The upholder of right views.
(२०) द्वे पुग्गला दुल्लभा लोकस्मि	Two persons who are rare in this world.
(२१) द्वे पुग्गला दुत्तप्पया	Two persons who are hard to satisfy.
(२२) द्वे पुग्गला सुतप्पया	Two persons who are easily satisfied.
(२३) द्विन्नं पुग्गलानं आसवा वड्ढन्ति	Two persons whose sinful tendencies increase.
(२४) द्विन्नं पुग्गलानं आसवा न वड्ढन्ति	Two persons whose sinful tendencies do not increase.
(२५) क. हीनाधिमुत्तो च	One having low inclination and
ख. पणीताधिमुत्तो च	One having good inclination.

---

१. हिरीमा — रो॰ ।

२. उपट्ठितसति — सी॰, रो॰ ।

(२६) क. तित्तो च	The gratified and
ख. तप्पेता च	The gratifier.

(३) तयो पुग्गला

Grouping of Human Types by Three

(१) क. [B.106; S.246] निरासो	The hopeless.
ख. आसंसो	The hopeful.
ग. विगतासो	One who has last hope.
(२) तयो गिलानूपमा पुग्गला	Three persons who. comparable to sick.
(३) क. कायसक्खी	The eye-witness.
ख. दिट्ठिप्पत्तो	One who has won vision.
ग. सद्धाविमुत्तो	One emancipated by faith.
(४) क. गूथभाणी	The foul-mouthed.
ख. पुप्फभाणी	The flower-speaker.
ग. मधुभाणी	The honey-tongued.
(५) क. अरुकूपमचित्तो[१] पुग्गलो	A cancer-minded person.
ख. विज्जूपमचित्तो पुग्गलो	A lightning-minded person.
ग. वजिरूपमचित्तो पुग्गलो	A diamond-minded person.
(६) क. अन्धो	The blind.
ख. एकचक्खु	The one-eyed.

---

१. अरुकुपमचित्तो — सी०; अरुणूपमचित्तो — रो०।

ग. द्विचक्खु[1] The two-eyed.

(७) क. [N.9]अवकुज्जपञ्ञो पुग्गलो A person of inverted intellect.

ख. उच्छङ्गपञ्ञो[2] पुग्गला A person of folded intellect.

ग. पुथुपञ्ञो पुग्गलो A person of wide intellect.

(८) क. [R.5] अत्थेकच्चो पुग्गलो कामेसु च भवेसु च अवीतरागो

A person not dispassionate as to sensual pleasures, as also to the states of rebirth.

ख. अत्थेकच्चो पुग्गलो कामेसु वीतरागो भवेसु अवीतरागो

A person dispassionate as to sensual pleasures, but not dispassionate as to rebirths.

ग. अत्थेकच्चो पुग्गलो कामेसु च भवेसु च वीतरागो

A person dispassionate as to both sensual pleasures and rebirths.

(९) क. पासाणलेखूपमो पुग्गलो A person comparable to a mark on stone.

ख. पथविलेखूपमो[3] पुग्गलो A person comparable to a mark on earth.

ग. उदकलेखूपमो पुग्गलो A person comparable to a mark on water.

(१०) तयो पोत्थकूपमा पुग्गला Three persons comparable to hempen cloth.

---

१. द्वेचक्खु — रो० ।

२. उच्चङ्गपञ्ञो — स्या० ।

३. पठवीलेखूपमो — स्या० ।

(११) तयो कासिकवत्थूपमा पुग्गला — Three persons comparable to Benares cloth.

(१२) क. सुप्पमेय्यो — One who is to be easily measured.

ख. दुप्पमेय्यो — One who is hard to be measured.

ग. अप्पमेय्यो — One who can not be measured.

(१३) क. अत्थेकच्चो पुग्गलो न सेवितब्बो न भजितब्बो न पयिरुपासितब्बो

A person not worthy to be served, to be devotedly served, to be worshipped.

ख. अत्थेकच्चो पुग्गलो सेवितब्बो भजितब्बो पयिरुपासितब्बो

A person worthy to be served, to be devotedly served, to be worshipped.

ग. अत्थेकच्चो पुग्गलो सक्कत्वा गरुं कत्वा सेवितब्बो भजितब्बो पयिरुपासितब्बो

A person worthy to be served with regard and esteem, to be devotedly served, to be worshipped.

(१४) क. [B.107] अत्थेकच्चो पुग्गलो जिगुच्छितब्बो, न सेवितब्बो न भजितब्बो न पयिरुपासितब्बो

A person who should be despised, not worthy to be served, to be devoted, to be worshipped.

ख. अत्थेकच्चो पुग्गलो अज्झुपेक्खितब्बो, न सेवितब्बो न भजितब्बो न पयिरुपासितब्बो

A person who should be treated with indifference, not worthy to be served, to be devotedly served, to be worshipped.

ग. अत्थेकच्चो पुग्गलो सेवितब्बो भजितब्बो पयिरुपासितब्बो

A person worthy to be served, to be devotedly served, to be worshipped.

(१५) क. [N.10; S.248] अत्थेकच्चो पुग्गलो सीलेसु परिपूरकारी,[१] समाधिस्मिं मत्तसो कारी, पञ्ञाय मत्तसो कारी

A person who fulfils the moral laws, but incompletely practises concentration and the way of insight.

ख. अत्थेकच्चो पुग्गलो सीलेसु च परिपूरकारी समाधिस्मिं च परिपूरकारी, पञ्ञाय मत्तसो कारी

A person who fulfils the moral laws and completes the practice of concentration, but incompletely practises the way of insight.

ग. अत्थेकच्चो पुग्गलो सीलेसु च परिपूरकारी समाधिस्मिं च परिपूरकारी पञ्ञाय च परिपूरकारी

A person who fulfils the moral laws and completes the practice of concentration and also completely practises the way of insight.

(१६) तयो सत्थारो — Three teachers.

(१७) अपरे पि तयो सत्थारो — Other three teachers.

(४) चत्तारो पुग्गला

Grouping of Human Types by Four

(१) क. असप्पुरिसो — The not a good man.

ख. असप्पुरिसेन असप्पुरिसतरो — More not a good man than the not good man.

ग. सप्पुरिसो — A good man.

घ. सप्पुरिसेन सप्पुरिसतरो — A better man than the good man.

(२) क. पापो — A wicked.

ख. पापेन पापतरो — More wicked than the wicked.

---

१. परिपूरीकारी — स्या०, एवमुपरि पि ।

	ग. कल्याणो	Lovely disposition.
	घ. कल्याणेन कल्याणतरो	More lovely than one of lovely disposition.
(३)	क. [R.6] पापधम्मो	A wicked nature.
	ख. पापधम्मेन पापधम्मतरो	A more wicked nature than the wicked nature.
	ग. कल्याणधम्मो	A lovely nature.
	घ. कल्याणधम्मेन कल्याणधम्मतरो	A more lovely nature than the lovely nature.
(४)	क. सावज्जो	The blameworthy.
	ख. वज्जबहुलो	One exceedingly blameworthy.
	ग. अप्पवज्जो[१]	One little blameworthy.
	घ. अनवज्जो	The blameless.
(५)	क. [N.11] उग्घटितञ्ञू	One of quick in acquiring.
	ख. विपञ्चितञ्ञू[२]	One learns by exposition.
	ग. नेय्यो	One who may be led.
	घ. पदपरमो	One with whom the word is the chief thing.

(६) क. [B.108] युत्तप्पटिभानो,[३] नो मुत्तप्पटिभानो One makes a fit but not a prompt reply.

ख. मुत्तप्पटिभानो, नो युत्तप्पटिभानो One makes a prompt but not a fit reply.

ग. युत्तप्पटिभानो च मुत्तप्पटिभानो च One makes a fit and prompt reply.

---

१. अप्पसावज्जो — स्या०, रो० ।

२. विपचितञ्ञू — सी०; विपच्चितञ्ञू — रो० ।

३. युत्तपटिभाणो — स्या०, रो०; युत्तपटिभानो — सी०, एवमुपरि पि ।

घ. नेव युत्तप्पटिभानो नो मुत्तप्पटिभानो One makes neither a fit nor a prompt reply.

(७) चत्तारो धम्मकथिका पुग्गला Four persons who are the preachers of Dhamma.

(८) चत्तारो वलाहकूपमा पुग्गला Four persons comparable to the cloud.

(९) चत्तारो मूसिकूपमा पुग्गला Four persons comparable to mice.

(१०) चत्तारो अम्बूपमा पुग्गला Four persons comparable to the mango.

(११) चत्तारो कुम्भूपमा पुग्गला Four persons comparable to a jar.

(१२) चत्तारो उदकरहदूपमा पुग्गला Four persons comparable to a pool of water.

(१३) चत्तारो बलीबद्दूपमा[१] पुग्गला Four persons comparable to the ox.

(१४) चत्तारो आसीविसूपमा[२] पुग्गला Four persons comparable to a serpent.

(१५) क. [S.250] अत्थेकच्चो पुग्गलो अननुविच्च अपरियोगाहेत्वा अवण्णारहस्स वण्णं भासिता होति

A person speaking in praise of an unworthy man without inquiry and scrutiny.

ख. अत्थेकच्चो पुग्गलो अननुविच्च अपरियोगाहेत्वा वण्णारहस्स अवण्णं भासिता होति

---

१. बलिवद्दूपमा — सी०, रो०; बलिबद्धूपमा — स्या० ।

२. आसिविसूपमा — सी०, स्या० ।

A person speaking in dispraise of a worthy man without inquiry and scrutiny.

ग. अत्थेकच्चो पुग्गलो[१] अननुविच्च अपरियोगाहेत्वा अप्पसादनीये ठाने पसादं उपदंसिता[२] होति

A person showing satisfaction in an unsatisfactory thing without inquiry and scrutiny.

घ. अत्थेकच्चो पुग्गलो अननुविच्च अपरियोगाहेत्वा पसादनीये ठाने अप्पसादं उपदंसिता होति

A person showing dissatisfaction in a satisfactory thing without inquiry and scrutiny.

(१६) क. [N.12] अत्थेकच्चो पुग्गलो अनुविच्च परियोगाहेत्वा अवण्णारहस्स अवण्णं भासिता होति

A person speaking in dispraise of an unworthy man after inquiry and scrutiny.

ख. अत्थेकच्चो पुग्गलो अनुविच्च परियोगाहेत्वा वण्णारहस्स वण्णं भासिता होति

A person speaking in praise of a praiseworthy man after inquiry and scrutiny.

ग. अत्थेकच्चो पुग्गलो अनुविच्च परियोगाहेत्वा अप्पसादनीये ठाने अप्पसादं उपदंसिता होति

A person finding dissatisfaction in an unsatisfactory thing after inquiry and scrutiny.

घ. अत्थेकच्चो पुग्गलो अनुविच्च परियोगाहेत्वा पसादनीये ठाने पसादं उपदंसिता होति

A person finding satisfaction in a satisfactory thing after inquiry and scrutiny.

---

१. रो० पोत्थके नत्थि।

२. उपधंसिता — सी०, एवमुपरि पि।

(१७) क. अत्थेकच्चो पुग्गलो अवण्णारहस्स अवण्णं भासिता होति भूतं तच्छं कालेन, नो च खो वण्णारहस्स वण्णं भासिता होति भूतं तच्छं कालेन

A person who speaks in dispraise of an unworthy man expressing the right and just thing at the right time but does not speak in praise of the praiseworthy expressing the right and the just thing at the right time.

ख. अत्थेकच्चो पुग्गलो वण्णारहस्स वण्णं [B.109] भासिता होति भूतं तच्छं कालेन, नो च खो अवण्णारहस्स अवण्णं भासिता होति भूतं तच्छं कालेन

A person who speaks in praise of a praiseworthy man expressing the right and the just thing at the right time, but does not speak in dispraise of the unworthy expressing the right and the just thing at the right time.

ग. अत्थेकच्चो पुग्गलो अवण्णारहस्स च अवण्णं भासिता होति [R.7] भूतं तच्छं कालेन, वण्णारहस्स च[१] वण्णं भासिता होति भूतं तच्छं कालेन

A person who speaks in dispraise of an unworthy man expressing the right and the just thing at the right time and he also speaks in praise of a praiseworthy expressing the right and the just thing at the right time.

घ. अत्थेकच्चो पुग्गलो नेव अवण्णारहस्स अवण्णं भासिता होति भूतं तच्छं कालेन, नो च[२] वण्णारहस्स वण्णं भासिता होति भूतं तच्छं कालेन

A person who neither speaks in dispraise of one unworthy of praise expressing the right and the just thing at the right time, nor he speaks in praise of the praiseworthy expressing the right and the just thing at the right time.

---

१. सी०, रो० पोत्थकेसु नत्थि।

२. पि — रो०।

(१८) क. [S.252] उट्ठानफलूपजीवी, नो पुञ्ञफलूपजीवी One living on the fruits of his exertion and not on the fruits of his previous merit.

ख. पुञ्ञफलूपजीवी, नो उट्ठानफलूपजीवी One living on the fruits of his previous merit, but not on the fruits of his exertion.

ग. उट्ठानफलूपजीवी च पुञ्ञफलूपजीवी च One living on the fruits of his exertion and on the fruits of his previous merit.

घ. नेव उट्ठानफलूपजीवी नो पुञ्ञफलूपजीवी One living neither on the fruits of his own exertion nor on the fruits of his previous merit.

(१९) क. [N.13] तमो तमपरायनो One who is in the dark and tends towards darkness.

ख. तमो जोतिपरायनो One who is in the dark but tends towards light.

ग. जोति तमपरायनो One who is in the light and tends towards darkness.

घ. जोति जोतिपरायनो One who is in the light and tends towards light.

(२०) क. ओणतोणतो The depressed and remain unprogressive.

ख. ओणतुण्णतो The depressed but remain progressive.

ग. उण्णतोणतो The prosperous but remain unprogressive.

घ. उण्णतुण्णतो The prosperous as well as the progressive.

(२१) चत्तारो रुक्खूपमा पुग्गला Four persons comparable to the tree.

(२२) क. रूपप्पमाणो[१] रूपप्पसन्नो One considering and esteeming the outward form.

ख. घोसप्पमाणो[२] घोसप्पसन्नो One considering and esteeming others' words.

ग. लूखप्पमाणो लूखप्पसन्नो One considering and esteeming outward austerity.

घ. धम्मप्पमाणो धम्मप्पसन्नो One considering and esteeming the Law.

(२३) क. अत्थेकच्चो पुग्गलो अत्तहिताय पटिपन्नो होति, नो परहिताय

A person who strives after his own welfare but not after that of others.

ख. अत्थेकच्चो पुग्गलो परहिताय पटिपन्नो होति, नो अत्तहिताय

A person who strives after others' welfare but not after his own.

ग. अत्थेकच्चो पुग्गलो अत्तहिताय चेव पटिपन्नो होति परहिताय च

A person who strives after his own welfare as well as that of others.

घ. अत्थेकच्चो पुग्गलो नेव अत्तहिताय पटिपन्नो होति नो परहिताय

A person who strives neither after his own welfare nor after that of others.

(२४) क. अत्थेकच्चो पुग्गलो अत्तन्तपो होति अत्तपरितापनानुयोगमनुयुत्तो

A person who is self-mortifying and is engaged in practices tending to self-mortification.

ख. अत्थेकच्चो पुग्गलो परन्तपो होति परपरितापनानुयोगमनुयुत्तो

A person who torments others and is engaged in practices tending to torment others.

---

१. रूपप्पमानो — सी० ।

२. घोसप्पमानो — सी० ।

ग. अत्थेकच्चो पुग्गलो अत्तन्तपो च होति [B.110] अत्तपरितापनानुयोगमनुयुत्तो, परन्तपो च परपरितापनानुयोगमनुयुत्तो

A person who is self-mortifying and is engaged in practices tending to self-mortification, and torments others and is engaged in practices tending to torment others.

घ. [N.14; S.254] अत्थेकच्चो पुग्गलो नेव अत्तन्तपो होति न अत्तपरितापनानुयोगमनुयुत्तो, न परन्तपो न परपरितापनानुयोगमनुयुत्तो — सो अनत्तन्तपो अपरन्तपो[१] दिट्ठेव धम्मे निच्छातो निब्बुतो सीतीभूतो[२] सुखप्पटिसंवेदी[३] ब्रह्मभूतेन अत्तना विहरति

A person who is neither self-mortifying nor is engaged in practices tending to self-mortification, and neither torments others nor is engaged in practices tending to torment others, he lives a higher life free from desire, calmed, appeased and happy in his present existence.

(२५) क. सरागो — One possessed of passion.

ख. सदोसो — One possessed of hatred.

ग. समोहो — One possessed of delusion.

घ. समानो — One possessed of pride.

(२६) क. अत्थेकच्चो पुग्गलो लाभी होति अज्झत्तं चेतोसमथस्स, न लाभी अधिपञ्ञाधम्मविपस्सनाय

A person who attains inner tranquillity of mind but not the higher wisdom of insight into things.

ख. [R.8] अत्थेकच्चो पुग्गलो लाभी होति अधिपञ्ञाधम्मविपस्सनाय, न लाभी अज्झत्तं चेतोसमथस्स

१. अपरन्तेहि — रो० ।

२. सीतिभूतो — सी०, रो० ।

३. सुखपटिसंवेदी — सी०, स्या०, रो० ।

A person who attains the higher wisdom of insight into things but not inner tranquillity of mind.

ग. अत्थेकच्चो पुग्गलो लाभी चेव होति अज्झत्तं चेतोसमथस्स, लाभी च अधिपञ्ञाधम्मविपस्सनाय

A person who attains inner tranquillity of mind and the higher wisdom of insight into things.

घ. अत्थेकच्चो पुग्गलो नेव लाभी होति अज्झत्तं चेतोसमथस्स, न लाभी अधिपञ्ञाधम्मविपस्सनाय

A person who attains neither inner tranquillity of mind nor the higher wisdom of insight into things.

(२७) क. अनुसोतगामी पुग्गलो — A person going along the stream.

ख. पटिसोतगामी पुग्गलो — A person going against the stream.

ग. ठितत्तो पुग्गलो — A person remaining stationary.

घ. तिण्णो पारङ्गतो[१] थले तिट्ठति ब्राह्मणो — A Brāhmaṇa who has crossed the stream and has gone to the other shore and is established in fruition.

(२८) क. अप्पस्सुतो,[२] सुतेन अनुपपन्नो — A person who does not act up to what little he has learnt.

ख. अप्पस्सुतो, सुतेन उपपन्नो — A person who acts up to what little he has learnt.

१. पारगतो — सी०, स्या०।

२. अप्पसुतो — रो०, एवमुपरि पि।

ग. [N.15] बहुस्सुतो, सुतेन अनुपपन्नो	A person who, though much learned, does not act up to his learning.
घ. बहुस्सुतो, सुतेन उपपन्नो	A person who is much learned and acts up to his learning.
(२९) क. समणमचलो	A recluse with a firm footing.
ख. समणपदुमो	A red-lotus-like recluse.
ग. समणपुण्डरीको	A white-lotus-like recluse.
घ. समणेसु समणसुखुमालो	A delicate recluse.

(५) पञ्च पुग्गला

Grouping of Human Types by Five

(१) क. [S.256] अत्थेकच्चो पुग्गलो आरभति[१] च विप्पटिसारी च होति, तं च चेतोविमुत्तिं पञ्ञाविमुत्तिं यथाभूतं नप्पजानाति, यत्थस्स ते उप्पन्ना [B.111] पापका अकुसला धम्मा अपरिसेसा निरुज्झन्ति

A person who acts and becomes remorseful but does not experience the emancipation of mind and the emancipation by insight as they really are, wherein the sinful and immoral states that have come into being, can completely cease to be.

ख. अत्थेकच्चो पुग्गलो आरभति न विप्पटिसारी च[२] होति, तं च चेतोविमुत्तिं पञ्ञाविमुत्तिं यथाभूतं नप्पजानाति, यत्थस्स ते उप्पन्ना पापका अकुसला धम्मा अपरिसेसा निरुज्झन्ति

A person who acts but does not become remorseful and does not experience the emancipation of mind and the emancipation by insight as they really are, wherein the sinful and

१. आरम्भति — स्या० ।

२. स्या०, रो० पोत्थकेसु नत्थि ।

immoral states that have come into being, can completely cease to be.

ग. अत्थेकच्चो पुग्गलो नारभति विप्पटिसारी च[1] होति, तं च चेतोविमुत्तिं पञ्ञाविमुत्तिं यथाभूतं नप्पजानाति, यत्थस्स ते उप्पन्ना पापका अकुसला धम्मा अपरिसेसा निरुज्झन्ति

A person who does not act but is remorseful and does not experience the emancipation of mind and the emancipation by insight as they really are, wherein the sinful and immoral states that have come into being, can completely cease to be.

घ. अत्थेकच्चो पुग्गलो नारभति न विप्पटिसारी होति, तं च चेतोविमुत्तिं पञ्ञाविमुत्तिं यथाभूतं नप्पजानाति, यत्थस्स ते उप्पन्ना पापका अकुसला धम्मा अपरिसेसा निरुज्झन्ति

A person who neither acts nor is remorseful and does not experience the emancipation of mind and the emancipation by insight as they really are, wherein the sinful and immoral states that have come into being, can completely cease to be.

ङ. अत्थेकच्चो[2] पुग्गलो नारभति न विप्पटिसारी होति, तं च चेतोविमुत्तिं पञ्ञाविमुत्तिं यथाभूतं पजानाति, यत्थस्स ते उप्पन्ना पापका अकुसला धम्मा अपरिसेसा निरुज्झन्ति[3]

A person who neither acts nor is remorseful and he experiences the emancipation of mind and the emancipation by insight as they really are, wherein the sinful and immoral states that have come into being, can completely cease to be.

---

१. सी० ,स्या० ,रो० पोत्थकेसु नत्थि ।

२. रो० पोत्थके न दिस्सति ।

३. रो० पोत्थके न दिस्सति ।

(२) क. [N.16; R.9] दत्वा अवजानाति	One who despises after giving.
ख. संवासेन अवजानाति	One who despises after living together.
ग. आधेय्यमुखो होति	One with a gape-mouth.
घ. लोलो[१] होति	One who is wobbler.
ङ. मन्दो मोमूहो होति	One who is dull and stupid.
(३) पञ्च योधाजीवूपमा पुग्गला	Five persons comparable to a professional warrior.
(४) पञ्च पिण्डपातिका	Five (persons) who live on alms.
(५) पञ्च खलुपच्छाभत्तिका	Five (persons) refusing to accept food after proper time.
(६) पञ्च एकासनिका	Five (persons) using one kind of seat.
(७) पञ्च पंसुकूलिका	Five (persons) wearing rags collected from refuse heaps.
(८) पञ्च तेचीवरिका	Five (persons) wearing threefold robs.
(९) पञ्च आरञ्ञिका	Five (persons) forest- dwellers.
(१०) पञ्च रुक्खमूलिका	Five who live under a tree.
(११) पञ्च अब्भोकासिका	Five who live under the open sky.
(१२) पञ्च नेसज्जिका	Five always seated or never lie down.
(१३) पञ्च यथासन्थतिका	Five using any seats that are offered.

१. लोको — रो० ।

(१४) पञ्च सोसानिका — Five who dwell in cemeteries.

(६) छ पुग्गला

Grouping of Human Types by Six

(१) क. [B.112; S.258] अत्थेकच्चो पुग्गलो पुब्बे अननुस्सुतेसु धम्मेसु सामं सच्चानि अभिसम्बुज्झति, तत्थ च सब्बञ्ञुतं पापुणाति बलेसु[१] च वसीभावं

A person who himself understands the truths in regard to the doctrines unheard of before, and obtains omniscience thereof as well as mastery over the powers (Balas).

ख. अत्थेकच्चो पुग्गलो पुब्बे अननुस्सुतेसु धम्मेसु सामं सच्चानि अभिसम्बुज्झति, न च तत्थ सब्बञ्ञुतं पापुणाति न च बलेसु[२] वसीभावं

A person who himself understands the truths in regard to the doctrines unheard of before, but does not obtain omniscience thereof as well as mastery over the powers (Balas).

ग. अत्थेकच्चो पुग्गलो पुब्बे अननुस्सुतेसु धम्मेसु सामं सच्चानि अनभिसम्बुज्झति,[३] दिट्ठेव[४] धम्मे दुक्खस्सन्तकरो होति सावकपारमिं च[५] पापुणाति

A person who himself does not understand the truths in regard to the doctrines unheard of before, but puts an end to suffering in his present conditions and attains the perfection of a disciple.

---

१. फलेसु — रो० ।

२. फलेसु — रो० ।

३. अभिसम्बुज्झति — रो० ।

४. दिट्ठे चेव — म० ।

५. सी० पोत्थके नत्थि ।

घ. [N.17] अत्थेकच्चो पुग्गलो पुब्बे अननुस्सुतेसु धम्मेसु सामं सच्चानि अनभिसम्बुज्झति, दिट्ठेव धम्मे दुक्खस्सन्तकरो होति, न च सावकपारमिं पापुणाति

A person who himself does not understand the truths in regard to the doctrines unheard of before, but puts an ends to suffering in his present conditions, but does not attain the perfection of a disciple.

ङ. अत्थेकच्चो पुग्गलो पुब्बे अननुस्सुतेसु धम्मेसु सामं सच्चानि अनभिसम्बुज्झति, न[१] च[२] दिट्ठेव धम्मे दुक्खस्सन्तकरो होति, अनागामी होति अनागन्ता[३] इत्थत्तं

A person who himself does not understand the truths in regard to the doctrines unheard of before, and he does not put an end to suffering in his present conditions, and becomes a never-returner not having to come back to this world.

च. अत्थेकच्चो पुग्गलो पुब्बे अननुस्सुतेसु धम्मेसु सामं सच्चानि अनभिसम्बुज्झति, न च दिट्ठेव धम्मे दुक्खस्सन्तकरो होति, आगामी[४] (सोतापन्नसकदागामी) होति आगन्ता इत्थत्तं

A person who himself does not understand the truths in regard to the doctrines unheard of before, and he does not put an end to suffering in his present conditions, and becomes a stream-attainer and once-returner having to come back to this world.

---

१. रो० पोत्थके नत्थि।

२. रो० पोत्थके नत्थि।

३. अनागन्त्वा — स्या०, रो० ।

४. सोतापन्नसकदागामी — स्या०; सकदागामी — रो० ।

(७) सत्त पुग्गला

Grouping of Human Types by Seven

(१)	[R.10] सत्त उदकूपमा पुग्गला	Seven persons to be compared with those immersed in water.
	क. सकिं निमुग्गो निमुग्गो व होति	One who once drowned is drowned.
	ख. उम्मुज्जित्वा निमुज्जति[1]	One who is drowned after emergence.
	ग. उम्मुज्जित्वा ठितो होति	One who remains stationary after emergence.
	घ. उम्मुज्जित्वा विपस्सति विलोकेति	One who looks around after emergence.
	ङ. उम्मुज्जित्वा पतरति	One who swims up after emergence.
	च. उम्मुज्जित्वा पटिगाधप्पत्तो[2] होति	One who obtains a firm footing after emergence.
	छ. उम्मुज्जित्वा तिण्णो होति पारङ्गतो थले तिट्ठति ब्राह्मणो	One who as a true Brāhmaṇa crosses after emergence and goes to the other shore and establishes himself in fruition.
(२)	क. [B.113] उभतोभागविमुत्तो	One emancipated in both ways.
	ख. पञ्ञाविमुत्तो	One emancipated by way of insight.
	ग. कायसक्खी	The eye-witness.
	घ. दिट्ठिप्पत्तो	One who has won vision.

१. निम्मुज्जति — स्या० ।

२. पटिगाधपत्तो — रो० ।

ङ. सद्धाविमुत्तो — One emancipated by faith.

च. [N.18] धम्मानुसारी — One conforming to the Law.

छ. सद्धानुसारी — One conforming by faith.

(८) अट्ठ पुग्गला

Grouping of Human Types by Eight

(१) [S.260] चत्तारो मग्गसमङ्गिनो, चत्तारो फलसमङ्गिनो पुग्गला।

Four persons identifiable with the path and four identifiable with the fruition.

(९) नव पुग्गला

Grouping of Human Types by Nine

(१) क. सम्मासम्बुद्धो — A Perfectly Enlightened One.

ख. पच्चेकसम्बुद्धो — One Enlightened for himself.

ग. उभतोभागविमुत्तो — One emancipated in both ways.

घ. पञ्ञाविमुत्तो — One emancipated by way of insight.

ङ. कायसक्खी — The eye-witness.

च. दिट्ठिप्पत्तो — One who has won vision.

छ. सद्धाविमुत्तो — One emancipated by faith.

ज. धम्मानुसारी — One conforming to the Law.

झ. सद्धानुसारी — One conforming by faith.

(१०) दस पुग्गला

Grouping of Human Types by Ten

(१) पञ्च पुग्गला इध निट्ठा, पञ्च पुग्गला इध विहाय निट्ठा।

मातिका उद्देसो निट्ठितो।

Five persons reaching perfection here and five reaching perfection hereafter.

Here ends the Table of Matrices.

पठमो परिच्छेदो

मातिकानिद्देसो

१. एककपुग्गलपञ्ञत्ति

(१) समयविमुत्तो पुग्गलो

१. [N.19; R.11; B.114; S.262] कतमो च पुग्गलो समयविमुत्तो ?

इधेकच्चो पुग्गलो कालेन कालं समयेन समयं अट्ठ विमोक्खे कायेन फुसित्वा[१] विहरति, पञ्ञाय चस्स दिस्वा एकच्चे आसवा परिक्खीणा होन्ति । अयं वुच्चति पुग्गलो "समयविमुत्तो" ।

CHAPTER ONE

Description of Matrices

1. Division of Human Types by One

(1) A person who is emancipated at times

1. What sort of person is one emancipated at times?

Here a certain person goes on experiencing the eight stages of emancipation from season to season and from time to time and dwells in touching with the body (Nāmakāya), and he having seen them through insight, some of his sinful tendencies (Āsavas) are completely destroyed. Such a person is said to be emancipated at times.

---

१. फस्सित्वा — सी०, एवमुपरि पि ।

(२) असमयविमुत्तो पुग्गलो

२. कतमो च पुग्गलो असमयविमुत्तो ?

इधेकच्चो पुग्गलो न हेव खो कालेन कालं समयेन समयं अट्ठ विमोक्खे कायेन फुसित्वा विहरति, पञ्ञाय चस्स दिस्वा आसवा परिक्खीणा होन्ति। अयं वुच्चति पुग्गलो "असमयविमुत्तो"। सब्बे पि अरियपुग्गला अरिये विमोक्खे असमयविमुत्ता।

(2) A person who is emancipated not at times

2. What sort of person is one emancipated not (only) at times?

Here a certain person goes on experiencing the eight stages of emancipation though not from season to season and time to time and dwells in touching with the body (Nāmakāya), and he having seen them through insight, his sinful tendencies (Āsavas) are completely destroyed. Such a person is said to be emancipated not (only) at times. Indeed, all persons who are Ariyas (noble) are so emancipated in matters of the higher emancipation.

(३) कुप्पधम्मो पुग्गलो

३. कतमो च पुग्गलो कुप्पधम्मो ?

इधेकच्चो पुग्गलो लाभी होति रूपसहगतानं वा अरूपसहगतानं वा समापत्तीनं। सो च खो न निकामलाभी होति न अकिच्छलाभी न अकसिरलाभी; न यत्थिच्छकं यदिच्छकं यावतिच्छकं समापज्जति पि वुट्ठाति पि। ठानं खो पनेतं विज्जति यं तस्स पुग्गलस्स पमादमागम्म ता समापत्तियो कुप्पेय्युं। अयं वुच्चति पुग्गलो "कुप्पधम्मो"।

(3) A person who is of perturbable nature

3. What sort of person is one of perturbable nature?

Here a certain person obtains the attainments (of ecstatic trance) whether accompanied by an idea of form or by an idea of formlessness, and he does not surely obtain them as he desires, nor without difficulty, nor without toil, neither does he get into, nor get up from them where he desires, when he desires, and as long as he desires; there is this possibility that indolence coming over him should perturb those attainments. Such a person is said to be of perturbable nature.

(४) अकुप्पधम्मो पुग्गलो

४. कतमो च पुग्गलो अकुप्पधम्मो ?

इधेकच्चो पुग्गलो लाभी होति रूपसहगतानं वा अरूपसहगतानं वा समापत्तीनं। सो च खो निकामलाभी होति अकिच्छलाभी अकसिरलाभी; यत्थिच्छकं यदिच्छकं यावतिच्छकं समापज्जति पि वुट्ठाति पि। अट्ठानमेतं अनवकासो यं तस्स पुग्गलस्स पमादमागम्म ता [N.20] समापत्तियो कुप्पेय्युं। अयं वुच्चति पुग्गलो "अकुप्पधम्मो"। सब्बे पि अरियपुग्गला अरिये विमोक्खे अकुप्पधम्मा।

(4) A person who is of imperturbable nature

4. What sort of person is one of imperturbable nature?

Here a certain person obtains the attainment (of ecstatic trance) whether accompanied by an idea of form or by an idea of formlessness, and he surely obtains them as he desires, without difficulty or toil, and he gets into and gets up from them where he desires, when he desires, and as long as he desires; there is no occasion and there is no opening that indolence coming over him should perturb the attainments of that person. Such a person is said to be of imperturbable nature. Indeed, all persons who are Ariyas (noble) are of imperturbable nature in matters of Ariyan emancipation.

(५) परिहानधम्मो पुग्गलो

५. [S.264] कतमो च पुग्गलो परिहानधम्मो ?

इधेकच्चो पुग्गलो लाभी होति रूपसहगतानं वा [R.12] अरूपसहगतानं वा समापत्तीनं। सो च खो न निकामलाभी होति न अकिच्छलाभी न अकसिरलाभी; [B.115] न यत्थिच्छकं यदिच्छकं यावतिच्छकं समापज्जति पि वुट्ठाति पि। ठानं खो पनेतं विज्जति यं सो पुग्गलो पमादमागम्म ताहि समापत्तीहि परिहायेय्य। अयं वुच्चति पुग्गलो "परिहानधम्मो"।

(5) A person who is of fallible nature

5. What sort of person is one of fallible nature?

Here a certain person obtains the attainments whether accompanied by an idea of form or by an idea of formlessness, and he surely does not obtain them as he desires, nor without difficulty, nor without toil, neither does he get into nor get up from them where he desires, when he desires, and as long as he desires; there is this possibility that indolence coming over him should cause him to give up his attainments. Such a person is said to be of fallible nature.

(६) अपरिहानधम्मो पुग्गलो

६. कतमो च पुग्गलो अपरिहानधम्मो ?

इधेकच्चो पुग्गलो लाभी होति रूपसहगतानं वा अरूपसहगतानं वा समापत्तीनं। सो च खो निकामलाभी होति अकिच्छलाभी अकसिरलाभी; यत्थिच्छकं यदिच्छकं यावतिच्छकं समापज्जति पि वुट्ठाति पि। अट्ठानमेतं अनवकासो यं सो पुग्गलो पमादमागम्म ताहि समापत्तीहि परिहायेय्य[१]। अयं वुच्चति पुग्गलो "अपरिहानधम्मो"। सब्बे पि अरियपुग्गला अरिये विमोक्खे अपरिहानधम्मा।

(6) A person who is of infallible nature

6. What sort of person is one of infallible nature?

Here a certain person obtains the attainments whether accompanied by an idea of form or by an idea of formlessness, and he surely obtains them as he

१. परिहारेय्य — रो०।

desires without difficulty and without toil, and he gets into and gets up from them where he desires, when he desires, and as long as he desires; there is no occasion and there is no opening that indolence coming over him should cause him to give up his attainments. Such a person is said to be of infallible nature. Indeed, all persons who are Ariyas (noble) are of infallible nature in matters of Ariyan emancipation.

(७) चेतनाभब्बो पुग्गलो

७. कतमो च पुग्गलो चेतनाभब्बो ?

इधेकच्चो पुग्गलो लाभी होति रूपसहगतानं वा अरूपसहगतानं वा समापत्तीनं। सो च खो न निकामलाभी होति न अकिच्छलाभी न अकसिरलाभी; न[१] यत्थिच्छकं यदिच्छकं यावतिच्छकं समापज्जति पि वुट्ठाति पि। सचे अनुसञ्चेतेति, न[२] परिहायति ताहि समापत्तीहि। सचे न अनुसञ्चेतेति, परिहायति ताहि समापत्तीहि। अयं वुच्चति पुग्गलो "चेतनाभब्बो"।

(7) A person who is competent in will

7. What sort of person is he who is competent in will?

Here a certain person obtains the attainments whether accompanied by an idea of form or by an idea of formlessness, and he does not surely obtain them as he desires, nor without difficulty, nor without toil, neither does he get into not get up from them where he desires, when he desires, and as long as he desires; if he follows this up by willing (not to fall away), he does not fall away from those attainments, if he does not so will, he does fall away from them. Such a person is said to be a person who is competent in will.

---

१. सी० पोत्थके नत्थि।

२. स्या० पोत्थके नत्थि।

(८) अनुरक्खणाभब्बो पुग्गलो

८. कतमो च पुग्गलो अनुरक्खणाभब्बो[१] ?

[N.21] इधेकच्चो पुग्गलो लाभी होति रूपसहगतानं वा अरूपसहगतानं वा समापत्तीनं। सो च खो न निकामलाभी होति न अकिच्छलाभी न अकसिरलाभी; न यत्थिच्छकं यदिच्छकं यावतिच्छकं समापज्जति पि वुट्ठाति पि। सचे अनुरक्खति, न परिहायति ताहि समापत्तीहि। सचे न अनुरक्खति, परिहायति ताहि समापत्तीहि। अयं वुच्चति पुग्गलो "अनुरक्खणाभब्बो"।

(8) A person who is competent in watchfulness

8. What sort of person is he who is competent in watchfulness?

Here a certain person obtains the attainments whether accompanied by an idea of form or by an idea of formlessness, and he does not surely obtain them as he desires, nor without difficulty or toil, neither does he get into nor get up from them where he desires, when he desires, and as long as he desires; if he is watchful, he does not fall away from those attainments; if he is not watchful, he does fall away from them. Such a person is said to be a person who is competent in watchfulness.

(९) पुथुज्जनो पुग्गलो

९. [S. 266] कतमो च पुग्गलो पुथुज्जनो ?

यस्स पुग्गलस्स तीणि संयोजनानि[२] अप्पहीनानि; न च तेसं धम्मानं पहानाय पटिपन्नो। अयं वुच्चति पुग्गलो "पुथुज्जनो"।

(9) A person who is an average person

9. What sort of person is said to be an average person?

---

१. अनुरक्खनाभब्बो — सी०, स्या०, एवमुपरि पि।

२. सञ्ञोजनानि — स्या०, रो०।

The person whose three fetters have not been put away and who is not proceeding to put these away— such a person is said to be an average person.

(१०) गोत्रभू पुग्गलो

१०. कतमो च पुग्गलो गोत्रभू ?

[R.13] येसं धम्मानं समनन्तरा अरियधम्मस्स अवक्कन्ति होति, तेहि धम्मेहि समन्नागतो[१] । अयं वुच्चति पुग्गलो "गोत्रभू" ।

(10) A person who is of the Ariya (noble) family

10. What sort of person is one become of the Ariya (noble) family?

The person who is endowed with those conditions immediately after which there is the advent of the Ariyan (noble) nature— such a person is said to be one become of the Ariya (noble) family.

(११-१२) भयूपरतो अभयूपरतो पुग्गलो

११. [B.116] कतमो च पुग्गलो भयूपरतो ?

सत्त सेक्खा[२] भयूपरता, ये च[३] पुथुज्जना सीलवन्तो । अरहा अभयूपरतो ।

(11-12) A person who is restrained by fear and who is not restrained by fear

11. What sort of person is restrained by fear?

The seven kinds of learners are restrained by fear and those average persons who observe the precepts. The Arahants are not restrained by fear.

(१३) अभब्बागमनो पुग्गलो

१२. कतमो च पुग्गलो अभब्बागमनो ?

---

१. समन्नागतो पुग्गलो — स्या०, रो० ।

२. सेखा — स्या० ।

३. च पुग्गला — स्या० ।

ये ते पुग्गला कम्मावरणेन समन्नागता, किलेसावरणेन समन्नागता, विपाकावरणेन समन्नागता, अस्सद्धा अच्छन्दिका दुप्पञ्ञा एळा,[१] अभब्बा नियामं ओक्कमितुं कुसलेसु धम्मेसु सम्मत्तं । इमे वुच्चन्ति पुग्गला "अभब्बागमना" ।

(13) A person who is incapable of progress

12. What sort of person is incapable of progress?

The persons who are covered with the veil of karma, covered with the veil of evil passions, covered with the veil of the consequences (thereof), who are devoid of faith, wanting in desire, are foolish, faulty, incapable of walking along what is recognised to be the true path in regard to things that are good: these persons are said to be incapable of progress.

(१४) भब्बागमनो पुग्गलो

१३. कतमो च पुग्गलो भब्बागमनो ?

ये ते पुग्गला न कम्मावरणेन समन्नागता न किलेसावरणेन समन्नागता न विपाकावरणेन समन्नागता, सद्धा छन्दिका पञ्ञवन्तो[२] [N.22] अनेळा,[३] भब्बा नियामं ओक्कमितुं कुसलेसु धम्मेसु सम्मत्तं । इमे वुच्चन्ति पुग्गला "भब्बागमना" ।

(14) A person who is capable of progress

13. What sort of person is capable of progress?

The persons who are not covered with the veil of karma, not covered with the veil of evil passions, not covered with the veil of the consequences (thereof), who have faith, who have desire, are wise, pure, capable of walking along what is recognised to be the true path in regard to things that are good: these persons are said to be capable of progress.

---

१. एला — सी० ; जळा — स्या०, रो० ।

२. पञ्ञवन्ता — सी० ।

३. सी०, रो० पोत्थकेसु नत्थि ।

(१५-१६) नियतो अनियतो पुग्गलो

१४. कतमो च पुग्गलो नियतो ?

पञ्च पुग्गला आनन्तरिका[१] ये च मिच्छादिट्ठिका नियता अट्ठ च अरियपुग्गला नियता। अवसेसा पुग्गला अनियता।

(15-16) A person who is with determined destiny and who is with undetermined destiny

14. What sort of person is one with determined destiny?

Five types of persons going forward to hell and those who hold erroneous views are persons with determined destiny. Eight types of noble persons are persons with determined destiny. The remaining persons are with undetermined destiny.

(१७-१८) पटिपन्नको फले ठितो पुग्गलो

१५. कतमो च पुग्गलो पटिपन्नको ?

चत्तारो मग्गसमङ्गिनो पुग्गला पटिपन्नका ; चत्तारो फलसमङ्गिनो पुग्गला फले[२] ठिता[२]।

(17-18) A person who is a path attainer and who is established in the fruition

15. What sort of person is a path-attainer?

The four persons who possess the path are path-attainers. The four persons who possess the fruition stage are established in the fruition.

(१९) समसीसी पुग्गलो

१६. कतमो च पुग्गलो समसीसी ?

यस्स पुग्गलस्स अपुब्बं अचरिमं आसवपरियादानं च होति जीवितपरियादानं च। अयं वुच्चति पुग्गलो "समसीसी"।

---

१. आनन्तरियका — सी०।

२-२. फलेट्ठिता — स्या०।

(19) A person who is equal-headed

16. What sort of person is he who is 'equal-headed'?

The person in whose case no sooner does the termination of sinful tendencies takes place than the life terminates. Such a person is said to be one who is 'equal-headed.'

(२०) ठितकप्पी पुग्गलो

१७. [S.268] कतमो च पुग्गलो ठितकप्पी ?

अयं च पुग्गलो सोतापत्तिफलसच्छिकिरियाय पटिपन्नो। अस्स कप्पस्स च उड्डय्हनवेला। अस्स नेव ताव कप्पो उड्डय्हेय्य यावायं पुग्गलो न सोतापत्तिफलं सच्छिकरोति। अयं वुच्चति पुग्गलो "ठितकप्पी"। [R.14] सब्बे पि मग्गसमङ्गिनो पुग्गला ठितकप्पिनो।

(20) A person who is aeon endures (arrester)

17. What sort of person is one for whom an aeon endures?

Should such a person strive for realisation of the fruition stage of a stream-attainer, and should it then be the time for the conflagration of the existing aeon, the aeon must not be burnt up until this person realised the desired state: this person is said to be one for whom an aeon endures. All persons who possess the path are such.

(२१-२२) अरियो अनरियो पुग्गलो

१८. कतमो च पुग्गलो अरियो ?

अट्ठ अरियपुग्गला अरिया। अवसेसा पुग्गला अनरिया।

(21-22) A person who is an Ariya (noble) and who is not an Ariya (noble)

18. What sort of person is an Ariya (noble)?

The eight types of Ariyan persons are the Ariyas. The remaining persons are not Ariyas.

(२३-२५) सेक्खो असेक्खो नेवसेक्खनासेक्खो पुग्गलो

१९. [B.117] कतमो च पुग्गलो सेक्खो ?

चत्तारो मग्गसमङ्गिनो तयो फलसमङ्गिनो पुग्गला "सेक्खा"। अरहा असेक्खो। अवसेसा पुग्गला नेवसेक्खनासेक्खा।

(23-25) A person who is learner, non-learner, neither learner nor non-learner

19. What sort of person is a learner?

The four persons who possess the path and the three persons who possess the fruition are learners. Arahants are non-learners. The remaining persons are neither learners nor non-learners.

(२६) तेविज्जो पुग्गलो

२०. [N.23] कतमो च पुग्गलो तेविज्जो ?

तीहि विज्जाहि समन्नागतो पुग्गलो "तेविज्जो"।

(26) A person who is a master of threefold lore

20. What sort of person is a master of threefold lore?

A person having three vijjās is a person endowed with the threefold lore.

(२७) छळभिञ्ञो पुग्गलो

२१. कतमो च पुग्गलो छळभिञ्ञो ?

छहि अभिञ्ञाहि समन्नागतो पुग्गलो "छळभिञ्ञो"।

(27) A person who is a possessor of the six superknowledges

21. What sort of person is a possessor of the six superknowledges?

A person having these is a person endowed with six superknowledges (supernormal exercise of thought and will).

(२८) सम्मासम्बुद्धो पुग्गलो

२२. कतमो च पुग्गलो सम्मासम्बुद्धो ?

इधेकच्चो पुग्गलो पुब्बे अननुस्सुतेसु धम्मेसु सामं सच्चानि अभिसम्बुज्झति ; तत्थ च सब्बञ्ञुतं पापुणाति, बलेसु[१] च वसीभावं । अयं वुच्चति पुग्गलो "सम्मासम्बुद्धो" ।

(28) A person who is a Perfectly Enlightened One

22. What sort of person is a Perfectly Enlightened One?

Here a certain person who himself thoroughly understands the truths in regard to doctrines unheard of before, and attains omniscience therein, as well as mastery over the powers (Balas)— this sort of person is said to be a Perfectly Enlightened One.

(२९) पच्चेकसम्बुद्धो पुग्गलो

२३. कतमो च पुग्गलो पच्चेकसम्बुद्धो ?

इधेकच्चो पुग्गलो पुब्बे अननुस्सुतेसु धम्मेसु सामं सच्चानि अभिसम्बुज्झति ; न च तत्थ सब्बञ्ञुतं पापुणाति, न च बलेसु वसीभावं । अयं वुच्चति पुग्गलो "पच्चेकसम्बुद्धो" ।

(29) A person who is Enlightened for himself

23. What sort of person is Enlightened himself?

Here a certain person himself thoroughly understands the truths in regard to doctrines unheard of before, but attains neither omniscience nor mastery over the powers (Balas) thereof— this sort of person is said to be one Enlightened for himself.

---

१. फलेसु — रो० ।

(३०) उभतोभागविमुत्तो पुग्गलो

२४. कतमो च पुग्गलो उभतोभागविमुत्तो ?

इधेकच्चो पुग्गलो अट्ठ विमोक्खे कायेन फुसित्वा विहरति ; पञ्ञाय चस्स दिस्वा आसवा परिक्खीणा होन्ति । अयं वुच्चति पुग्गलो "उभतोभागविमुत्तो" ।

(30) A person who is emancipated in both ways

24. What sort of person is emancipated in both ways?

Here a certain person goes on himself experiencing the eight stages of emancipation, and dwells in touching with the body (Nāmakāya), and having seen them through insight, his sinful tendencies (Āsavas) are completely destroyed. This sort of person is said to be emancipated in both ways.

(३१) पञ्ञाविमुत्तो पुग्गलो

२५. [S.270] कतमो च पुग्गलो पञ्ञाविमुत्तो ?

इधेकच्चो पुग्गलो न हेव खो अट्ठ विमोक्खे कायेन फुसित्वा विहरति ; पञ्ञाय चस्स दिस्वा आसवा परिक्खीणा होन्ति। अयं वुच्चति पुग्गलो "पञ्ञाविमुत्तो" ।

(31) A person who is emancipated by way of insight

25. What sort of person is emancipated by way of insight?

Here a certain person without experiencing the eight stages of emancipation, and dwells in touching with the body (Nāmakāya), but having perceived them through insight, has his sinful tendencies (Āsavas) completely destroyed. This sort of person is said to be emancipated by insight.

(३२) कायसक्खी पुग्गलो

२६. [N.24] कतमो च पुग्गलो कायसक्खी ?

इधेकच्चो पुग्गलो अट्ठ विमोक्खे कायेन फुसित्वा [R.15] विहरति ; पञ्ञाय चस्स दिस्वा एकच्चे आसवा परिक्खीणा होन्ति । अयं वुच्चति पुग्गलो "कायसक्खी" ।

(32) A person who is an eye-witness

26. What sort of person is an 'eye-witness'?

Here when a certain person lives experiencing the eight stages of emancipation, and dwells in touching with the body (Nāmakāya), and having seen them through insight, some of his sinful tendencies (Āsavas) are completely destroyed. This sort of person is said to be an 'eye-witness'.

(३३) दिट्ठिप्पत्तो पुग्गलो

२७. कतमो च पुग्गलो दिट्ठिप्पत्तो ?

इधेकच्चो पुग्गलो "इदं दुक्खं"ति यथाभूतं पजानाति, "अयं दुक्खसमुदयो"ति यथाभूतं पजानाति, "अयं दुक्खनिरोधो"ति यथाभूतं पजानाति, "अयं दुक्खनिरोधगामिनी पटिपदा"ति यथाभूतं पजानाति । तथागतप्पवेदिता [B.118] चस्स धम्मा पञ्ञाय वोदिट्ठा होन्ति वोचरिता । पञ्ञाय चस्स दिस्वा एकच्चे आसवा परिक्खीणा होन्ति । अयं वुच्चति पुग्गलो "दिट्ठिप्पत्तो" ।

(33) A person who has won vision

27. What sort of person is one who has won vision?

Here a certain person truly understands that "this is suffering", truly understands that "this is the origin of suffering", truly understands that "this is the cessation of suffering", and truly understands that "this is the path leading to the cessation of suffering". The doctrines promulgated by the *Tathāgata* are perceived by him through insight as well as practised; and having seen them through insight, some of his sinful tendencies are completely extinct. This sort of person is said to be one who has won vision.

(३४) सद्धाविमुत्तो पुग्गलो

२८. कतमो च पुग्गलो सद्धाविमुत्तो ?

इधेकच्चो पुग्गलो "इदं दुक्खं"ति यथाभूतं पजानाति, "अयं दुक्खसमुदयो"ति यथाभूतं पजानाति, "अयं दुक्खनिरोधो"ति यथाभूतं पजानाति, "अयं दुक्खनिरोधगामिनी पटिपदा"ति यथाभूतं पजानाति। तथागतप्पवेदिता चस्स धम्मा पञ्ञाय वोदिट्ठा होन्ति वोचरिता। पञ्ञाय चस्स दिस्वा एकच्चे आसवा परिक्खीणा होन्ति, नो च खो यथा दिट्ठिप्पत्तस्स। अयं वुच्चति पुग्गलो "सद्धाविमुत्तो"।

(34) A person who is emancipated by faith

28. What sort of person is emancipated by faith?

Here a certain person truly understands that "this is suffering," truly understands that "this is the origin of suffering," truly understands that "this is the cessation of suffering," and truly understands that "this is the path leading to the cessation of suffering." The doctrines promulgated by the *Tathāgata* are perceived by him through insight as well as practised, and having seen them through insight, some of his sinful tendencies are completely destroyed, though not in the same way as in the case of one who has won vision. This sort of person is said to be one emancipated by faith.

(३५) धम्मानुसारी पुग्गलो

२९. कतमो च पुग्गलो धम्मानुसारी ?

यस्स पुग्गलस्स सोतापत्तिफलसच्छिकिरियाय पटिपन्नस्स पञ्ञिन्द्रियं अधिमत्तं होति, पञ्ञावाहिं पञ्ञापुब्बङ्गमं अरियमग्गं भावेति। अयं वुच्चति पुग्गलो "धम्मानुसारी"। सोतापत्तिफलसच्छिकिरियाय पटिपन्नो पुग्गलो धम्मानुसारी फले ठितो दिट्ठिप्पत्तो।

(35) A person who is one conforming to the Law

29. What sort of person is 'one conforming to the Law'?

The faculty of insight of a person proceeding to realise the fruition stage of 'stream-attaining' develops to a large extent. He cultivates the Noble Path carrying with it insight, preceded by insight— this sort of person is said to be 'one conforming to the Law.' Such a person practising the fruition stage of a stream-attainer is one conforming to the Law; while the same person established in the fruition is one who has won vision.

(३६) सद्धानुसारी पुग्गलो

३०. [S.272] कतमो च पुग्गलो सद्धानुसारी ?

[N.25] यस्स पुग्गलस्स सोतापत्तिफलसच्छिकिरियाय पटिपन्नस्स सद्धिन्द्रियं अधिमत्तं होति, सद्धावाहिं[१] सद्धापुब्बङ्गमं अरियमग्गं भावेति। अयं वुच्चति पुग्गलो "सद्धानुसारी"। सोतापत्तिफलसच्छिकिरियाय पटिपन्नो पुग्गलो सद्धानुसारी फले ठितो सद्धाविमुत्तो।

(36) A person who is one conforming by faith

30. What sort of person is 'one conforming by faith'?

The believing faculty of a person proceeding to realise the fruition stage of 'stream-attaining' develops to a large extent. He cultivates the Noble Path carrying with it faith, preceded by faith— this sort of person is said to be 'one conforming by faith.' Such a person striving after the fruition stage of a stream-attainer is one conforming by faith; while the same person established in the fruition is emancipated by faith.

(३७) सत्तक्खत्तुपरमो पुग्गलो

३१. कतमो च पुग्गलो सत्तक्खत्तुपरमो ?

इधेकच्चो पुग्गलो तिण्णं संयोजनानं परिक्खया [R.16] सोतापन्नो[२] होति अविनिपातधम्मो नियतो सम्बोधिपरायनो[३]। सो सत्तक्खत्तुं देवे च मानुसे[४]

---

१. पञ्ञावाहि — सी०, एवमुपरि पि।

२. पटिपन्नो — रो०।

३. सम्बोधिपरायणो — सी०।

४. मनुस्से — सी०; मानुस्से — रो०।

च सन्धावित्वा संसरित्वा दुक्खस्सन्तं करोति। अयं वुच्चति पुग्गलो "सत्तक्खत्तुपरमो"।

(37) A person who undergoes rebirth seven times

31. What sort of person is he who undergoes rebirth (not more than) seven times?

Here a certain person, having completely destroyed the three fetters, becomes a 'stream-attainer'; he is no more liable to fall into a woeful state, but is destined to succeed and has enlightenment as his final end or aim; he running on and transmigrating seven times amongst devas and men makes an end of suffering. Such a person is said to be one not undergoing rebirth more than seven times.

(३८) कोलङ्कोलो पुग्गलो

३२. कतमो च पुग्गलो कोलङ्कोलो ?

इधेकच्चो पुग्गलो तिण्णं संयोजनानं परिक्खया सोतापन्नो होति अविनिपातधम्मो [B.119] नियतो सम्बोधिपरायनो। सो द्वे वा तीणि वा कुलानि सन्धावित्वा संसरित्वा दुक्खस्सन्तं करोति। अयं वुच्चति पुग्गलो "कोलङ्कोलो"।

(38) A person who transmigrates from family to family

32. What sort of person is he who transmigrates from family to good family?

Here a certain person having completely destroyed the three fetters, becomes a 'stream-attainer'; he is no more liable to fall into a woeful state, but is destined to succeed, and has enlightenment as his final end or aim; he running on and transmigrating through two or three good families makes an end of suffering. Such a person is said to be one who migrates from family to good family.

(३९) एकबीजी पुग्गलो

३३. कतमो च पुग्गलो एकबीजी ?

इधेकच्चो पुग्गलो तिण्णं संयोजनानं परिक्खया सोतापन्नो होति अविनिपातधम्मो नियतो सम्बोधिपरायनो। सो एकंयेव[१] मानुसकं[२] भवं निब्बत्तेत्वा दुक्खस्सन्तं करोति। अयं वुच्चति पुग्गलो "एकबीजी"।

(39) A person who is single-seeded

33. What sort of person is 'single-seeded'?

Here a certain person, having completely destroyed the three fetters, becomes a 'stream-attainer'; he is no more liable to fall into a woeful state, but is destined to succeed and has enlightenment as his final end or aim; he having returned to the state of human existence makes an end of suffering. Such a person is said to be 'single-seeded.'

(४०) सकदागामी पुग्गलो

३४. कतमो च पुग्गलो सकदागामी?

इधेकच्चो पुग्गलो तिण्णं संयोजनानं परिक्खया रागदोसमोहानं तनुत्ता सकदागामी होति, सकिदेव इमं लोकं आगन्त्वा दुक्खस्सन्तं करोति। अयं वुच्चति पुग्गलो "सकदागामी"।

(40) A person who is a once-returner

34. What sort of person is a 'once-returner'?

Here a certain person, having completely destroyed the three fetters, having weakened passions, hatred and delusion, becomes a once-returner; coming back once only to this world, he makes an end of suffering. Such a person is said to be a 'once-returner.'

(४१) अनागामी पुग्गलो

३५. [N.26] कतमो च पुग्गलो अनागामी?

इधेकच्चो पुग्गलो पञ्चन्नं ओरम्भागियानं संयोजनानं परिक्खया ओपपातिको होति तत्थ परिनिब्बायी अनावत्तिधम्मो तस्मा लोका। अयं वुच्चति पुग्गलो "अनागामी"।

---

१. एतंयेव — रो०।

२. मानुस्सकं — रो०।

(41) A person who is never-returner

35. What sort of person is a 'never-returner'?

Here a certain person, having completely destroyed the five fetters causing rebirth in the lower worlds, becomes a 'being of apparitional rebirth'; attaining the final release in the self-same state, he is not liable to return from that region. Such a person is said to be a 'never-returner.'

(४२) अन्तरापरिनिब्बायी पुग्गलो

३६. [S.274] कतमो च पुग्गलो अन्तरापरिनिब्बायी ?

इधेकच्चो पुग्गलो पञ्चन्नं ओरम्भागियानं संयोजनानं परिक्खया ओपपातिको होति तत्थ परिनिब्बायी अनावत्तिधम्मो तस्मा लोका। सो उपपन्नं[१] वा समनन्तरा अप्पत्तं वा वेमज्झं आयुप्पमाणं अरियमग्गं सञ्जनेति उपरिट्ठिमानं संयोजनानं पहानाय। अयं वुच्चति पुग्गलो "अन्तरापरिनिब्बायी"।

(42) A person who attains Nirvāṇa before reaching the middle of the term of life in the Brahma World

36. What sort of person is one who dies and attains Nirvāṇa before half the age he should have lived in a Brahma World expires?

Here a certain person, having completely destroyed the five fetters, causing rebirth into the lower worlds, becomes a 'being of apparitional rebirth'; attaining the final release in the self-same state, he is not liable to return from that region; he, either immediately after his advent, or before reaching the middle of this span of life, brings forth the Noble Path that so he may put away the fetters of the higher nature. Such a person is said to be one who dies and attains Nirvāṇa before half the age he should have lived in a Brahma World expires.

---

१. उप्पन्नं — सी०, स्या०।

(४३) उपहच्चपरिनिब्बायी पुग्गलो

३७. कतमो च पुग्गलो उपहच्चपरिनिब्बायी ?

इधेकच्चो पुग्गलो पञ्चन्नं ओरम्भागियानं [R.17] संयोजनानं परिक्खया ओपपातिको होति तत्थ परिनिब्बायी अनावत्तिधम्मो तस्मा लोका। सो अतिक्कमित्वा वेमज्झं आयुप्पमाणं उपहच्च वा कालकिरियं[१] अरियमग्गं सञ्जनेति उपरिट्ठिमानं संयोजनानं पहानाय। अयं वुच्चति पुग्गलो "उपहच्चपरिनिब्बायी"।

(43) A person who is a term-curtailing decedent

37. What sort of person is a 'term-curtailing decedent'?

Here a certain person, having completely destroyed the five fetters, causing rebirth in the lower worlds, becomes a 'being of apparitional rebirth'; attaining the final release in the self-same state, not liable to return from that region; he stepping out of the middle of the span of his life and advancing towards decease brings forth the Noble Path that so he may but away the fetters of the higher nature. Such a person is said to be a 'term-curtailing decedent'.

(४४) असङ्खारपरिनिब्बायी पुग्गलो

३८. कतमो च पुग्गलो असङ्खारपरिनिब्बायी ?

इधेकच्चो पुग्गलो पञ्चन्नं ओरम्भागियानं संयोजनानं परिक्खया ओपपातिको होति तत्थ [B.120] परिनिब्बायी अनावत्तिधम्मो तस्मा लोका। सो असङ्खारेन अरियमग्गं सञ्जनेति उपरिट्ठिमानं संयोजनानं पहानाय। अयं वुच्चति पुग्गलो "असङ्खारपरिनिब्बायी"।

(44) A person who is automatically decedent

38. What sort of person is 'automatically decedent'?

Here a certain person having completely destroyed the five fetters, causing rebirth in the lower worlds, becomes a 'being of apparitional rebirth'; attaining the final release in the self-same state, not liable to return

---

१. काळकिरियं — सी०।

from that region; he automatically brings forth the Noble Path that so he may put away the fetters of the higher nature. Such a person is said to be 'automatically decedent.'

(४५) ससङ्खारपरिनिब्बायी पुग्गलो

३९. कतमो च पुग्गलो ससङ्खारपरिनिब्बायी ?

[N.27] इधेकच्चो पुग्गलो पञ्चन्नं ओरम्भागियानं संयोजनानं परिक्खया ओपपातिको होति तत्थ परिनिब्बायी अनावत्तिधम्मो तस्मा लोका। सो ससङ्खारेन अरियमग्गं सञ्जनेति उपरिट्ठिमानं संयोजनानं पहानाय। अयं वुच्चति पुग्गलो "ससङ्खारपरिनिब्बायी"।

(45) A person who is attaining Nirvāṇa through strenuous exertion

39. What sort of person is one attaining Nirvāṇa through strenuous exertion?

Here a certain person, having completely destroyed the five fetters, causing rebirth in the lower worlds, becomes a 'being of apparitional rebirth'; attaining the final release in the self-same state, not liable to return from that region; he by a strenuous effort of his will produces the Noble Path with a view to putting away the fetters of the higher nature. Such a person is said to be one attaining Nirvāṇa through strenuous exertion.

(४६) उद्धंसोतो अकनिट्ठगामी पुग्गलो

४०. कतमो च पुग्गलो उद्धंसोतो अकनिट्ठगामी ?

इधेकच्चो पुग्गलो पञ्चन्नं ओरम्भागियानं संयोजनानं परिक्खया ओपपातिको होति तत्थ परिनिब्बायी अनावत्तिधम्मो तस्मा लोका। सो अविहा चुतो अतप्पं गच्छति, अतप्पा चुतो सुदस्सं गच्छति, सुदस्सा चुतो सुदस्सिं गच्छति, सुदस्सिया[१] चुतो अकनिट्ठं गच्छति; अकनिट्ठे अरियमग्गं सञ्जनेति उपरिट्ठिमानं संयोजनानं पहानाय। अयं वुच्चति पुग्गलो "उद्धंसोतो अकनिट्ठगामी"।

---

१. सुदस्सा — सी०।

(46) A person who is one proceeding upstream to the Akaniṭṭha region

40. What sort of person is one proceeding upstream to the Akaniṭṭha region?

Here a certain person, having completely destroyed the five fetters, causing rebirth, in the lower region, becomes a 'being of apparitional rebirth'; attaining the final release in the self-same state, not liable to return from that region; he having deceased from Aviha (the immobile gods) goes to Atappa (serene gods), having deceased from Atappa goes to Sudassa (beautiful gods), having deceased from Sudassa goes to Sudassi (clearsighted gods), having deceased from Sudassi goes to Akaniṭṭha (the supreme gods), in the Akaniṭṭha abode he brings forth the Noble Path that so he may put away the fetters of the higher nature. Such a person is said to be one proceeding upstream to the Akaniṭṭha region.

(४७-४८) सोतापन्नो सोतापत्तिफलसच्छिकिरियाय पटिपन्नो पुग्गलो

४१. कतमो[१] च पुग्गलो सोतापन्नो सोतापत्तिफलसच्छिकिरियाय पटिपन्नो[१] ?

[S.276] तिण्णं संयोजनानं पहानाय पटिपन्नो पुग्गलो सोतापत्तिफलसच्छिकिरियाय पटिपन्नो। यस्स पुग्गलस्स तीणि संयोजनानि पहीनानि— अयं वुच्चति पुग्गलो "सोतापन्नो"।

(47-48) A person who is a stream-attainer and who is one striving for realisation of the fruition stage

41. What sort of person is a 'stream-attainer', and what sort of person is one striving for realisation of the fruition stage?

१-१. सी०, रो० पोत्थकेसु नत्थि।

A person who works for putting away the three fetters is one working for realisation of the fruition stage of a 'stream-attainer'; the person whose three fetters have been put away is said to be a 'stream-attainer'.

(४९-५०) सकदागामी सकदागामिफलसच्छिकिरियाय पटिपन्नो पुग्गलो

४२. कामरागब्यापादानं तनुभावाय पटिपन्नो पुग्गलो सकदागामिफलसच्छिकिरियाय पटिपन्नो। यस्स पुग्गलस्स कामरागब्यापादा तनुभूता— अयं वुच्चति पुग्गलो "सकदागामी"।

(49-50) A person who is a once-returner and who is one striving for realisation of the fruition stage

42. (What sort of person is a 'once-returner', and what sort of person is one striving for realisation of the fruition stage?)

A person who is working for the destruction of attachment to sensual pleasures and malevolence is one working for realisation of the fruition stage of a 'once-returner'; the person whose attachment to sensual pleasures and malevolence has been destroyed is to be a 'once-returner'.

(५१-५२) अनागामी अनागामिफलसच्छिकिरियाय पटिपन्नो पुग्गलो

४३. कामरागब्यापादानं अनवसेसप्पहानाय पटिपन्नो [R.18] पुग्गलो अनागामिफलसच्छिकिरियाय पटिपन्नो। यस्स पुग्गलस्स कामरागब्यापादा अनवसेसा पहीना— अयं वुच्चति पुग्गलो "अनागामी"।

(51-52) A person who is a never-returner and who is one striving for realisation of the fruition stage

43. (What sort of person is a 'never-returner', and what sort of person is one striving for realisation of the fruition stage?)

A person working for putting away the attachment to sensual pleasures and malevolence without a residuum is one working for realisation of the fruition stage of a 'non-returner.' The person whose attachment to sensual pleasure and malevolence has been entirely put away is said to be a 'never-returner.'

(५३-५४) अरहा अरहत्तफलसच्छिकिरियाय पटिपन्नो पुग्गलो

४४. [N.28] रूपरागअरूपरागमानउद्धच्चअविज्जाय अनवसेसप्पहानाय पटिपन्नो पुग्गलो अरहत्तफलसच्छिकिरियाय पटिपन्नो। यस्स पुग्गलस्स [B.121] रूपरागो अरूपरागो मानो उद्धच्चं अविज्जा अनवसेसा पहीना— अयं वुच्चति पुग्गलो "अरहा"।

एककनिद्देसो निट्ठितो।

(53-54) A person who is an Arahant and who is one striving for realisation of the fruition stage

44. (What sort of person is an Arahant, and what sort of person is one striving for realisation of the fruition stage?)

A person working for putting away attachment to form and the formless, to pride, haughtiness, and ignorance without any residuum is one working for the fruition stage of Arahantship. The person whose attachment to form and the formless, to pride, haughtiness and ignorance has been entirely put away is said to be an Arahant.

Here ends the specification of grouping by one.

दुतियो परिच्छेदो

२. दुकपुग्गलपञ्ञत्ति[1]

(१. क) कोधनो पुग्गलो

१. [N.29; S.278] कतमो च पुग्गलो कोधनो ?

तत्थ कतमो कोधो ?

यो कोधो कुज्झना कुज्झितत्तं दोसो दुस्सना[2] दुस्सितत्तं[3] ब्यापत्ति ब्यापज्जना[4] ब्यापज्जितत्तं[5] विरोधो पटिविरोधो चण्डिक्कं[6] असुरोपो अनत्तमनता चित्तस्स— अयं वुच्चति 'कोधो'। यस्स पुग्गलस्स अयं कोधो अप्पहीनो[7]— अयं वुच्चति पुग्गलो "कोधनो"।

CHAPTER TWO

2. Divison of Human Types by Two

(1. A) A person who is angry

1. What sort of person is angry?

What then is anger?

---

१. दुकनिद्देसो — सी०, स्या०; द्वे पुग्गला — रो०।

२. दूसना — स्या०।

३. दूसितत्तं — स्या०।

४. व्यापज्जना — सी०, रो०, एवमुपरि पि।

५. रो० पोत्थके नत्थि।

६. चण्डित्तं — रो०।

७. अप्पहीणो — सी०।

That which is anger, being angry, and the state of being angry, hatred, hating, hatefulness, malice, the act of being malicious, maliciousness, hostility, enmity, rudeness, abruptness, resentment of mind— this is called anger. He who has not got rid of this anger is said to be an angry person.

(ख) उपनाही पुग्गलो

२. कतमो च पुग्गलो उपनाही ?

तत्थ कतमो उपनाहो ?

पुब्बकालं कोधो अपरकालं उपनाहो। यो एवरूपो उपनाहो उपनय्हना[१] उपनय्हितत्तं[२] अट्ठपना[३] ठपना सण्ठपना अनुसंसन्दना[४] अनुप्पबन्धना[५] दळ्हीकम्मं[६] कोधस्स— अयं वुच्चति 'उपनाहो'। यस्स पुग्गलस्स अयं[७] उपनाहो अप्पहीनो— अयं वुच्चति पुग्गलो "उपनाही"।

(B) A person who is vengeful

2. What sort of person is said to be vengeful?

What then is vengeance?

First comes anger, after that comes vengeance. That which is vengeance as this is, the act of revenging and the state of being vengeful, the fixing, settling, establishing, grounding and following up, the violent act of anger is called vengeance. He whose vengeance remains unremoved is said to be vengeful.

---

१. उपनहना — स्या०।
२. उपनाहितत्तं — स्या०।
३. अठपना — रो०।
४. अनुपसण्ठपना — रो०।
५. अनुपबन्धना — रो०।
६. दळ्हिकम्मं — रो०।
७. रो० पोत्थके नत्थि।

(२. क) मक्खी पुग्गलो

३. कतमो च पुग्गलो मक्खी ?

तत्थ कतमो मक्खो ?

यो मक्खो मक्खायना[१] मक्खायितत्तं[२] निट्ठुरियं[३] निट्ठुरियकम्मं[४]— अयं वुच्चति 'मक्खो'। [N.30] यस्स पुग्गलस्स अयं मक्खो अप्पहीनो— अयं वुच्चति पुग्गलो "मक्खी"।

(2. A) A person who is a slanderer

3. What sort of person is a slanderer?

What then is slander?

That which is slander, that which is slandering, that which is the state of being a slanderer, that which is hypocrisy, work of hypocrisy. This is said to be slander. He in whom this slander remains unremoved is said to be a slanderer.

(ख) पळासी पुग्गलो

४. कतमो च पुग्गलो पळासी[५] ?

तत्थ कतमो पळासो ?

यो पळासो पळासायना [R.19] पळासायितत्तं पळासाहारो[६] विवादट्ठानं युद्धग्गाहो[७] अप्पटिनिस्सग्गो[८]— अयं वुच्चति 'पळासो'। यस्स पुग्गलस्स अयं पळासो अप्पहीना— अयं वुच्चति पुग्गलो "पळासी"।

---

१. मक्खीयना — सी॰।

२. मक्खीयितत्तं — सी॰।

३. निद्धुनीयं — रो॰।

४. निद्धुनीयकम्मं — रो॰।

५. पलासी — सी॰, स्या॰, एवमुपरि पि।

६. पळासाकारो — रो॰।

७. युगग्गाहो — ना॰, म॰।

८. अपरिनिस्सग्गो — रो॰।

(B) A person who is quarrelsome

4. What sort of person is quarrelsome?

What then is quarrelling?

That which is a quarrel, that which is quarrelling, and that which is quarrelsomeness, the way of quarrel, the point of dispute, the coming to fight, unrelenting— this is called quarrelling. A person in whom such quarrelling remains unremoved is said to be a quarrelsome person.

(३. क) इस्सुकी पुग्गलो

५. [B.122] कतमो च पुग्गलो इस्सुकी ?

तत्थ कतमा इस्सा ?

या परलाभसक्कारगरुकारमाननवन्दनपूजनासु इस्सा इस्सायना इस्सायितत्तं उसूया[१] उसूयना[२] उसूयितत्तं[३]— अयं वुच्चति 'इस्सा'। यस्स पुग्गलस्स अयं इस्सा अप्पहीना— अयं वुच्चति पुग्गलो "इस्सुकी"।

(3. A) A person who is envious

5. What sort of person is envious?

What then is envy?

That which is envying, enviousness, jealousy, regarding with jealousy, the state of being jealous with regard to the gain, honour, respect, reverence, salutation and worship paid to others— this is said to be envy. A person in whom this envy is unremoved is said to be envious person.

(ख) मच्छरी पुग्गलो

६. कतमो च पुग्गलो मच्छरी ?

तत्थ कतमं मच्छरियं ?

---

१. उस्सुया — रो॰ ।

२. उस्सुयना — रो॰ ।

३. उस्सुयितत्तं — रो॰ ।

पञ्च मच्छरियानि— आवासमच्छरियं, कुलमच्छरियं, लाभमच्छरियं, वण्णमच्छरियं, धम्ममच्छरियं। यं एवरूपं मच्छेरं[१] मच्छरायना मच्छरायितत्तं वेविच्छं— कदरियं कटुकञ्चुकता अग्गहितत्तं चित्तस्स— इदं वुच्चति 'मच्छरियं'। [N.31] यस्स पुग्गलस्स इदं मच्छरियं अप्पहीनं— अयं वुच्चति पुग्गलो "मच्छरी"।

(B) A person who is avaricious

6. What sort of person is avaricious?

What is meant by avarice?

There are five forms of avarice— avarice with regard to residence, descent, gain, beauty, and merit (dhamma), that which is avarice of this nature, harbouring avarice, avariciousness, inordinate longing, covetousness, presenting a harsh appearance, unrestraint of mind— this is said to be avarice. The person in whom this avarice remains unremoved is said to be an avaricious person.

(४. क) सठो पुग्गलो

७. [S.280] कतमो च पुग्गलो सठो[२] ?

तत्थ कतमं साठेय्यं ?

इधेकच्चो सठो[३] होति परिसठो। यं तत्थ सठं सठता साठेय्यं कक्करता[४] कक्करियं[५] परिक्खतता[६] पारिक्खत्तियं[७]— इदं वुच्चति 'साठेय्यं'। यस्स पुग्गलस्स इदं साठेय्यं अप्पहीनं— अयं वुच्चति पुग्गलो "सठो"।

१. मच्छरियं — रो०।
२. सथो — स्या०, एवमुपरि पि।
३. पुग्गलो सठो — सी०; पुग्गलो सथो — स्या०।
४. कक्खलता — स्या०।
५. कक्खलियं — स्या०।
६. परिक्खतता — स्या०, रो०।
७. परिक्खत्तियं — सी०, रो०; परिक्खतियं — स्या०।

(4. A) A person who is crafty

7. What sort of person is crafty?

What is meant by craftiness?

Here a person becomes crafty and cunning. That which is craft, craftiness, stage of being crafty, hardness, toughness, counterfeit, sham— this is said to be craftiness. The person in whom this craftiness remains unremoved is said to be a crafty person.

(ख) मायावी पुग्गलो

८. कतमो च पुग्गलो मायावी ?

तत्थ कतमा माया ?

इधेकच्चो कायेन दुच्चरितं चरित्वा वाचाय दुच्चरितं चरित्वा मनसा दुच्चरितं चरित्वा तस्स पटिच्छादनहेतु पापिकं[१] इच्छं पणिदहति । "मा मं जञ्ञा" ति इच्छति । "मा मं जञ्ञा" ति सङ्कप्पति[२] । "मा मं जञ्ञा" ति वाचं भासति । "मा मं जञ्ञा" ति कायेन परक्कमति । या एवरूपा माया मायाविता अच्चासरा[३] वञ्चना निकति विकिरणा[४] परिहरणा गूहना[५] परिगूहना[६] छादना पटिच्छादना[७] अनुत्तानीकम्मं अनाविकम्मं वोच्छादना[८] पापकिरिया— अयं वुच्चति 'माया' । यस्स पुग्गलस्स अयं माया अप्पहीना— अयं वुच्चति पुग्गलो "मायावी" ।

(B) A person who is deceitful

8. What sort of person is deceitful?

What is deception in that case?

---

१. पापकं — रो० ।

२. सङ्कप्पेति — सी०, रो० ।

३. अच्चसरा — सी०; अच्छादना — रो० ।

४. निकिरणा — सी०; विकीरणा — स्या०; निकरणा — रो० ।

५. गुहना — स्या०, रो० ।

६. परिगुहना — स्या०, रो० ।

७. परिछादना — सी०; परिच्छादना — स्या०, रो० ।

८. विच्छादना — रो० ।

Here someone misbehaves by body, misbehaves by word, and misbehaves in thought, and with a view to hide that, entertains a sinful desire. He desires thus: "Let none know me"! He resolves thus: "Let none know me"! He says thus: "Let none know me"! He acts thus: "Let none know me"! That which is this deception, deceitfulness, pride, cheating, guile, scattering, avoiding, closing up, closing up completely, screening, screening perfectly, unrevealing, undisclosing, and suppressing particularly— this sinful act is called deception. The person in whom this deception is not destroyed is said to be a deceitful person.

(५. क) अहिरिको पुग्गलो

९. [N.32] कतमो च पुग्गलो अहिरिको ?

तत्थ कतमं अहिरिकं ?

[R.20] यं न हिरीयति[१] हिरियितब्बेन[२] न हिरीयति पापकानं अकुसलानं धम्मानं समापत्तिया— इदं वुच्चति 'अहिरिकं'। इमिना अहिरिकेन समन्नागतो पुग्गलो "अहिरिको"।

(5. A) A person who is shameless

9. What sort of person is shameless?

What then is shamelessness?

That which is the not being ashamed where one should be ashamed, the not being ashamed of acquiring sinful and immoral qualities— this is said to be shamelessness. A person who is possessed of this shamelessness is said to be a shameless person.

(ख) अनोत्तप्पी पुग्गलो

१०. [B.123] कतमो च पुग्गलो अनोत्तप्पी ?

---

१. हिरियति — स्या०, रो०।

२. हिरीयितब्बेन — सी०।

तत्थ कतमं अनोत्तप्पं ?

यं न ओत्तप्पति ओत्तप्पितब्बेन न ओत्तप्पति पापकानं अकुसलानं धम्मानं समापत्तिया— इदं वुच्चति 'अनोत्तप्पं'। इमिना अनोत्तप्पेन समन्नागतो पुग्गलो "अनोत्तप्पी"।

(B) A person who is impudent

10. What sort of person is impudent?

What then is impudence?

Not repenting where one ought to, not repenting of the acquiring sinful and immoral qualities— this is said to be impudence. A person who is possessed of impudence as this is, is said to be impudent.

(६. क) दुब्बचो पुग्गलो

११. कतमो च पुग्गलो दुब्बचो ?

तत्थ कतमो दोवचस्सता ?

सहधम्मिके वुच्चमाने दोवचस्सायं दोवचस्सियं दोवचस्सता विप्पटिकुलग्गाहिता[१] विपच्चनीकसातता[२] अनादरियं अनादरियता अगारवता अप्पतिस्सवता[३]— अयं वुच्चति 'दोवचस्सता'। इमाय[४] दोवचस्सताय[४] समन्नागतो पुग्गलो "दुब्बचो"।

(6. A) A person who is disobedient

11. What sort of person is disobedient?

What then is disobedience?

Disobedience, want of obedience, absence of obedience, the taking up of a hostile attitude, persisting in antagonism, want of respect, disrespect, irreverence,

---

१. विप्पटिकूलगाहिता — सी०, स्या०, रो०।

२. विपच्चनिक० — सी०।

३. अप्पटिस्सवता — स्या०।

४-४. ताय — सी०।

unruliness (insubordination) when the matter of the observance of duties is spoken of— this is said to be disobedience. One who is possessed of such disobedience is said to be a disobedient person.

(ख) पापमित्तो पुग्गलो

१२. [S.282] कतमो च पुग्गलो पापमित्तो ?

तत्थ कतमा पापमित्तता ?

ये ते पुग्गला अस्सद्धा दुस्सीला अप्पस्सुता [N.33] मच्छरिनो दुप्पञ्ञा, या तेसं सेवना निसेवना संसेवना भजना सम्भजना भत्ति सम्भत्ति सम्पवङ्कता[१]— अयं वुच्चति 'पापमित्तता'। इमाय पापमित्तताय समन्नागतो पुग्गलो "पापमित्तो"।

(B) A person who is associate of the wicked

12. What sort of person is said to be the associate of the wicked?

What then is association with the wicked?

Serving, following, attending on, devotion to, honouring, reverence, veneration for, leaning towards those men who are faithless, wicked, uneducated, avaricious and foolish— this is said to be association with the wicked. One who has such a sinful association is said to be an associate of the wicked.

(७. क) इन्द्रियेसु अगुत्तद्वारो पुग्गलो

१३. कतमो च पुग्गलो इन्द्रियेसु अगुत्तद्वारो ?

तत्थ कतमा इन्द्रियेसु अगुत्तद्वारता ?

इधेकच्चो पुग्गलो[२] चक्खुना रूपं दिस्वा निमित्तग्गाही होति अनुब्यञ्जनग्गाही; यत्वाधिकरणमेनं चक्खुन्द्रियं असंवुतं विहरन्तं अभिज्झादोमनस्सा पापका अकुसला धम्मा अन्वास्सवेय्युं, तस्स संवराय न पटिपज्जति न रक्खति चक्खुन्द्रियं चक्खुन्द्रिये न संवरं आपज्जति। सोतेन सद्दं

---

१. तं सम्पवङ्कता — सी०।

२. सी०, स्या० पोत्थकेसु नत्थि।

सुत्वा ... पे० ... घानेन गन्धं घायित्वा ... पे० ... जिव्हाय रसं सायित्वा ... पे० ... कायेन फोट्ठब्बं फुसित्वा ... पे०... मनसा धम्मं विञ्ञाय निमित्तग्गाही होति अनुब्यञ्जनग्गाही; यत्वाधिकरणमेनं मनिन्द्रियं असंवुतं विहरन्तं अभिज्झादोमनस्सा पापका अकुसला धम्मा अन्वास्सवेय्युं, तस्स संवराय न पटिपज्जति न रक्खति मनिन्द्रियं [R.21] मनिन्द्रिये न संवरं आपज्जति । या इमेसं छन्नं इन्द्रियानं अगुत्ति अगोपना अनारक्खो असंवरो— अयं वुच्चति 'इन्द्रियेसु अगुत्तद्वारता' । इमाय इन्द्रियेसु अगुत्तद्वारताय समन्नागतो पुग्गलो "इन्द्रियेसु अगुत्तद्वारो" ।

(7. A) A person who is unguarded as to the sense-doors

13. What sort of person is unguarded as to the 'sense-doors'?

What then is unguardedness as to the 'sense-doors'?

Here a person sees an object with the eye and is enamoured of its form and beauty. And whereas if he lives with his sense of sight unrestrained, the sinful and wicked mental conditions— namely, covetousness and dejection— will flow in, he does not strive to restrain, he does not guard the sense of sight, nor does he get control over the faculty of sight. (In the same way) he hears a sound with his ears ...pe... smells an odour with the nose ...pe... tastes with the tongue ...pe... feels a tangible thing with the body ...pe... knows a mental state with the mind and is enamoured of its form and beauty; whereas if he lives unrestrained as to the faculty of mind, the sinful and wicked mental conditions— viz., covetousness and dejection— will flow in, he does not strive to restrain, nor does he guard the faculty of mind, nor does he get control over the faculty of mind. That which is not guarding, not restraining, not protecting, and not controlling these six faculties— this is said to be unguarding as to the 'sense-doors.' A person who has such unguarding of sense-doors is said to be unguarded as to 'sense-doors'.

(ख) भोजने अमत्तञ्ञू पुग्गलो

१४. कतमो च पुग्गलो भोजने अमत्तञ्ञू ?

तत्थ कतमा भोजने अमत्तञ्ञुता ?

[N.34] इधेकच्चो पुग्गलो अप्पटिसङ्खा अयोनिसो [B.124] आहारं आहारेति दवाय मदाय मण्डनाय विभूसनाय, या तत्थ असन्तुट्ठिता अमत्तञ्ञुता अप्पटिसङ्खा भोजने— अयं वुच्चति 'भोजने अमत्तञ्ञुता'। इमाय भोजने अमत्तञ्ञुताय समन्नागतो पुग्गलो "भोजने अमत्तञ्ञु"।

(B) A person who is immoderate as to food

14. What sort of person is immoderate as to food?

What then is immoderation in food?

Here somebody thoughtlessly and unwisely takes food for the sake of amusement, pride, decoration, ornamentation, insatiability, immoderation, and thoughtlessness as to food— this is said to be immoderation as to food. A person having this immoderation as to food is said to be immoderate as to food.

(८. क) मुट्ठस्सति पुग्गलो

१५. [S.284] कतमो च पुग्गलो मुट्ठस्सति ?

तत्थ कतमं मुट्ठस्सच्चं[१] ?

या अस्सति[२] अननुस्सति अप्पटिस्सति अस्सति[३] अस्सरणता[४] अधारणता पिलापनता[५] सम्मुसनता[६]— इदं वुच्चति 'मुट्ठस्सच्चं'। इमिना मुट्ठस्सच्चेन समन्नागतो पुग्गलो "मुट्ठस्सति"।

---

१. मुट्ठसच्चं — सी०, स्या०, एवमुपरि पि।

२. असति — सी०, रो०, एवमुपरि पि।

३. रो० पोत्थके नत्थि।

४. असरणता — सी०, स्या०, रो०।

५. विलापनता — रो०।

६. सम्मुस्सनता — सी०, रो०।

(8. A) A person who is forgetful

15. What sort of person is forgetful?

What then is forgetfulness?

That which is forgetfulness, failing of memory, non-remembrance, non-recollection, unretentiveness, inattention, oblivion— this is said to be forgetfulness. A person possessed of such forgetfulness is said to be forgetful.

(ख) असम्पजानो पुग्गलो

१६. कतमो च पुग्गलो असम्पजानो ?

तत्थ कतमं असम्पजञ्ञं ?

यं अञ्ञाणं अदस्सनं अनभिसमयो अननुबोधो असम्बोधो अप्पटिवेधो असङ्गाहणा[१] अपरियोगाहणा असमपेक्खणा अपच्चवेक्खणा अपच्चक्खकम्मं[२] दुम्मेज्झं बाल्यं असम्पजञ्ञं मोहो पमोहो सम्मोहो अविज्जा अविज्जोघो अविज्जायोगो अविज्जानुसयो अविज्जापरियुट्ठानं अविज्जालङ्गी मोहो अकुसलमूलं— इदं वुच्चति 'असम्पजञ्ञं'। इमिना असम्पजञ्ञेन समन्नागतो पुग्गलो "असम्पजानो"।

(B) A person who is unmindful

16. What sort of person is unmindful?

What then is unmindfulness?

That which is want of knowledge, want of vision, want of comprehension, want of understanding, want of perfect knowledge, want of penetration, the not grasping, not diving deep, not surveying, not reflecting, absence of work of reflection, dullness, foolishness, want of intelligence, delusion, infatuation, bewilderment, ignorance, the flood of ignorance, the bond of ignorance, the propensity of ignorance, the accession of ignorance, the barrier of ignorance, dullness, a root

१. असङ्गाहना — सी०, स्या०, रो०, एवमुपरि पि।

२. अपच्चवेक्खकम्मं — रो०।

of evil. A person who is possessed of such unmindfulness is said to be unmindful.

(९. क) सीलविपन्नो पुग्गलो

१७. कतमो च पुग्गलो सीलविपन्नो ?

[N.35] तत्थ कतमा सीलविपत्ति ?

कायिको वीतिक्कमो वाचसिको वीतिक्कमो कायिकवाचसिको वीतिक्कमो— अयं वुच्चति सीलविपत्ति[१]। सब्बं पि दुस्सील्यं सीलविपत्ति। इमाय सीलविपत्तिया[२] समन्नागतो पुग्गलो "सीलविपन्नो"।

(9. A) A person who is an infringer of moral law

17. What sort of person is an infringer of moral law?

What then is infringement of moral law?

Transgression with regard to the body, with regard to speech, and with regard to both— this is said to be infringement of moral law. Immorality of every description is an infringement of moral law. A person who is possessed of such an infringement as this, is said to be an infringer of moral law.

(ख) दिट्ठिविपन्नो पुग्गलो

१८. कतमो च पुग्गलो दिट्ठिविपन्नो ?

तत्थ कतमा दिट्ठिविपत्ति ?

"नत्थि दिन्नं, नत्थि यिट्ठं, नत्थि हुतं, नत्थि सुकतदुक्कटानं[३] कम्मानं फलं विपाको, नत्थि अयं [R.22] लोको, नत्थि परो लोको, नत्थि माता, नत्थि पिता, नत्थि सत्ता ओपपातिका, नत्थि लोके समणब्राह्मणा सम्मग्गता[४] सम्मापटिपन्ना ये इमं च लोकं परं च लोकं सयं अभिञ्ञा सच्छिकत्वा पवेदेन्ती"ति— या एवरूपा दिट्ठि

---

१. सीलविप्पत्ति — रो० ।

२. सीलविपत्ति — रो० ।

३. सुकतदुक्कतानं — सी० ; सुकटदुक्कटानं — स्या० ।

४. समग्गता — रो० ।

दिट्ठिगतं दिट्ठिगहनं दिट्ठिकन्तारो दिट्ठिविसूकायिकं[१] दिट्ठिविप्फन्दितं दिट्ठिसंयोजनं गाहो पटिग्गाहो[२] अभिनिवेसो परामासो कुम्मग्गो मिच्छापथो मिच्छत्तं तित्थायतनं विपरियासग्गाहो[३] [B.125] अयं वुच्चति 'दिट्ठिविपत्ति'। सब्बा पि मिच्छादिट्ठि दिट्ठिविपत्ति। इमाय दिट्ठिविपत्तिया समन्नागतो पुग्गलो "दिट्ठिविपन्नो"।

(B) A person who is an upholder of wrong views

18. What sort of person is an upholder of wrong views?

What then is upholding of wrong views?

"There is no merit in charity, sacrificial rites and sacrificial offerings, and there is no fruit nor results of good or of bad deeds. There is neither the present nor a future world. There is neither mother nor father, nor beings who are born without them. There are no recluses or Brahmins in this world who have attained peace of mind and are acting their best, who having by their own effort known and seen this world and the next make known to others": views like this, the way of opinion, the wilderness of opinion, this disorder of heresy, this fluttering of opinion, this fetter of opinion, this seizing and grasping, the devotion to it, its conduct, this bad path, this wrong way, this falsehood, the "landing place," this holding the contrary aim— all this is said to be wrong views. Wrong opinion of every description is known as wrong views. A person who is taken by a wrong view such as this, is said to be an upholder of wrong views.

(१०. क) अज्झत्तसंयोजनो पुग्गलो

१९. [S.286] कतमो च पुग्गलो अज्झत्तसंयोजनो ?

---

१. दिट्ठिविसूकायितं — सी०।

२. पतिट्ठाहो — सी०।

३. विपरियेसगाहो — सी०; विपरियेसग्गाहो — स्या०, रो०।

यस्स पुग्गलस्स पञ्चोरम्भागियानि संयोजनानि अप्पहीनानि— अयं वुच्चति पुग्गलो "अज्झत्तसंयोजनो"।

(10. A) A person who is with internal fetters

19. What sort of person is with internal fetters?

A person in whom the five fetters tying him down to the lower worlds remain unremoved is said to be a person with internal fetters.

(ख) बहिद्धासंयोजनो पुग्गलो

२०. कतमो च पुग्गलो बहिद्धासंयोजनो ?

[N.36] यस्स पुग्गलस्स पञ्चुद्धम्भागियानि संयोजनानि अप्पहीनानि— अयं वुच्चति पुग्गलो "बहिद्धासंयोजनो"।

(B) A person who is with external fetters

20. What sort of person is with external fetters?

A person in whom the five fetters restraining him to the upper worlds remain unremoved is said to be one with external fetters.

(११. क) अक्कोधनो पुग्गलो

२१. कतमो च पुग्गलो अक्कोधनो ?

तत्थ कतमो कोधो ?

यो कोधो कुज्झना कुज्झितत्तं दोसो दुस्सना दुस्सितत्तं ब्यापत्ति ब्यापज्जना ब्यापज्जितत्तं विरोधो पटिविरोधो चण्डिक्कं असुरोपो अनत्तमनता चित्तस्स— अयं वुच्चति 'कोधो'। यस्स पुग्गलस्स अयं कोधो पहीनो— अयं वुच्चति पुग्गलो "अक्कोधनो"।

(11. A) A person who is without anger

21. What sort of person is without anger?

What then is the word 'anger'?

That which is wrath, being wrathful, and the state of being angry, hatred, hating, hatefulness, malice, the act of being malicious, maliciousness, hostility, enmity, rudeness, abruptness, resentment of mind— this is said to be anger. A person in whom such anger has been put away is said to be a person without anger.

(ख) अनुपनाही पुग्गलो

२२. कतमो च पुग्गलो अनुपनाही?

तत्थ कतमो उपनाहो?

पुब्बकालं कोधो अपरकालं उपनाहो। यो एवरूपो उपनाहो उपनय्हना उपनय्हितत्तं अट्ठपना ठपना सण्ठपना अनुसंसन्दना अनुप्पबन्धना दळ्हीकम्मं कोधस्स— अयं वुच्चति 'उपनाहो'। यस्स पुग्गलस्स अयं उपनाहो पहीनो— अयं वुच्चति पुग्गलो "अनुपनाही"।

(B) A person who is unrevengeful

22. What sort of person is unrevengeful?

What then is revenge?

First comes anger, after that comes vengeance. That which is vengeance as this is, the act of revenging and the state of being vengeful, the fixing, settling, establishing, grounding and following up, the violent at of anger— this is said to be revenge. The person in whom revenge as this is has been put away is said to be an unrevengeful person.

(१२. क) अमक्खी पुग्गलो

२३. कतमो च पुग्गलो अमक्खी?

तत्थ कतमो मक्खो?

यो मक्खो मक्खायना मक्खायितत्तं निट्ठुरियं निट्ठुरियकम्मं— अयं वुच्चति 'मक्खो'। यस्स पुग्गलस्स अयं मक्खो पहीनो— अयं वुच्चति पुग्गलो "अमक्खी"।

(12. A) A person who is not a slanderer

23. What sort of person is not a slanderer?

What then is 'slander'?.

That which is slander, that which is practising slander, that which is the state of being a slanderer, that which is hypocrisy, work of hypocrisy— this is said to be slander. A person in whom such slander is put away is said to be not a slanderer.

(ख) अपळासी पुग्गलो

२४. कतमो च पुग्गलो अपळासी ?

[N.37] तत्थ कतमो पळासो ?

यो पळासो पळासायना पळासायितत्तं पळासाहारो विवादट्ठानं युद्धग्गाहो अप्पटिनिस्सग्गो— अयं वुच्चति 'पळासो'। यस्स पुग्गलस्स अयं पळासो पहीनो— अयं वुच्चति पुग्गलो "अपळासी"।

(B) A person who is not quarrelsome

24. What sort of person is not quarrelsome?

What then is quarreling?

That which is quarrel, that which is quarrelling, and that which is quarrelsomeness, the way of quarrel, the point of dispute, the coming to fight, unrelenting— this is called quarrelling. A person in whom quarrelling like this is put away is said to be not quarrelsome person.

(१३. क) अनिस्सुकी पुग्गलो

२५. [R.23; B.126; S.288] कतमो च पुग्गलो अनिस्सुकी ?

तत्थ कतमा इस्सा ?

या परलाभसक्कारगरुकारमाननवन्दनपूजनासु इस्सा इस्सायना इस्सायितत्तं उसूया उसूयना उसूयितत्तं— अयं वुच्चति 'इस्सा'। यस्स पुग्गलस्स अयं इस्सा पहीना— अयं वुच्चति पुग्गलो "अनिस्सुकी"।

(13. A) A person who is unenvious

25. What sort of person is unenvious?

What then is envy?

That which is envying, the state of being envious, that which is jealousy, the act of jealousy and the state of being jealous about the gain, honour, respect, reverence, salutation, and worship paid to others— this is said to be envy. A person in whom such envy is put away is said to be unenvious person.

(ख) अमच्छरी पुग्गलो

२६. कतमो च पुग्गलो अमच्छरी?

तत्थ कतमं मच्छरियं?

पञ्च मच्छरियानि— आवासमच्छरियं, कुलमच्छरियं, लाभमच्छरियं, वण्णमच्छरियं, धम्ममच्छरियं। यं एवरूपं मच्छेरं मच्छरायना मच्छरायितत्तं वेविच्छं कदरियं कटुकञ्चुकता अग्गहितत्तं चित्तस्स— इदं वुच्चति 'मच्छरियं'। यस्स पुग्गलस्स इदं मच्छरियं पहीनं— अयं वुच्चति पुग्गलो "अमच्छरी"।

(B) A person who is unavaricious

26. What sort of person is unavaricious?

What then is avarice?

There are five forms of avarice— avarice with regard to residence, descent, gain, beauty, and merit (dhamma), that which is avarice of this nature, harbouring avarice, avariciousness, inordinate longing, covetousness, presenting a harsh appearance, unrestraint of mind— this is said to be avarice. The person in whom such an avarice has been put away is said to be an unavaricious person.

(१४. क) असठो पुग्गलो

२७. कतमो च पुग्गलो असठो?

तत्थ कतमं साठेय्यं?

इधेकच्चो सठो[१] होति परिसठो। यं तत्थ [N.38] सठं सठता साठेय्यं कक्करता कक्करियं परिक्खत्तता पारिक्खत्तियं— इदं वुच्चति 'साठेय्यं'। यस्स पुग्गलस्स इदं साठेय्यं पहीनं— अयं वुच्चति पुग्गलो "असठो"।

(14. A) A person who is not crafty

27. what sort of person is one who is not crafty? What then is craftiness?

Here a person becomes crafty and cunning— that which is craft, craftiness, state of being crafty, hardness, toughness, counterfeit, sham— this is said to be craftiness. The person in whom such craftiness has been put away is said to be one not crafty person.

(ख) अमायावी पुग्गलो

२८. कतमो च पुग्गलो अमायावी?

तत्थ कतमा माया?

इधेकच्चो पुग्गलो कायेन दुच्चरितं चरित्वा वाचाय दुच्चरितं चरित्वा मनसा दुच्चरितं चरित्वा तस्स पटिच्छादनहेतु पापिकं इच्छं पणिदहति। "मा मं जञ्ञा" ति इच्छति। "मा मं जञ्ञा"ति सङ्कप्पति। "मा मं जञ्ञा"ति वाचं भासति। "मा मं जञ्ञा"ति कायेन परक्कमति। या एवरूपा माया मायाविता अच्चासरा[२] वञ्चना निकति विकिरणा[३] परिहरणा गूहना परिगूहना छादना पटिच्छादना[४] अनुत्तानीकम्मं अनाविकम्मं वोच्छादना[५] पापकिरिया— अयं वुच्चति 'माया'। यस्स पुग्गलस्स अयं माया पहीना— अयं वुच्चति पुग्गलो "अमायावी"।

(B) A person who is undeceiving

28. What sort of person is undeceiving?

What then is deception?

---

१. पुग्गलो सठो — सी०, रो०; पुग्गलो सथो — स्या०।

२. अच्चसरा — सी०।

३. निकिरणा — सी०; विकीरणा — स्या०; निकरणा — रो०।

४. परिछादना — सी०; परिच्छादना — स्या०, रो०।

५. विच्छादना — रो०।

Here some person misbehaves by body, misbehaves by word, and misbehaves in thought and with a view to hide that, entertains a sinful desire. He desires thus: "Let none know me"! He resolves thus: "Let none know me"! He says thus: " Let none know me"! He acts thus: "Let none know me"! That which is this deception, deceitfulness, pride, cheating, guile, scattering, avoiding, closing up, closing up completely, screening, screening perfectly, unrevealing, undisclosing, and suppressing particularly— this sinful act is called deception. The person in whom this deception has been put away is said to be undeceiving person.

(१५. क) हिरिमा पुग्गलो

२९. [S.290] कतमो च पुग्गलो हिरिमा ?

तत्थ कतमा[१] हिरी[२] ?

[R.24] यं हिरीयति[३] हिरियितब्बेन हिरीयति पापकानं अकुसलानं धम्मानं समापत्तिया— अयं वुच्चति 'हिरी'। इमाय हिरिया समन्नागतो पुग्गलो "हिरिमा"।

(15. A) A person who is scrupulous

29. What sort of person is scrupulous ?

What then is scruple?

That which is being scrupulous where one should be, the being scrupulous as to doing a sinful and immoral act— this is said to be scruple. A person who is possessed of scruple like this is said to be scrupulous.

(ख) ओत्तप्पी पुग्गलो

३०. [N.39] कतमो च पुग्गलो ओत्तप्पी ?

---

१. कतमं — स्या०।

२. हिरि — स्या०।

३. हिरि हिरीयति — सी०; हिरियति — स्या०, रो०।

तत्थ कतमं ओत्तप्पं ?

यं ओत्तप्पति ओत्तप्पितब्बेन ओत्तप्पति पापकानं अकुसलानं धम्मानं समापत्तिया— इदं वुच्चति 'ओत्तप्पं'। इमिना ओत्तप्पेन समन्नागतो पुग्गलो "ओत्तप्पी"।

(B) A person who is discreet

30. What sort of person is discreet?

What then is discretion?

Being discreet where one ought to be, discretion as to doing a sinful and immoral act— this is said to be discretion. A person who is possessed of discretion like this is said to be a discreet person.

(१६. क) सुवचो पुग्गलो

३१. [B.127] कतमो च पुग्गलो सुवचो ?

तत्थ कतमा सोवचस्सता ?

सहधम्मिके वुच्चमाने सोवचस्सायं सोवचस्सियं सोवचस्सता अविप्पटिकुलग्गाहिता[१] अविपच्चनीकसातता सादरियं[२] सादरियता[२] सगारवता सप्पतिस्सवता[३]— अयं वुच्चति 'सोवचस्सता'। इमाय सोवचस्सताय समन्नागतो पुग्गलो "सुवचो"।

(16. A) A person who is obedient

31. What sort of person is obedient?

What then is obedience?

Obedience, obeying, the habit of obeying, not taking up a hostile attitude, not persisting in antagonism, respecting, respect, reverence, subordination— this is said to be obedience when the observance of duties is

१. अविप्पटिकूलगाहिता — सी०; अप्पटिकूलगाहिता — स्या०, रो०।

२-२. सी० पोत्थके नत्थि; सादरता — स्या०।

३. सप्पटिस्सवता — स्या०, रो०।

spoken of. A person who is possessed of such obedience is said to be an obedient person.

(ख) कल्याणमित्तो पुग्गलो

३२. कतमो च पुग्गलो कल्याणमित्तो ?

तत्थ कतमा कल्याणमित्तता ?

ये ते पुग्गला सद्धा सीलवन्तो बहुस्सुता चागवन्तो पञ्ञवन्तो, या तेसं सेवना निसेवना संसेवना भजना सम्भजना भत्ति सम्भत्ति सम्पवङ्कता— अयं वुच्चति 'कल्याणमित्तता'। इमाय कल्याणमित्तताय समन्नागतो पुग्गलो "कल्याणमित्तो"।

(B) A person who is associate of the good

32. What sort of person is the associate of the good?

What then is association with the good?

Serving, respecting, revering, honouring, love, reverence, friendship for those people who are faithful, virtuous, learned, possessed of devotion and candour— this is said to be meant by association with the good. A person who has such an association with the good is said to be an associate of the good.

(१७. क) इन्द्रियेसु गुत्तद्वारो पुग्गलो

३३. कतमो च पुग्गलो इन्द्रियेसु गुत्तद्वारो ?

तत्थ कतमा इन्द्रियेसु गुत्तद्वारता ?

[N.40] इधेकच्चो पुग्गलो चक्खुना रूपं दिस्वा न निमित्तग्गाही होति नानुब्यञ्जनग्गाही; यत्वाधिकरणमेनं चक्खुन्द्रियं असंवुतं विहरन्तं अभिज्झादोमनस्सा पापका अकुसला धम्मा अन्वास्सवेय्युं, तस्स संवराय पटिपज्जति रक्खति चक्खुन्द्रियं चक्खुन्द्रिये संवरं आपज्जति। सोतेन सद्दं सुत्वा ...पे०... घानेन गन्धं घायित्वा ...पे०... जिव्हाय रसं सायित्वा ...पे०...कायेन फोट्ठब्बं फुसित्वा ...पे०... मनसा धम्मं विञ्ञाय न निमित्तग्गाही होति नानुब्यञ्जनग्गाही; यत्वाधिकरणमेनं मनिन्द्रियं असंवुतं विहरन्तं अभिज्झादोमनस्सा पापका अकुसला धम्मा अन्वास्सवेय्युं, तस्स संवराय पटिपज्जति रक्खति मनिन्द्रियं मनिन्द्रिये संवरं

आपज्जति। या इमेसं छन्नं इन्द्रियानं गुत्ति गोपना आरक्खो [R.25] संवरो— अयं वुच्चति 'इन्द्रियेसु गुत्तद्वारता'। इमाय इन्द्रियेसु गुत्तद्वारताय समन्नागतो पुग्गलो "इन्द्रियेसु गुत्तद्वारो"।

(17. A) A person who is guarded as to the sense-doors

33. What sort of person is guarded as to the 'sense-doors'?

What then is guarding the 'sense-doors'?

Here a certain person sees an object with the eye, but is not enamoured of its form and beauty. And whereas if he lives with his sense of sight unrestrained, the sinful and wicked mental conditions— viz., covetousness and dejection— will flow in, he strives after its restraint, he guards the sense of sight and exercises control over the faculty of sight; (in the same way) he hears a sound with his ears...pe... smells an odour with his nose...pe... tastes with his tongue...pe... feels an external object with his body...pe... apprehends a mental phenomenon with his mind, but is not enamoured of its form and beauty, whereas if he lives unrestrained as to the faculty of mind, the sinful and wicked mental conditions— viz., covetousness and dejection— will flow in, he strives after its restraint, guards the faculty of mind and exercises control over it. That which is guarding, restraining, protecting, and controlling of these six faculties— this is said to be guarding the 'sense-doors'. A person who has such a vigilance over the sense-doors is said to be guarded as to his 'sense-doors'.

(ख) भोजने मत्तञ्ञू पुग्गलो

३४. [S.292] कतमो च पुग्गलो भोजने मत्तञ्ञू?

तत्थ कतमा भोजने मत्तञ्ञुता?

इधेकच्चो पुग्गलो पटिसङ्खा योनिसो आहारं आहारेति— "नेव दवाय, न मदाय, न मण्डनाय, न विभूसनाय; यावदेव इमस्स कायस्स ठितिया यापनाय विहिंसूपरतिया[१] ब्रह्मचरियानुग्गहाय। इति पुराणं च वेदनं पटिहङ्खामि, नवं च वेदनं न उप्पादेस्सामि, यात्रा च मे भविस्सति अनवज्जता च फासुविहारो चा" ति। या तत्थ सन्तुट्ठिता [B.128] मत्तञ्ञुता पटिसङ्खा भोजने— अयं वुच्चति 'भोजने मत्तञ्ञुता'। [N.41] इमाय भोजने मत्तञ्ञुताय समन्नागतो पुग्गलो "भोजने मत्तञ्ञू"।

(B) A person who is moderate as to food

34. What sort of person is moderate as to food? What then is moderation in food?

Here somebody wisely thinking takes food not for the sake of amusement, not for pride, not for decoration, not for ornamentation, so far as it is necessary for the preservation and keeping up of the body and for the sake of relieving the distress of hunger, helping the cause of a holy life: 'thus I shall put an end to my past feelings and shall not give occasion to new feelings; thus shall come to me sustenance, purity, and peaceful life'; that which is contentment, moderation, thoughtfulness as to food—this is said to be moderation in food. A person possessing such temperance is said to be moderate as to food.

(१८. क) उपट्ठितस्सति पुग्गलो

३५. कतमो च पुग्गलो उपट्ठितस्सति?

तत्थ कतमा सति?

या सति अनुस्सति पटिस्सति सति सरणता धारणता अपिलापनता असम्मुसनता[२] सति सतिन्द्रियं सतिबलं सम्मासति— अयं वुच्चति 'सति'। इमाय सतिया समन्नागतो पुग्गलो "उपट्ठितस्सति"।

---

१. विहिंसुपरतिया — स्या०।

२. अपम्मुस्सनता — सी०।

(18. A) A person who is alert

35. What sort of person is alert?

What then is mindfulness?

The mindfulness which is remembering, which is remembrance, recollection, retentiveness, non-forgetting, non-disorder of memory, mindfulness, a faculty called mindfulness, the power called mindfulness, and perfect mindfulness— this is said to be mindfulness. A person who possesses mindfulness like this is said to be an alert person.

(ख) सम्पजानो पुग्गलो

३६. कतमो च पुग्गलो सम्पजानो ?

तत्थ कतमं सम्पजञ्ञं ?

या पञ्ञा पजानना विचयो पविचयो धम्मविचयो सल्लक्खणा उपलक्खणा पच्चुपलक्खणा[१] पण्डिच्चं कोसल्लं नेपुञ्ञं वेभब्या[२] चिन्ता उपपरिक्खा भूरी मेधा परिणायिका विपस्सना सम्पजञ्ञं पतोदो पञ्ञा पञ्ञिन्द्रियं पञ्ञाबलं पञ्ञासत्थं पञ्ञापासादो[३] पञ्ञाआलोको पञ्ञाओभासो पञ्ञापज्जोतो पञ्ञारतनं अमोहो धम्मविचयो सम्मादिट्ठि— इदं वुच्चति 'सम्पजञ्ञं'। इमिना सम्पजञ्ञेन समन्नागतो पुग्गलो "सम्पजानो"।

(B) A person who understands

36. What sort of person understands?

What then is understanding?

That which is knowledge, knowing, discrimination, investigation of the truth, observing, remarking, and discernment, erudition, expertness, adroitness, superior thinking, examination, reason, intellect that leads, introspection, mindfulness, goad, insight, the faculty of insight, the power of insight, weapon of insight, palace

---

१. पच्चूपलक्खणा — सी० ।

२. वेभव्या — सी०, रो० ।

३. पञ्ञापसादो — रो० ।

of insight, light of insight, brightness of insight, splendour of insight, jewel of insight, disillusionment, investigation into the truth, perfect vision— this is said to be mindfulness. A person who is possessed of such understanding understands.

(१९. क) सीलसम्पन्नो पुग्गलो

३७. कतमो च पुग्गलो सीलसम्पन्नो ?

तत्थ कतमा सीलसम्पदा ?

कायिको अवीतिक्कमो वाचसिको अवीतिक्कमो कायिकवाचसिको अवीतिक्कमो— अयं वुच्चति 'सीलसम्पदा'। सब्बो पि सीलसंवरो सीलसम्पदा। इमाय सीलसम्पदाय समन्नागतो पुग्गलो "सीलसम्पन्नो"।

(19. A) A person who is an observer of the moral law

37. What sort of person is an observer of the moral law?

What then is observance of the moral law?

Non-transgression with regard to body and to speech and with regard to both— this is said to be observance of the moral law; all restraints under moral law are its observance. Any person equipped with this observance of the moral law is said to be the observer of the moral law.

(ख) दिट्ठिसम्पन्नो पुग्गलो

३८. [N.42; S.294] कतमो च पुग्गलो दिट्ठिसम्पन्नो ?

[R.26] तत्थ कतमा दिट्ठिसम्पदा ?

"अत्थि दिन्नं, अत्थि यिट्ठं, अत्थि हुतं, अत्थि सुकतदुक्कटानं कम्मानं फलं विपाको, अत्थि अयं लोको, अत्थि परो लोको, अत्थि माता, अत्थि पिता, अत्थि सत्ता ओपपातिका, अत्थि लोके समणब्राह्मणा सम्मग्गता[१] सम्मापटिपन्ना ये इमं च लोकं परं च लोकं सयं अभिञ्ञा सच्छिकत्वा पवेदेन्ती" ति। या एवरूपा पञ्ञा पजानना

१. समग्गता — रो०।

...पे०... अमोहो धम्मविचयो सम्मादिट्ठि— अयं वुच्चति 'दिट्ठिसम्पदा'। सब्बा पि सम्मादिट्ठि दिट्ठिसम्पदा। इमाय दिट्ठिसम्पदाय समन्नागतो पुग्गलो "दिट्ठिसम्पन्नो"।

(B) A person who is the upholder of right views

38. What sort of person is the upholder of right views?

What is then the upholding of right views?

"There is merit in charity, in sacrificial rites, and sacrificial offerings. There is fruit, and there is result of good and bad deeds done. There exists this world, there is also the next world, there is mother and there is father and there are those beings who are born without their union. There are true recluses and brahmins in this world who have attained peace of mind and are acting their best, and who, having personally known and realised what this world is as well as the next, make known to others"— such knowledge and such knowing...pe... absence of ignorance discernment of the truth, right vision— this is said to be upholding of right views. All right views are classed under right views. A person who is endowed with this upholding of right views is said to be the upholder of right views.

(२०) द्वे दुल्लभा पुग्गला

३९. कतमे द्वे पुग्गला दुल्लभा लोकस्मिं ?

यो च पुब्बकारी, यो च कतञ्ञू कतवेदी— इमे द्वे पुग्गला दुल्लभा लोकस्मिं।

(20) Two persons who are rare

39. Which two persons are rare in this world?

He who does good first and he who recognises it— these two persons are rare in this world.

(२१) द्वे दुत्तप्पया पुग्गला

४०. [B.129] कतमे द्वे पुग्गला दुत्तप्पया?

यो च लद्धं लद्धं निक्खिपति, यो च लद्धं लद्धं विस्सज्जेति[१]— इमे द्वे पुग्गला "दुत्तप्पया"।

(21) Two persons who are hard to satisfy

40. Which two persons are hard to satisfy?

He who stores up whatever he gets and he who gives away whatever he gets— these two persons are hard to satisfy.

(२२) द्वे सुतप्पया पुग्गला

४१. कतमे द्वे पुग्गला सुतप्पया?

यो च लद्धं लद्धं न निक्खिपति, यो च लद्धं लद्धं न विस्सज्जेति— इमे द्वे पुग्गला "सुतप्पया"।

(22) Two persons who are easily satisfied

41. Which two persons are easily satisfied?

He who does not store up whatever he gets and he who does not give away whatever he gets— these two persons are easily satisfied.

(२३) द्विन्नं आसवा वड्ढन्ति

४२. कतमेसं द्विन्नं पुग्गलानं आसवा वड्ढन्ति?

[N.43] यो च न कुक्कुच्चायितब्बं कुक्कुच्चायति, यो च कुक्कुच्चायितब्बं न कुक्कुच्चायति— इमेसं द्विन्नं पुग्गलानं आसवा वड्ढन्ति।

(23) Two's sins increase

42. Of which two persons do the sins (Āsavā) increase?

१. विसज्जेति — स्या०, रो०।

He who doubts where he should not and he who does not disbelieve where he ought to— of these two persons the sins go on increasing.

(२४) द्विन्नं आसवा न वड्ढन्ति

४३. कतमेसं द्विन्नं पुग्गलानं आसवा न वड्ढन्ति ?

यो च न कुक्कुच्चायितब्बं न कुक्कुच्चायति, यो च कुक्कुच्चायितब्बं कुक्कुच्चायति— इमेसं द्विन्नं पुग्गलानं आसवा न वड्ढन्ति ।

(24) Two's sins do not increase

43. Of which two persons do the sins not increase?

He who does not doubt where it is not proper to doubt and he who doubts where he ought to do so— of these two persons the sins do not increase.

(२५. क) हीनाधिमुत्तो पुग्गलो

४४. [S.296] कतमो च पुग्गलो हीनाधिमुत्तो ?

इधेकच्चो पुग्गलो दुस्सीलो होति पापधम्मो । सो अञ्ञं दुस्सीलं पापधम्मं सेवति भजति पयिरुपासति । अयं वुच्चति पुग्गलो "हीनाधिमुत्तो" ।

(25. A) A person who is one having low inclination

44. What sort of person is one having low inclination?

Here is a person who, himself morally wicked and evil by nature, serves, follows, and worships another person who is also wicked and of evil disposition— this is said to be a person having low inclination.

(ख) पणीताधिमुत्तो पुग्गलो

४५. कतमो च पुग्गलो पणीताधिमुत्तो ?

इधेकच्चो पुग्गलो सीलवा होति कल्याणधम्मो । सो अञ्ञं सीलवन्तं कल्याणधम्मं सेवति भजति पयिरुपासति । अयं वुच्चति पुग्गलो "पणीताधिमुत्तो" ।

(B) A person who is one having good inclination

45. What sort of person is one having good inclination?

Here a certain person who, morally good and of virtuous habits, serves, follows, and reveres another person of the same nature— he is said to be a person having good inclination.

(२६. क-ख) तित्तो पुग्गलो तप्पेता च

४६. [R.27] कतमो च पुग्गलो तित्तो ?

पच्चेकसम्बुद्धा[१] ये च तथागतस्स सावका अरहन्तो तित्ता। सम्मासम्बुद्धो तित्तो च तप्पेता च[२]।

दुकनिद्देसो निट्ठितो।

(26. A-B) A person who is the gratified and who is the gratifier

46. What sort of person is the gratified?

Those who are Enlightened for themselves and those of the disciples of the *Tathāgata* who are Arahants are the gratified. The Perfectly Enlightened One is both gratified and a gratifier.

Here ends the specification of grouping by two.

१. पच्चेकबुद्धो — सी०।

२. 'अयं वुच्चति पुग्गलो तित्तो' ति — सी० पोत्थके अधिको पाठो दिस्सति।

ततियो परिच्छेदो

३. तिकपुग्गलपञ्ञत्ति

(१. क) निरासो पुग्गलो

१. [N.44; S.298] कतमो च पुग्गलो निरासो ?

इधेकच्चो पुग्गलो दुस्सीलो होति पापधम्मो असुचि सङ्कस्सरसमाचारो पटिच्छन्नकम्मन्तो [B.130] अस्समणो[१] समणपटिञ्ञो अब्रह्मचारी ब्रह्मचारिपटिञ्ञो[२] अन्तोपूति[३] अवस्सुतो कसम्बुजातो[४]। सो सुणाति—"इत्थन्नामो किर भिक्खु आसवानं खया अनासवं चेतोविमुत्तिं पञ्ञाविमुत्तिं दिट्ठेव धम्मे सयं अभिञ्ञा सच्छिकत्वा उपसम्पज्ज विहरती"ति। तस्स न एवं होति— "कुदास्सु[५] नामाहं पि आसवानं खया अनासवं चेतोविमुत्तिं पञ्ञाविमुत्तिं दिट्ठेव धम्मे सयं अभिञ्ञा सच्छिकत्वा उपसम्पज्ज विहरिस्सामी" ति ? अयं वुच्चति पुग्गलो "निरासो"।

CHAPTER THREE

3. Division of Human Types by Three

(1. A) A person who is hopeless

1. What sort of person is hopeless?

---

१. असमणो — रो०।

२. ब्रह्मचारीपटिञ्ञो — सी०, स्या०, रो०।

३. अन्तोपूती — रो०।

४. कसम्बुकजातो — स्या०, रो०।

५. कुदस्सु — सी०, एवमुपरि पि।

Here a certain person who is immoral and is of evil disposition, who is of impure habits and who is the doer of deeds (which must be) concealed, professes to be a Samaṇa, although he is not one; being unchaste, he professes to live the holy life; is corrupt within, is filled with desire, and is one in whom foulness has accumulated, and when he hears thus— "a monk of such and such a name, on the dissolution of sinful tendencies lives in the attainment of emancipation by way of insight and by means of higher wisdom of emancipation of thought which is devoid of sinful tendencies, after he has by himself known and realised them in this life." He does not think thus— "When shall I too on the dissolution of sinful tendencies live, in the attainment of emancipation by way of insight and by means of higher wisdom of emancipation of thought which is devoid of sinful tendencies, after he has by himself known and realised them in the life"? Such a person is said to be a hopeless person.

(ख) आसंसो पुग्गलो

२. कतमो च पुग्गलो आसंसो ?

इधेकच्चो पुग्गलो सीलवा होति कल्याणधम्मो। सो सुणाति— "इत्थन्नामो किर भिक्खु आसवानं खया अनासवं चेतोविमुत्तिं पञ्ञाविमुत्तिं दिट्ठेव धम्मे सयं अभिञ्ञा सच्छिकत्वा उपसम्पज्ज विहरती"ति। तस्स एवं होति—"कुदास्सु नामाहं पि आसवानं खया अनासवं चेतोविमुत्तिं पञ्ञाविमुत्तिं दिट्ठेव धम्मे सयं अभिञ्ञा सच्छिकत्वा उपसम्पज्ज विहरिस्सामी"ति ? अयं वुच्चति पुग्गलो "आसंसो"।

(B) A person who is hopeful

2. What sort of person is hopeful?

Here a certain person who is moral and is of good disposition. He hears thus— "a monk of such and such a name, on the dissolution of sinful tendencies, lives in the attainment of emancipation by way of insight and of emancipation of thought which is devoid of the sinful tendencies, after he has by himself known and realised them by means of higher wisdom in this life." He thereupon thinks— "When shall I too on the dissolution of sinful tendencies, lives in the attainment of emancipation by way of insight and of emancipation of thought which is devoid of the sinful tendencies (Āsavas), after he has by himself known and realised them by means of higher wisdom in this life"? Such a person is said to be hopeful.

(ग) विगतासो पुग्गलो

३. कतमो च पुग्गलो विगतासो ?

इधेकच्चो पुग्गलो आसवानं खया अनासवं चेतोविमुत्तिं पञ्ञाविमुत्तिं दिट्ठेव धम्मे सयं अभिञ्ञा सच्छिकत्वा उपसम्पज्ज विहरति । सो सुणाति— "इत्थन्नामो किर भिक्खु आसवानं खया अनासवं चेतोविमुत्तिं पञ्ञाविमुत्तिं दिट्ठेव धम्मे सयं अभिञ्ञा सच्छिकत्वा [N.45] उपसम्पज्ज विहरती"ति । तस्स न एवं होति— "कुदास्सु नामाहं पि आसवानं खया अनासवं चेतोविमुत्तिं पञ्ञाविमुत्तिं दिट्ठेव धम्मे सयं अभिञ्ञा सच्छिकत्वा उपसम्पज्ज विहरिस्सामी"ति ? तं किस्स हेतु ? या हिस्स पुब्बे अविमुत्तस्स विमुत्तासा, सा पटिप्पस्सद्धा । अयं वुच्चति पुग्गलो "विगतासो" ।

(C) A person who has lost hope

3. What sort of person is he who has lost hope?

Here a certain person, having known and realised by himself in this life, by means of higher wisdom, the emancipation that comes through insight and emancipation of thought, which is the being rid of evil tendencies. He hears thus— "a bhikkhu of such and such a name lives in this world, having personally come to know and realise, by means of higher knowledge, the emancipation that comes through insight and emancipation of thought, which is the being rid of evil tendencies". He thereupon does not think thus— "When shall I too on the dissolution of sinful tendencies lives in the attainment of emancipation by way of insight and by means of higher wisdom of emancipation of thought which is devoid of sinful tendencies, after he has by himself known and realised them in this life"? To what is this due? Because that aspiration to attain emancipation, which he entertained when he was still unemancipated, has been stilled. Such a person is said to be one who has lost hope.

(२) तयो गिलानूपमा पुग्गला

४. [S.300] तत्थ कतमे तयो गिलानूपमा पुग्गला ?

तयो गिलाना— (१) इधेकच्चो गिलानो लभन्तो वा सप्पायानि [R.28] भोजनानि अलभन्तो वा सप्पायानि भोजनानि, लभन्तो वा सप्पायानि भेसज्जानि अलभन्तो वा सप्पायानि भेसज्जानि, लभन्तो वा पतिरूपं[1] उपट्ठाकं अलभन्तो वा पतिरूपं उपट्ठाकं, नेव वुट्ठाति तम्हा आबाधा ।

(2) Three persons who are comparable to sick

4. Who are the three persons that may be likened to a sick person?

There are three kinds of sick persons— (1) Here there is some sick person who, whether or not he gets proper diet, some sick person who, whether or not he gets good medicines, some sick person who, whether or not he gets an able nurse, fail to recover from his illness.

(२) इध पनेकच्चो गिलानो लभन्तो वा सप्पायानि भोजनानि अलभन्तो वा सप्पायानि भोजनानि, लभन्तो वा सप्पायानि [B.131] भेसज्जानि अलभन्तो वा सप्पायानि भेसज्जानि, लभन्तो वा पतिरूपं उपट्ठाकं अलभन्तो वा पतिरूपं उपट्ठाकं, वुट्ठाति तम्हा आबाधा ।

(2) Here again there is some sick person who, whether or not gets proper diet, some sick person who, whether or not gets good medicines, some sick person

---

१. पटिरूपं — स्या०, रो०, एवमुपरि पि ।

who, whether or not gets an able nurse, recovers from his illness.

(३) इध पनेकच्चो गिलानो लभन्तो सप्पायानि भोजनानि नो अलभन्तो, लभन्तो सप्पायानि भेसज्जानि नो अलभन्तो, लभन्तो पतिरूपं उपट्ठाकं नो अलभन्तो, वुट्ठाति तम्हा आबाधा।

(3) Here again there is some sick person who, getting proper diet but not without getting, some sick person who, getting good medicines but not without getting, some sick person who, getting an able nurse, recovers from his illness.

तत्र य्वायं गिलानो लभन्तो सप्पायानि भोजनानि नो अलभन्तो, लभन्तो सप्पायानि भेसज्जानि नो अलभन्तो, लभन्तो पतिरूपं उपट्ठाकं नो अलभन्तो, वुट्ठाति तम्हा आबाधा, इमं गिलानं पटिच्च भगवता[१] गिलानभत्तं अनुञ्ञातं गिलानभेसज्जं अनुञ्ञातं गिलानुपट्ठाको अनुञ्ञातो। इमं च पन गिलानं पटिच्च अञ्ञे पि गिलाना उपट्ठातब्बा।

For the last class of patients i.e. those who can recover from a disease if he gets proper diet but not without getting, he gets good medicines but not without getting, he gets an able nurse but not without getting; here the Blessed One has prescribed diet (fit for the sick), prescribed medicine (worthy of the sick), prescribed an able nurse (fit for the sick), for them. Other patients are to be attended to because of this class of patients.

एवमेवं[२] तयो गिलानूपमा पुग्गला सन्तो संविज्जमाना लोकस्मिं। कतमो तयो?

(१) इधेकच्चो पुग्गलो लभन्तो वा तथागतं दस्सनाय अलभन्तो वा तथागतं दस्सनाय, लभन्तो वा तथागतप्पवेदितं धम्मविनयं सवणाय[३] अलभन्तो वा

१. सी० पोत्थके नत्थि।

२. एवमेव — सी०, स्या०।

३. सवनाय — स्या०, एवमुपरि पि।

तथागतप्पवेदितं धम्मविनयं सवणाय, नेव ओक्कमति नियामं कुसलेसु धम्मेसु सम्मत्तं ।

Like these three sick persons there dwell in this world three types of persons. Which three?

(1) Here a certain persons, whether or not he sees the Tathāgata and whether or not he listens to the doctrine and the discipline thereof as expounded by the Tathāgata, does not enter upon the accepted order (niyāma) in things that are good.

(२) [N.46] इध पनेकच्चो पुग्गलो लभन्तो वा तथागतं दस्सनाय अलभन्तो वा तथागतं दस्सनाय, लभन्तो वा तथागतप्पवेदितं धम्मविनयं सवणाय अलभन्तो वा तथागतप्पवेदितं धम्मविनयं सवणाय, ओक्कमति नियामं कुसलेसु धम्मेसु सम्मत्तं ।

(2) Here again a certain person, whether or not he sees the Tathāgata with his own eyes and whether or not he hears the doctrine and the discipline thereof as expounded by the Tathāgata, enters upon the accepted order in things that are good.

(३) इध पनेकच्चो पुग्गलो लभन्तो तथागतं दस्सनाय नो अलभन्तो, लभन्तो तथागतप्पवेदितं धम्मविनयं सवणाय नो अलभन्तो, ओक्कमति नियामं कुसलेसु धम्मेसु सम्मत्तं ।

(3) Here again another person only when he is able to see the Tathāgata and to listen to the doctrine and the discipline thereof as expounded by the Tathāgata enters upon the accepted order in things that are good, but not otherwise.

तत्र य्वायं पुग्गलो लभन्तो तथागतं दस्सनाय नो अलभन्तो, लभन्तो तथागतप्पवेदितं धम्मविनयं सवणाय नो [B.132] अलभन्तो, ओक्कमति नियामं कुसलेसु धम्मेसु सम्मत्तं, इमं पुग्गलं पटिच्च भगवता धम्मदेसना अनुञ्ञाता, इमं तयो च पुग्गलं[१] पटिच्च [R.29] अञ्ञेसं पि धम्मो देसेतब्बो । इमे तयो गिलानूपमा पुग्गला सन्तो संविज्जमाना लोकस्मिं ।

---

१. पन पुग्गलं — सी०, स्या०, रो० ।

In the case of the person of the last type— namely, one who enters upon the accepted order in things that are good only when he comes to see the Tathāgata and hears the doctrine and discipline imparted by him, but not otherwise— for him has the Blessed One prescribed religious discourse, and because of this person the doctrine should be imparted to others. These are the three persons in this world who are comparable to sick men.

(३. क) कायसक्खी पुग्गलो

५. [S.302] कतमो च पुग्गलो कायसक्खी?

इधेकच्चो पुग्गलो अट्ठ विमोक्खे कायेन फुसित्वा[१] विहरति, पञ्ञाय चस्स दिस्वा एकच्चे आसवा परिक्खीणा होन्ति— अयं वुच्चति पुग्गलो "कायसक्खी"।

(3. A) A person who is an eye-witness

5. What sort of person is an 'eye-witness'?

Here a person goes on himself experiencing the eight stages of emancipation, and dwells in touching with the body (Nāmakāya), and having seen them through insight, some of his sinful tendencies (Āsavas) are completely destroyed. This sort of person is said to be an 'eye-witness'.

(ख) दिट्ठिप्पत्तो पुग्गलो

६. कतमो च पुग्गलो दिट्ठिप्पत्तो?

इधेकच्चो पुग्गलो "इदं दुक्खं"ति यथाभूतं पजानाति, "अयं दुक्खसमुदयो" ति यथाभूतं पजानाति, "अयं दुक्खनिरोधो" ति यथाभूतं पजानाति, "अयं दुक्खनिरोधगामिनी पटिपदा" ति यथाभूतं पजानाति, तथागतप्पवेदिता चस्स धम्मा पञ्ञाय वोदिट्ठा होन्ति वोचरिता। पञ्ञाय चस्स दिस्वा एकच्चे आसवा परिक्खीणा होन्ति। अयं वुच्चति पुग्गलो "दिट्ठिप्पत्तो"।

---

१. फस्सित्वा — सी०, एवमुपरि पि।

(B) A person who has won vision

6. What sort of person is one who has won vision?

Here a person truly understands that "this is suffering", truly understands that "this is the origin of suffering", truly understands that "this is the cessation of suffering", truly understands that "this is the path leading to the cessation of suffering." The doctrines promulgated by the Tathāgata are perceived by him through insight as well as practised; and having seen them through insight, some of his sinful tendencies (Āsavas) are completely destroyed. This sort of person is said to be one who has won vision.

(ग) सद्धाविमुत्तो पुग्गलो

७. कतमो च पुग्गलो सद्धाविमुत्तो ?

इधेकच्चो पुग्गलो "इदं दुक्खं"ति यथाभूतं पजानाति, "अयं दुक्खसमुदयो"ति यथाभूतं पजानाति, "अयं दुक्खनिरोधो"ति यथाभूतं पजानाति, "अयं दुक्खनिरोधगामिनी पटिपदा"ति यथाभूतं पजानाति, [N.47] तथागतप्पवेदिता चस्स धम्मा पञ्ञाय वोदिट्ठा होन्ति वोचरिता, पञ्ञाय चस्स दिस्वा एकच्चे आसवा परिक्खीणा होन्ति, नो च खो यथादिट्ठिप्पत्तस्स। अयं वुच्चति पुग्गलो "सद्धाविमुत्तो"।

(C) A person who is emancipated by faith

7. What sort of person is emancipated by faith?

Here a person truly understands that "this is suffering", truly understands that "this is the origin of suffering", truly understands that "this is the cessation of suffering", and truly understands that "this is the path leading to the cessation of suffering." The doctrines promulgated by the Tathāgata are perceived by him through insight as well as practised, and having seen them through insight, some of his sinful tendencies are completely destroyed, though not in the same way as in the case of the person who has won vision. This sort of person is said to be one emancipated by faith.

(४. क) गूथभाणी पुग्गलो

८. कतमो च पुग्गलो गूथभाणी ?

इधेकच्चो पुग्गलो मुसावादी होति। सभग्गतो वा परिसग्गतो वा ञातिमज्झगतो वा पूगमज्झगतो वा राजकुलमज्झगतो वा अभिनीतो सक्खिपुट्ठो— "एहम्भो,[१] पुरिस, यं जानासि तं वदेही" ति, सो अजानं वा आह[२] — "जानामी"ति, जानं वा आह— "न जानामी" ति, अपस्सं वा आह—"पस्सामी" ति, पस्सं वा आह—"न पस्सामी"ति। इति अत्तहेतु वा परहेतु वा आमिसकिञ्चिक्खहेतु वा सम्पजानमुसा भासिता होति। अयं वुच्चति पुग्गलो "गूथभाणी"।

(4. A) A person who is foul-mouthed

8. What sort of person is 'foul-mouthed'?

Here a certain person who is a liar, being brought into an assembly, into the midst of a meeting, or into the midst of his relations, or into a congregation, or into the prince's council, and interrogated as a witness thus: "Come, good man, just tell us what you know about it"; he would say, "I know" when he does not know, and knowing he would say, "I do not know". He would say he saw those things which he never saw, and would not say which things he actually witnessed; thus either for his own sake, or for the sake of others, or for the sake of any least gain to him, he would speak untruth consciously. Such a person is said to be 'foul-mouthed.'

(ख) पुप्फभाणी पुग्गलो

९. [B.133; S.304] कतमो च पुग्गलो पुप्फभाणी ?

इधेकच्चो पुग्गलो मुसावादं पहाय मुसावादा पटिविरतो होति, सभग्गतो वा परिसग्गतो वा ञातिमज्झगतो वा पूगमज्झगतो वा राजकुलमज्झगतो वा अभिनीतो सक्खिपुट्ठो— "एहम्भो, पुरिस, यं जानासि तं वदेही"ति, सो अजानं वा

१. एहि भो — स्या०, रो०।

२. अहं — सी०, रो०, एवमुपरि पि।

आह— "न जानामी"ति, जानं वा आह— "जानामी"ति, अपस्सं वा आह— "न पस्सामी"ति, पस्सं वा आह— "पस्सामी"ति। इति अत्तहेतु वा परहेतु वा आमिसकिञ्चिक्खहेतु वा न सम्पजानमुसा भासिता होति। अयं वुच्चति पुग्गलो "पुप्फभाणी"।

(B) A person who is a flower-speaker

9. What sort of person is a 'flower-speaker'?

Here a certain person giving up falsehood refrains from speaking the same and, when he is brought into an assembly, or into the midst of a meeting, or into the midst of his relatives, or into a congregation, or into the prince's council, interrogated as witness thus: "Come, good man, tell us what you know about it"; if he does not know it, he says that he does not know it, if, on the other hand, he knows it, he confesses that he knows, if he has not seen it, he at once says that he has not seen it, but on the contrary if he has seen it, he says what he has seen. Thus neither for his own sake, nor for the sake of others, nor for the sake of any least gain to him would he speak untruth consciously. Such a person is said to be a 'flower-speaker.'

(ग) मधुभाणी पुग्गलो

१०. कतमो च पुग्गलो मधुभाणी ?

इधेकच्चो पुग्गलो या सा वाचा नेला[१] कण्णसुखा [R.30] पेमनिया[२] हदयङ्गमा पोरी बहुजनकन्ता बहुजनमनापा, तथारूपिं वाचं भासिता होति। अयं वुच्चति पुग्गलो "मधुभाणी"।

(C) A person who is honey-tongued

10. What sort of person is 'honey-tongued'?

---

१. नेळा — स्या० रो०।

२. पेमनीया — स्या०।

Here a certain person speaks those words that are blameless, pleasing to the ear, lovely, appealing to the heart, urbane, coveted by many and fascinating to many. Such a person is said to be 'honey-tongued.'

(५. क) अरुकूपमचित्तो पुग्गलो

११. [N.48] कतमो च पुग्गलो अरुकूपमचित्तो ?

इधेकच्चो पुग्गलो कोधनो होति उपायासबहुलो, अप्पं पि वुत्तो समानो अभिसज्जति कुप्पति ब्यापज्जति पतित्थीयति[१], कोपं च दोसं च अप्पच्चयं च पातुकरोति। सेय्यथापि नाम दुट्ठारुको कट्ठेन वा कठलाय वा घट्टितो भिय्योसो मत्ताय आसवं देति, एवमेवं इधेकच्चो पुग्गलो कोधनो होति उपायासबहुलो, अप्पं पि वुत्तो समानो अभिसज्जति कुप्पति ब्यापज्जति पतित्थीयति, कोपं च दोसं च अप्पच्चयं च पातुकरोति। अयं वुच्चति पुग्गलो "अरुकूपमचित्तो"।

(5. A) A person who is cancer-minded

11. What sort of person is 'cancer-minded'?

Here a certain person who is angry, full of despair, gets wrathful and enraged and becomes out of sorts and stubborn when something, however little, is spoken to him. He gives vent to his rage, to the spirit of enmity and suspicion. In the same manner as a gangrenous sore, when it is poked with a wooden stick or a stone, discharges putrid matter largely, so also there is a certain person who is angry, full of despair, gets wrathful and enraged and becomes out of sorts and gives vent to his rage, to the spirit of enmity and suspicion at the slightest provocation. Such a person is said to be 'cancer-minded.'

(ख) विज्जूपमचित्तो पुग्गलो

१२. कतमो च पुग्गलो विज्जूपमचित्तो ?

इधेकच्चो पुग्गलो "इदं दुक्खं"ति यथाभूतं पजानाति, "अयं दुक्खसमुदयो"ति यथाभूतं पजानाति, "अयं दुक्खनिरोधो"ति यथाभूतं पजानाति,

---

१. पतिट्ठीयति — स्या०, रो०, एवमुपरि पि।

"अयं दुक्खनिरोधगामिनी पटिपदा"ति यथाभूतं पजानाति। सेय्यथापि नाम चक्खुमा पुरिसो रत्तन्धकारतिमिसाय[१] विज्जन्तरिकाय रूपानि पस्सेय्य, एवमेवं इधेकच्चो पुग्गलो "इदं दुक्खं"ति यथाभूतं पजानाति, "अयं दुक्खसमुदयो"ति यथाभूतं पजानाति, "अयं दुक्खनिरोधो"ति यथाभूतं पजानाति, [B.134] "अयं दुक्खनिरोधगामिनी पटिपदा"ति यथाभूतं पजानाति। अयं वुच्चति पुग्गलो "विज्जूपमचित्तो"।

(B) A person who is lightning-minded

12. What sort of person is 'lightning-minded'?

Here a certain person truly understands that "this is suffering", truly understands that "this is the origin of suffering", truly understands that "this is the cessation of suffering", and truly understands that "this is the path leading to the cessation of suffering". Just as a person, possessed of sight, can see things by the flash of lightning in the darkness of night, so also there is a certain person who truly understands that "this is suffering", truly understands that "this is the origin of suffering", truly understands that "this is the cessation of suffering", and truly understands that "this is the path leading to the cessation of suffering". Such a person is said to be 'lightning-minded'.

(ग) वजिरूपमचित्तो पुग्गलो

१३. [S.306] कतमो च पुग्गलो वजिरूपमचित्तो ?

इधेकच्चो पुग्गलो आसवानं खया अनासवं चेतोविमुत्तिं पञ्ञाविमुत्तिं दिट्ठेव धम्मे सयं अभिञ्ञा सच्छिकत्वा उपसम्पज्ज विहरति। सेय्यथापि नाम वजिरस्स नत्थि किञ्चि अभेज्जं मणि[२] वा पासाणो[३] वा, एवमेवं इधेकच्चो पुग्गलो

---

१. रत्तन्धकारतिमिसायं — सी०।

२. मणी — सी०; नाम मणि — स्या०।

३. पासानो — सी०।

आसवानं खया अनासवं चेतोविमुत्तिं पञ्ञाविमुत्तिं दिट्ठेव धम्मे सयं अभिञ्ञा सच्छिकत्वा उपसम्पज्ज विहरति। अयं वुच्चति पुग्गलो "वजिरूपमचित्तो"।

(C) A person who is diamond-minded

13. What sort of person is diamond-minded?

Here a certain person, on the destruction of his sinful tendencies, lives having come to know and realise sinless emancipation of mind and of insight even in the present existence. Just as there is nothing which cannot be pierced by a diamond, be it a precious or ordinary stone, so also there is a certain person who, on the destruction of his sinful tendencies, lives having come to know and realise sinless emancipation of mind and of insight even in the present existence.

(६. क) अन्धो पुग्गलो

१४. [N.49] कतमो च पुग्गलो अन्धो?

इधेकच्चस्स पुग्गलस्स तथारूपं चक्खु न होति यथारूपेन चक्खुना अनधिगतं वा भोगं अधिगच्छेय्य, अधिगतं वा भोगं फातिं करेय्य; तथारूपं पिस्स[१] चक्खु न होति यथारूपेन चक्खुना कुसलाकुसले धम्मे जानेय्य, सावज्जानवज्जे धम्मे जानेय्य, हीनप्पणीते धम्मे जानेय्य, कण्हसुक्कसप्पटिभागे धम्मे जानेय्य। अयं वुच्चति पुग्गलो "अन्धो"।

(6. A) A person who is blind

14. What sort of person is blind?

Here a certain person does not possess that sight whereby he can discover and attain that wealth which has not been attained, or can augment it, he has not even that insight whereby he can distinguish good and bad, the blameworthy and the blameless, the superior and the inferior states and the admixture of dark and light qualities. Such a person is said to be blind.

---

१. पनस्स — सी०।

(ख) एकचक्खु पुग्गलो

१५. कतमो च पुग्गलो एकचक्खु ?

इधेकच्चस्स पुग्गलस्स तथारूपं चक्खु होति, यथारूपेन चक्खुना अनधिगतं वा भोगं अधिगच्छेय्य, [R.31] अधिगतं वा भोगं फातिं करेय्य; तथारूपं पिस्स चक्खु न होति यथारूपेन चक्खुना कुसलाकुसले धम्मे जानेय्य, सावज्जानवज्जे धम्मे जानेय्य, हीनप्पणीते धम्मे जानेय्य, कण्हसुक्कसप्पटिभागे धम्मे जानेय्य। अयं वुच्चति पुग्गलो "एकचक्खु"।

(B) A person who is one-eyed

15. What sort of person is 'one-eyed'?

Here a certain person who has the eye of knowledge whereby he can attain that wealth which he could not attain before and can moreover augment it, does not possess that mental vision whereby he can distinguish between the good and the bad, the blameworthy and the blameless, the superior and the inferior states as well as discover the admixture of dark and light qualities. Such a person is said to be 'one-eyed'.

(ग) द्विचक्खु पुग्गलो

१६. कतमो च पुग्गलो द्विचक्खु ?

इधेकच्चस्स पुग्गलस्स तथारूपं चक्खु होति यथारूपेन चक्खुना अनधिगतं वा भोगं अधिगच्छेय्य, अधिगतं वा भोगं फातिं करेय्य; तथारूपं पिस्स चक्खु होति यथारूपेन चक्खुना कुसलाकुसले धम्मे जानेय्य, सावज्जानवज्जे धम्मे जानेय्य, हीनप्पणीते धम्मे जानेय्य, कण्हसुक्कसप्पटिभागे धम्मे जानेय्य। अयं वुच्चति पुग्गलो "द्विचक्खु"।

(C) A person who is two-eyed

16. What sort of person is 'two-eyed'?

Here a person posseses that eye which can help him to bring that wealth which he could not attain before and also to increase it, as well as that insight which makes it possible for him to know the good and the bad, the blameworthy and the blameless, the superior and the inferior states, and the admixture of dark and light qualities. Such a person is said to be 'two-eyed'.

(७. क) अवकुज्जपञ्ञो पुग्गलो

१७. [B.135; S.308] कतमो च पुग्गलो अवकुज्जपञ्ञो ?

इधेकच्चो पुग्गलो आरामं गन्ता[१] होति अभिक्खणं भिक्खूनं सन्तिके धम्मस्सवणाय[२]। तस्स भिक्खू धम्मं देसेन्ति आदिकल्याणं मज्झेकल्याणं परियोसानकल्याणं सात्थं सब्यञ्जनं, केवलपरिपुण्णं परिसुद्धं ब्रह्मचरियं पकासेन्ति। सो तस्मिं आसने निसिन्नो तस्सा कथाय [N.50] नेव आदिं मनसि करोति, न मज्झं मनसि करोति, न परियोसानं मनसि करोति। वुट्ठितो पि तम्हा आसना तस्सा कथाय नेव आदिं मनसि करोति, न मज्झं मनसि करोति, न परियोसानं मनसि करोति। सेय्यथापि नाम कुम्भो निक्कुज्जो[३] तत्र उदकं आसित्तं विवट्टति,[४] नो सण्ठाति; एवमेवं इधेकच्चो पुग्गलो आरामं गन्ता होति अभिक्खणं भिक्खूनं सन्तिके धम्मस्सवणाय। तस्स भिक्खू धम्मं देसेन्ति आदिकल्याणं मज्झेकल्याणं परियोसानकल्याणं सात्थं सब्यञ्जनं, केवलपरिपुण्णं परिसुद्धं ब्रह्मचरियं पकासेन्ति। सो तस्मिं आसने निसिन्नो तस्सा कथाय नेव आदिं मनसि करोति, न मज्झं मनसि करोति, न परियोसानं मनसि करोति। वुट्ठितो पि तम्हा आसना तस्सा कथाय नेव आदिं मनसि करोति, न मज्झं मनसि करोति, न परियोसानं मनसि करोति। अयं वुच्चति पुग्गलो "अवकुज्जपञ्ञो"।

(7. A) A person who is of inverted intelligence

17. What sort of person is of 'inverted-intelligence'?

Here a certain person goes to a monastery in order to listen to religious discourse from the monks. The monks give instructions to him in the doctrine

१. गतो — सी०; गन्त्वा — स्या०, रो०।

२. धम्मसवणाय — सी०; धम्मस्सवनाय — स्या०; धम्मसवनाय — रो०।

३. निकुज्जो — स्या०।

४. विवत्तति — स्या०, रो०।

that is beneficial at the beginning, beneficial at the middle, and beneficial at the end, and enunciate to him the perfectly pure holy life that is full of meaning, suitably worded and in its fulness and entirety. Seated in that seat, he does not mind the discourse when it was told, nor when it was continued, nor when it was finished; in the same manner, having got up from his seat, he pays no heed to the discourse, neither at the beginning, nor at the middle, nor at the end. Even as when a jar is kept upside down, the water that is poured upon it does not accumulate but streams down, so aslo there is a certain person who goes to a monastery in order to listen to the religious discourse from the monks. The monks give instructions to him in the doctrine that is beneficial at the beginning, beneficial at the middle, and beneficial at the end, and enunciate to him the perfectly pure holy life that is full of meaning, suitably worded and in its fulness and entirety. Seated in that seat, he does not mind the discourse when it was told, nor when it was continued, nor when it was finished. In the same manner, having got up from his seat, he pays no heed to the discourse, neither at the begining, nor at the middle, nor at the end. Such a person is said to the of 'inverted-intelligence'.

(ख) उच्छङ्गपञ्ञो पुग्गलो

१८. कतमो च पुग्गलो उच्छङ्गपञ्ञो[१] ?

इधेकच्चो पुग्गलो आरामं गन्ता होति अभिक्खणं भिक्खूनं सन्तिके धम्मस्सवणाय। तस्स भिक्खू धम्मं देसेन्ति आदिकल्याणं मज्झेकल्याणं परियोसानकल्याणं सात्थं सब्यञ्जनं, केवलपरिपुण्णं परिसुद्धं ब्रह्मचरियं पकासेन्ति। सो तस्मिं आसने निसिन्नो तस्सा कथाय आदिं पि मनसि करोति, मज्झं पि मनसि करोति, परियोसानं पि मनसि करोति। वुट्ठितो च खो तम्हा आसना तस्सा कथाय

१. उच्चङ्गपञ्ञो — स्या०।

नेव आदिं मनसि करोति, न मज्झं मनसि करोति, न परियोसानं मनसि करोति। सेय्यथापि नाम पुरिसस्स उच्छङ्गे[१] नानाखज्जकानि आकिण्णानि— [R.32] तिला तण्डुला मोदका बदरा। सो तम्हा आसना वुट्ठहन्तो सतिसम्मोसा पकिरेय्य। एवमेवं इधेकच्चो पुग्गलो आरामं गन्ता होति अभिक्खणं भिक्खूनं सन्तिके धम्मस्सवणाय। तस्स भिक्खू धम्मं देसेन्ति आदिकल्याणं मज्झेकल्याणं [B.136] परियोसानकल्याणं सात्थं सब्यञ्जनं, केवलपरिपुण्णं परिसुद्धं ब्रह्मचरियं पकासेन्ति। सो तस्मिं आसने निसिन्नो तस्सा कथाय आदिं पि मनसि करोति, मज्झं पि मनसि करोति, परियोसानं पि मनसि करोति। [N.51] वुट्ठितो च[२] खो[३] तम्हा आसना तस्सा कथाय नेव आदिं पि मनसि करोति, न मज्झं[४] पि मनसि करोति, न परियोसानं पि मनसि करोति। अयं वुच्चति पुग्गलो "उच्छङ्गपञ्ञो"।

(B) A person who is of folded intelligence

18. What sort of person is of 'folded intelligence'?

Here a certain person goes to a monastery to listen to the religious discourse from the monks. The monks give instructions to him in the doctrine that is beneficial at the beginning, beneficial at the middle, and beneficial at the end, enunciate to him the perfectly pure holy life that is full of meaning, suitably worded and in its fulness and entirety. Seated in that seat he minds the discourse at the beginning, at the middle, and at the end, but having got up from his seat, he pays no heed to the discourse, neither at the beginning, nor at the middle, nor at the end. Just as a person who has in the fold of a lap of his cloth placed many kinds of food whether sesamum seed or rice, modaka (sweets) and plums, and when he rises from his seat, they are all scattered through lapse of memory. In the like manner there is a person goes to the monastery

---

१. उच्चङ्गेपि — स्या०।

२. सी० पोत्थके नत्थि।

३. सी० पोत्थके नत्थि।

४. मज्झि — सी०।

to listen to the religious discourse from the monks. The monks give instructions to him in the doctrine that is beneficial at the beginning, beneficial at the middle, and beneficial at the end, enunciate to him the perfectly pure holy life that is full of meaning, suitable worded and in its fulness and entirety. Seated in that seat he minds the discourse at the beginning, at the middle, and at the end, but having got up from his seat, he pays no heed to the discourse, neither at the beginning, nor at the middle, nor at the end. Such a person is said to be one of 'folded intelligence.'

(ग) पुथुपञ्ञो पुग्गलो

१९. [S.310] कतमो च पुग्गलो पुथुपञ्ञो ?

इधेकच्चो पुग्गलो आरामं गन्ता होति अभिक्खणं भिक्खूनं सन्तिके धम्मस्सवणाय। तस्स भिक्खू धम्मं देसेन्ति आदिकल्याणं मज्झेकल्याणं परियोसानकल्याणं सात्थं सब्यञ्जनं, केवलपरिपुण्णं परिसुद्धं ब्रह्मचरियं पकासेन्ति। सो तस्मिं आसने निसिन्नो तस्सा कथाय आदिं पि मनसि करोति, मज्झं पि मनसि करोति, परियोसानं पि मनसि करोति। वुट्ठितो पि तम्हा आसना तस्सा कथाय आदिं पि मनसि करोति, मज्झं पि मनसि करोति, परियोसानं पि मनसि करोति। सेय्यथापि नाम कुम्भो उक्कुज्जो तत्र[१] उदकं आसित्तं सण्ठाति, नो विवट्टति; एवमेवं इधेकच्चो पुग्गलो आरामं गन्ता होन्ति अभिक्खणं भिक्खूनं सन्तिके धम्मस्सवणाय। तस्स भिक्खू धम्मं देसेन्ति आदिकल्याणं मज्झेकल्याणं परियोसानकल्याणं सात्थं सब्यञ्जनं, केवलपरिपुण्णं परिसुद्धं ब्रह्मचरियं पकासेन्ति। सो तस्मिं आसने निसिन्नो तस्सा कथाय आदिं पि मनसि करोति, मज्झं पि मनसि करोति, परियोसानं पि मनसि करोति। वुट्ठितो पि तम्हा आसना तस्सा कथाय आदिं पि मनसि करोति, मज्झं पि मनसि करोति, परियोसानं पि मनसि करोति। अयं वुच्चति पुग्गलो "पुथुपञ्ञो"।

(C) A person who is of wide intelligence

19. What sort of person is of 'wide intelligence'?

---

१. तत्थ — स्या०।

Here a certain person goes to a monastery and remains listening to religious discourse from the monks. The monks give instructions to him in the doctrine that is beneficial at the beginning, beneficial at the middle, and beneficial at the end, enunciate to him the perfectly pure holy life that is full of meaning, suitably worded and in its fulness and entirety. Seated in that seat, he pays heed to the discourse at the beginning, at the middle, and at the end. When he having got up from his seat, he pays heed to the discourse at the beginning, at the middle and at the end. For example, when a jar is kept upright, the water that may be poured into it persists and does not flow away. So a certain person goes to a monastery to listen to the religious discourse from the monks. The monks give instructions to him in the doctrine that is beneficial at the beginning, beneficial at the middle, and beneficial at the end, enunciate to him the perfectly pure holy life that is full of meaning, suitably worded and in its fulness and entirety. Seated in that seat, he pays heed to the discourse at the beginning, at the middle, and at the end. When he having got up from his seat, he pays heed to the discourse at the beginning, at the middle and at the end. Such is the person who is said to be a person of 'wide intelligence'.

(८. क) कामेसु च भवेसु च अवीतरागो पुग्गलो

२०. कतमो च पुग्गलो कामेसु च भवेसु च अवीतरागो ?

सोतापन्नसकदागामिनो— इमे वुच्चन्ति पुग्गला "कामेसु च भवेसु च अवीतरागा"[१] ।

(8. A) A person who is not dispassionate as to sensual pleasures and rebirths

20. What sort of person is not dispassionate as to sensual pleasures and rebirths?

---

१. अवीतरागो — सी० ।

The 'stream-attainer' as well as the 'once-returner'– these are the person who are not dispassionate as to sensual pleasures and rebirths.

(ख) कामेसु वीतरागो भवेसु अवीतरागो पुग्गलो

२१. कतमो च पुग्गलो कामेसु वीतरागो, भवेसु अवीतरागो ?

[N.52] अनागामी— अयं वुच्चति पुग्गलो "कामेसु वीतरागो, भवेसु अवीतरागो"।

(B) A person who is dispassionate as to sensual pleasures but not dispassionate as to rebirths

21. What sort of person is dispassionate as to sensual pleasures but not dispassionate as to rebirths?

The 'never-returner'— he is said to be a person who is dispassionate as to sensual pleasures and not dispassionate as to rebirths.

(ग) कामेसु च भवेसु च वीतरागो पुग्गलो

२२. कतमो च पुग्गलो कामेसु च भवेसु च वीतरागो ?

अरहा— अयं वुच्चति पुग्गलो "कामेसु च भवेसु च वीतरागो"।

(C) A person who is dispassionate as to both sensual pleasures and rebirths

22. What sort of person is dispassionate as to both sensual pleasures and rebirths?

The 'Arahant'— he is said to be a person who is dispassionate as to both sensual pleasures and rebirths.

(९. क) पासाणलेखूपमो पुग्गलो

२३. [B.137] कतमो च पुग्गलो पासाणलेखूपमो ?

इधेकच्चो पुग्गलो अभिण्हं कुज्झति। सो च ख्वस्स कोधो चिरं दीघरत्तं अनुसेति। सेय्यथापि नाम पासाणे लेखा न खिप्पं लुज्जति वातेन वा उदकेन वा,

चिरट्ठितिका होति; एवमेवं इधेकच्चो पुग्गलो अभिण्हं कुज्झति। सो च ख्वस्स कोधो चिरं दीघरत्तं अनुसेति। अयं वुच्चति पुग्गलो "पासाणलेखूपमो"।

(9. A) A person who may be compared to a mark drawn on stone

23. What sort of person may be compared to a mark drawn on stone?

Here a certain person becomes repeatedly angry and that anger endures for a long time, just as a mark inscribed on a stone is so indelible that it cannot be effaced soon either by wind or by water, but lasts long. So also there is a person who becomes repeatedly angry and that anger endures for a long time. Such is the person who may be compared to a mark drawn on stone.

(ख) पथविलेखूपमो पुग्गलो

२४. [S.312] कतमो च पुग्गलो पथविलेखूपमो[१] ?

इधेकच्चो पुग्गलो अभिण्हं कुज्झति। सो च ख्वस्स कोधो न[२] चिरं दीघरत्तं अनुसेति। सेय्यथापि नाम पथविया लेखा खिप्पं लुज्जति वातेन वा उदकेन वा, न चिरट्ठितिका होति; एवमेवं इधेकच्चो पुग्गलो अभिण्हं कुज्झति। सो च ख्वस्स कोधो न चिरं दीघरत्तं अनुसेति। अयं वुच्चति पुग्गलो "पथविलेखूपमो"।

(B) A person who may be compared to a mark drawn on earth

24. What sort of person may be compared to a mark drawn on earth?

Here certain person gets angry repeatedly, but this passion does not last for a long time; for instance, a mark on earth disappears quickly either by wind or by water and does not last long; in the same manner

---

१. पठविलेखूपमो — सी०; पठवीलेखूपमो — स्या०, रो०, एवमुपरि पि।

२. स्या० पोत्थके नत्थि।

there is a certain person who gets angry repeatedly, but this passion does not last for a long time. Such is the person who may be compared to a mark drawn on earth.

(ग) उदकलेखूपमो पुग्गलो

२५. कतमो च पुग्गलो उदकलेखूपमो ?

इधेकच्चो पुग्गलो आगाळ्हेन[१] पि वुच्चमानो फरुसेन पि वुच्चमानो अमनापेन पि वुच्चमानो संसन्दतिमेव[२] सन्धियतिमेव[३] सम्मोदतिमेव[४] । सेय्यथापि नाम [R.33] उदके लेखा खिप्पं लुज्जति, न चिरट्ठितिका होति; एवमेवं इधेकच्चो पुग्गलो आगाळ्हेन पि वुच्चमानो फरुसेन पि वुच्चमानो [N.53] अमनापेन पि वुच्चमानो संसन्दतिमेव सन्धियतिमेव सम्मोदतिमेव। अयं वुच्चति पुग्गलो "उदकलेखूपमो"।

(C) A person who may be compared to a mark drawn on water

25. What sort of person may be compared to a mark drawn on water?

Here a certain person who, even if he is spoken to in a strong and harsh and unpleasant manner, is connected and coherent, and makes himself agreeable. Just as a mark on water disappears quickly and does not last long, so also a certain person who, even if he is spoken to in a strong and harsh and unpleasant manner, is connected and coherent, and makes himself agreeable. Such is the person who may be compared to a mark drawn on water.

(१०) तयो पोत्थकूपमा पुग्गला

२६. तत्थ कतमे तयो पोत्थकूपमा पुग्गला ?

---

१. अगाळ्हेन — सी०, स्या०, रो० ।

२. संसन्दतिचेव — स्या०, रो० ।

३. सन्धीयतिमेव — सी०; सन्धीयति चेव — स्या०, रो० ।

४. सम्मोदति चेव — स्या०, रो०, एवमुपरि पि ।

तयो पोत्थका— नवो पि पोत्थको दुब्बण्णो चेव होति दुक्खसम्फस्सो च अप्पग्घो च, मज्झिमो पि पोत्थको दुब्बण्णो चेव होति दुक्खसम्फस्सो च अप्पग्घो च, जिण्णो पि पोत्थको दुब्बण्णो चेव होति दुक्खसम्फस्सो च अप्पग्घो च। जिण्णं पि पोत्थकं उक्खलिपरिमज्जनं वा करोन्ति सङ्कारकूटे वा नं छड्डेन्ति।

(10) Three persons who are comparable to hempen cloth

26. What are the three types of persons comparable to three kinds of hempen cloth?

There are three kinds of hempen cloth— One, although new, is of bad colour, of rough texture and cheap. Another is of bad colour, rough to the touch and cheap. (The last one) which is tattered cloth, of bad colour, coarse to the touch and cheap; they use this tattered hempen cloth to cleanse the rice-boiling pot, or throw it away into the rubbish-heap.

एवमेवं तयोमे पोत्थकूपमा पुग्गला सन्तो संविज्जमाना भिक्खूसु। कतमे तयो?

नवो चे पि भिक्खु होति दुस्सीलो पापधम्मो, इदमस्स[१] दुब्बण्णताय। सेय्यथापि सो पोत्थको दुब्बण्णो, [B.138] तथूपमो अयं पुग्गलो। ये खो पनस्स सेवन्ति भजन्ति पयिरुपासन्ति दिट्ठानुगतिं आपज्जन्ति, तेसं तं होति दीघरत्तं अहिताय दुक्खाय। इदमस्स दुक्खसम्फस्सताय। सेय्यथापि सो पोत्थको दुक्खसम्फस्सो, तथूपमो अयं पुग्गलो। येसं खो पन सो[२] पटिग्गण्हाति[३] चीवरपिण्डपातसेनासनगिलानप्पच्चयभेसज्जपरिक्खारं, तेसं तं न महप्फलं होति न महानिसंसं। [S.314] इदमस्स अप्पग्घताय। सेय्यथापि सो पोत्थको अप्पग्घो, तथूपमो अयं पुग्गलो।

In the same manner there exist among the monks three types of persons comparable to these hempen cloths. What are the three?

---

१. इमस्स — म०।

२. सी०, स्या०, रो० पोत्थकेसु नत्थि।

३. पतिगण्हाति — सी०; पटिगण्हाति — रो०, एवमुपरि पि।

If a certain young Buddhist monk happens to be immoral and wicked, this is due to his want of grace. Just as a hempen cloth is of bad colour, so also is this person. Those who serve him, respect him, worship him, come to hold his views, which turn out to be harmful and a cause of suffering for them for a long time. This is due to his coarseness. Just as a hempen cloth is rough to the touch, so also is this person. There does not arise any great benefit or great advantage to those from whom he accepts clothing, food, bed, seat, clinical requisites and medicines— this is owing to the little worth of the person. Just as a hempen cloth is of little value, so also is this person.

मज्झिमो चे पि भिक्खु होति ...पे०... थेरो चे पि भिक्खु होति दुस्सीलो पापधम्मो, इदमस्स दुब्बण्णताय। सेय्यथापि सो पोत्थको दुब्बण्णो, तथूपमो अयं पुग्गलो। ये खो पनस्स सेवन्ति भजन्ति पयिरुपासन्ति दिट्ठानुगतिं आपज्जन्ति, तेसं तं होति दीघरत्तं अहिताय दुक्खाय। इदमस्स दुक्खसम्फस्सताय। सेय्यथापि सो पोत्थको दुक्खसम्फस्सो, तथूपमो अयं पुग्गलो। येसं खो पन सो पटिग्गण्हाति चीवरपिण्डपातसेनासनगिलानप्पच्चयभेसज्जपरिक्खारं, तेसं तं न महप्फलं होति न महानिसंसं। इदमस्स अप्पग्घताय। सेय्यथापि सो पोत्थको अप्पग्घो, तथूपमो अयं पुग्गलो।

If a middle-aged monk ... pe ... If a senior monk happens to be immoral and wicked, this is because of his want of grace. Just as a hempen cloth is of bad colour, so also is this person. Those who serve him, respect him, worship him, come to hold his views: this turns out to be harmful and a cause of suffering for them for a long time. This is due to his coarseness. Just as a hempen cloth is rough to the touch, so also is this person. There 'does not arise any great benefit or great advantage to those from whom such a person accepts clothing, food, bed, seat, clinical requisites and medicines. This is due to the little worth of the person. Just as that piece of cloth is of little value, so also is this person.

एवरूपो च थेरो भिक्खु सङ्घमज्झे भणति। तमेनं भिक्खू एवमाहंसु— [N.54] "किं नु खो तुय्हं बालस्स अब्यत्तस्स भणितेन, त्वं पि नाम भणितब्बं मञ्ञसी"ति! सो कुपितो[१] अनत्तमनो तथारूपिं वाचं निच्छारेति यथारूपाय वाचाय सङ्घो तं[२] उक्खिपति, सङ्कारकूटेन नं पोत्थकं। [R.34] इमे तयो पोत्थकूपमा पुग्गला सन्तो संविज्जमाना भिक्खूसु।

If such a middle-aged or elder monk speaks in the assembly, the bhikkhus will remark thus— "What is the good of your speaking, fool and inexperienced as you are, that you consider that you should speak!" He gets angry and becomes displeased and gives out such words whereby the assembly of monks ousts him in the same manner as a piece of hempen cloth is thrown on to a rubbish-heap. These are the three types of persons who live and have their being among the bhikkhus, that are comparable to a piece of hempen cloth.

(११) तयो कासिकवत्थूपमा पुग्गला

२७. तत्थ कतमे तयो कासिकवत्थूपमा पुग्गला?

तीणि कासिकवत्थानि— नवं पि कासिकवत्थं वण्णवन्तं चेव होति सुखसम्फस्सं च महग्घं च, मज्झिमं पि कासिकवत्थं वण्णवन्तं चेव होति सुखसम्फस्सं च महग्घं च, जिण्णं पि कासिकवत्थं वण्णवन्तं चेव होति सुखसम्फस्सं च महग्घं च। जिण्णं पि कासिकवत्थं रतनपलिवेठनं वा करोन्ति गन्धकरण्डके वा नं निक्खिपन्ति।

(11) Three persons who are comparable to Benares cloth

27. What are the three types of persons comparable to Benares cloth?

There are three kinds of Benares cloth— one brand-new, beautifully coloured, smooth to the touch

१. कुप्पितो — स्या०, रो०।

२. सी०, स्या० पोत्थकेसु नत्थि।

and valuable; another cloth is neither new nor old but of fine colour and smooth to the touch and of much value; another is worn out yet beautiful in colour and pleasant to the touch. They use the worn Benares cloth for enwrapping jewellery, or they throw it into the perfumed chest.

[B.139] एवमेवं तयोमे कासिकवत्थूपमा पुग्गला सन्तो संविज्जमाना भिक्खूसु। कतमे तयो?

नवो चे पि भिक्खु होति सीलवा कल्याणधम्मो, इदमस्स सुवण्णताय। सेय्यथापि तं कासिकवत्थं वण्णवन्तं, तथूपमो अयं पुग्गलो। ये खो पनस्स सेवन्ति भजन्ति पयिरुपासन्ति दिट्ठानुगतिं आपज्जन्ति, तेसं तं होति दीघरत्तं हिताय सुखाय। इदमस्स सुखसम्फस्सताय। [S.316] सेय्यथापि तं कासिकवत्थं सुखसम्फस्सं, तथूपमो अयं पुग्गलो। येसं खो पन सो पटिग्गण्हाति चीवरपिण्डपातसेनासनगिलानप्पच्चयभेसज्जपरिक्खारं, तेसं तं महप्फलं होति महानिसंसं। इदमस्स महग्घताय। सेय्यथापि तं कासिकवत्थं महग्घं, तथूपमो अयं पुग्गलो।

In the same manner there exist among the monks three types of persons comparable to Benares cloth. Which are the three?

If a new Buddhist monk happens to be virtuous and lovely, it is as beauty of colour in him. Just as Benares cloth is beatifully coloured, so is this person. Those who serve him, respect him, worship him, entertain the same views with him, this will be for their good and happiness for a long time. This is owing to the pleasure of contact with him. Just as a Benares cloth is pleasant to the touch, in the same way should this person be figured. It comes to be of good consequence and great advantage to those from whom he accepts clothing, food, bed, seat, clinical requisites and medicines. This is owing to the great worth of the person. Just as Benares cloth is valuable, so also is this person.

मज्झिमो चे पि भिक्खु ...पे०... थेरो चे पि भिक्खु होति सीलवा कल्याणधम्मो, इदमस्स सुवण्णताय। सेय्यथापि तं कासिकवत्थं वण्णवन्तं, तथूपमो अयं पुग्गलो। ये खो पनस्स सेवन्ति भजन्ति पयिरुपासन्ति दिट्ठानुगतिं आपज्जन्ति, तेसं तं होति दीघरत्तं हिताय सुखाय। इदमस्स सुखसम्फस्सताय। सेय्यथापि तं कासिकवत्थं सुखसम्फस्सं, तथूपमो अयं पुग्गलो। येसं खो पन सो पटिग्गण्हाति चीवरपिण्डपातसेनासनगिलानप्पच्चयभेसज्जपरिक्खारं, तेसं तं महप्फलं होति महानिसंसं। इदमस्स महग्घताय। सेय्यथापि तं कासिकवत्थं महग्घं, तथूपमो अयं पुग्गलो।

If a middle aged monk ...pe... If an elderly monk happens to be virtuous and good natured, this is because of his virtue. Just as a Benares cloth is of beautiful colour, so also is this person. Those who either serve him, respect him, worship him, entertain the same views as he, this will long be for their good and happiness. This is owing to the pleasure of contact with him. Just as a Benares cloth is pleasant to the touch, so also this person is amiable in disposition. It comes to be of great benefit and advantage to those from whom such a person accepts clothing, food, bed and seat, clinical requisites and medicines. This is due to the great worth of the person. Just as Benares cloth is of considerable value, so also is this person.

[N.55] एवरूपो चे[१] थेरो भिक्खु सङ्घमज्झे भणति, तमेनं भिक्खू एवमाहंसु— "अप्पसद्दा आयस्मन्तो होथ, थेरो भिक्खु धम्मं च विनयं च भणती"ति। तस्स तं वचनं आधेय्यं गच्छति, [R.35] गन्धकरण्डकेव नं कासिकवत्थं। इमे तयो कासिकवत्थूपमा पुग्गला सन्तो संविज्जमाना भिक्खूसु।

If such a senior monk happens to say something in an assembly of monks, then the monks would address the assembly thus— "Let the venerable brethren make less noise, this monk is speaking about the doctrine and the discipline," and his words will be laid to heart just in the same way as Benares cloth is deposited in

१. च — सी०।

the perfumed chest. These are the three types of person present among the bhikkhus who are comparable to Benares cloth.

(१२. क) सुप्पमेय्यो पुग्गलो

२८. कतमो च पुग्गलो सुप्पमेय्यो?

इधेकच्चो पुग्गलो उद्धतो होति उन्नळो[1] चपलो मुखरो विकिण्णवाचो मुट्ठस्सति असम्पजानो असमाहितो विब्भन्तचित्तो पाकटिन्द्रियो[2]। अयं वुच्चति पुग्गलो "सुप्पमेय्यो"।

(12. A) A person who is to be easily measured

28. What sort of person is one to be easily measured?

Here is a certain person who is haughty, insolent, fickle, garrulous, irrelevant in speech, having the memory confused, unmindful, of unsettled and erring mind with his senses out of hand. Such a person is one who may be easily measured.

(ख) दुप्पमेय्यो पुग्गलो

२९. कतमो च पुग्गलो दुप्पमेय्यो?

इधेकच्चो पुग्गलो अनुद्धतो होति अनुन्नळो अचपलो अमुखरो अविकिण्णवाचो [B.140] उपट्ठितस्सति सम्पजानो समाहितो एकग्गचित्तो संवुतिन्द्रियो। अयं वुच्चति पुग्गलो "दुप्पमेय्यो"।

(B) A person who is hard to be measured

29. What sort of person is one hard to be measured?

Here is a certain person who is not haughty, not insolent, not fickle, not garrulous, not irrelevant in speech, having the memory collected, mindful, composed and concentrated in mind and his senses

---

१. उन्नलो — सी०, रो०, एवमुपरि पि।

२. असंवुतिन्द्रियो — सी०।

controlled. Such a person is one who is hard to be measured.

(ग) अप्पमेय्यो पुग्गलो

३०. कतमो च पुग्गलो अप्पमेय्यो ?

इधेकच्चो पुग्गलो आसवानं खया अनासवं चेतोविमुत्तिं पञ्ञाविमुत्तिं दिट्ठेव धम्मे सयं अभिञ्ञा सच्छिकत्वा उपसम्पज्ज विहरति । अयं वुच्चति पुग्गलो "अप्पमेय्यो" ।

(C) A person who cannot be measured

30. What sort of person cannot be measured?

Here is a certain person who on the wearing out of the sinful tendencies, devoid of these, having by himself come to know and realise even in this life, emancipation of mind and emancipation of insight, lives in attainment thereof. Such a person is one who cannot be measured.

(१३. क) न सेवितब्बो पुग्गलो

३१. [S.318] कतमो च पुग्गलो न सेवितब्बो न भजितब्बो न पयिरुपासितब्बो ।

इधेकच्चो पुग्गलो हीनो होति सीलेन समाधिना पञ्ञाय । एवरूपो पुग्गलो न सेवितब्बो न भजितब्बो न पयिरुपासितब्बो, अञ्ञत्र अनुद्दया अञ्ञत्र अनुकम्पा ।

(13. A) A person who is not to be served

31. What sort of person should not be served nor respected nor waited upon?

Here a certain person happens to be inferior in respect of morals, concentration, and insight. Such a person should not be served, nor respected, nor waited upon except out of compassion.

(ख) सेवितब्बो पुग्गलो

३२. कतमो च पुग्गलो सेवितब्बो भजितब्बो पयिरुपासितब्बो ?

[N.56] इधेकच्चो पुग्गलो सदिसो होति सीलेन समाधिना पञ्ञाय। एवरूपो पुग्गलो सेवितब्बो भजितब्बो पयिरुपासितब्बो। तं किस्स हेतु? "सीलसामञ्ञगतानं सतं सीलकथा च नो भविस्सति, सा च नो फासु भविस्सति, सा च नो पवत्तिनी[1] भविस्सति; समाधिसामञ्ञगतानं सतं समाधिकथा च नो भविस्सति, सा च नो फासु भविस्सति, सा च नो पवत्तिनी भविस्सति; पञ्ञासामञ्ञगतानं सतं पञ्ञाकथा च नो भविस्सति, सा च नो फासु भविस्सति, सा च नो पवत्तिनी भविस्सती"ति। एवरूपो पुग्गलो सेवितब्बो भजितब्बो पयिरुपासितब्बो।

(B) A person who is to be served

32. What sort of person is to be served, respected, waited upon?

Here a certain person happens to be quite an equal in respect of morals, concentration, and insight. Such a person is to be served, respected, waited upon and for what reason? "Because of the common possession of virtue there will be virtuous discourse between us and that will be to our benefit and that will be conducive to our advance; and because of the common possession of concentration there will also be virtuous discourse on concentration; that will be to our benefit and will be conducive to our advance. And lastly, because of the common possession of insight, there will be virtuous discourse between us on insight— that will be to our benefit and it will be conducive to our advance." And it is for this reason that such a person ought to be served, cultivated, waited upon.

(ग) सक्कत्वा सेवितब्बो पुग्गलो

३३. कतमो च पुग्गलो सक्कत्वा गरुं कत्वा सेवितब्बो भजितब्बो पयिरुपासितब्बो?

---

१. पवत्तनी — सी०, एवमुपरि पि।

इधेकच्चो पुग्गलो अधिको होति सीलेन समाधिना पञ्ञाय। एवरूपो पुग्गलो सक्कत्वा गरुं कत्वा सेवितब्बो भजितब्बो पयिरुपासितब्बो। तं किस्स हेतु? "अपरिपूरं वा सीलक्खन्धं परिपूरेस्सामि, परिपूरं वा सीलक्खन्धं [R.36] तत्थ तत्थ पञ्ञाय अनुग्गहेस्सामि[१]; अपरिपूरं वा समाधिक्खन्धं परिपूरेस्सामि, परिपूरं वा समाधिक्खन्धं तत्थ तत्थ पञ्ञाय अनुग्गहेस्सामि; अपरिपूरं वा पञ्ञाक्खन्धं परिपूरेस्सामि, परिपूरं वा पञ्ञाक्खन्धं तत्थ तत्थ पञ्ञाय अनुग्गहेस्सामी"ति। तस्मा एवरूपो पुग्गलो सक्कत्वा गरुं कत्वा सेवितब्बो भजितब्बो पयिरुपासितब्बो।

(C) A person who is waited upon with respect

33. What sort of person having been honoured, revered, is to be served, cultivated, waited upon?

Here a certain person happens to be greater (than we are) in respect of virtue, concentration, insight. Such a person is to be honoured, served, waited upon. For what reason? "Because I shall fulfil the body of those precepts which are unfulfilled or I shall learn such and such precepts that I have fulfilled. Or I shall fulfil the branches of concentration which are unfulfilled, or I shall learn this and that branch by insight which I have fulfilled; lastly, because I shall do likewise as to the cultivation of insight." Therefore such a person, having been honoured, revered, should be served, cultivated and waited upon.

(१४. क) जिगुच्छितब्बो न सेवितब्बो पुग्गलो

३४. [B.141; S.320] कतमो च पुग्गलो जिगुच्छितब्बो न सेवितब्बो न भजितब्बो न पयिरुपासितब्बो?

इधेकच्चो पुग्गलो दुस्सीलो होति पापधम्मो असुचि सङ्कस्सरसमाचारो पटिच्छन्नकम्मन्तो अस्समणो समणपटिञ्ञो अब्रह्मचारी ब्रह्मचारिपटिञ्ञो अन्तोपूति अवस्सुतो कसम्बुजातो। एवरूपो पुग्गलो जिगुच्छितब्बो न सेवितब्बो न भजितब्बो न पयिरुपासितब्बो। तं किस्स हेतु? किञ्चापि एवरूपस्स पुग्गलस्स

१. अनुग्गहिस्सामि — स्या०, रो०, एवमुपरि पि।

न दिट्ठानुगतिं आपज्जति, [N.57] अथ खो नं पापको कित्तिसद्दो अब्भुग्गच्छति— “पापमित्तो पुरिसपुग्गलो पापसहायो पापसम्पवङ्को”ति। सेय्यथापि नाम अहि गूथगतो किञ्चापि न डंसति अथ खो नं मक्खेति, एवमेवं किञ्चापि एवरूपस्स पुग्गलस्स न दिट्ठानुगतिं आपज्जति, अथ खो नं पापको कित्तिसद्दो अब्भुग्गच्छति— “पापमित्तो पुरिसपुग्गलो पापसहायो पापसम्पवङ्को”ति ! तस्मा एवरूपो पुग्गलो जिगुच्छितब्बो न सेवितब्बो न भजितब्बो न पयिरुपासितब्बो।

(14. A) A person who is to be abhorred, not to be served

34. What sort of person is to be abhorred, not to be served, not to be cultivated, not to be waited upon?

Here a certain person happens to be immoral, wicked, of impure habits and conduct, doer of deeds which are concealed; unworthy of being a monk, he passes for a monk; not leading a holy life, he passes for one who leads a holy life; corrupt within, filled with sinful desires, he is one in whom foulness has accumulated. Such a person should be abhorred, not served, nor respected nor waited upon. What is the reason? Even though such a person does not entertain a heretical view, still his notoriety spreads; this person is a friend of the sinner, an associate of the sinner and is entangled with the sinner. Just as a serpent falling into filth, although it will not bite, will be besmeared with it, in the same way even though such a person does not entertain heretical views, still his notoriety spreads; this person is a friend of the sinner, an associate of the sinner and is entangled with the sinner. Therefore, such a person should be abhorred, not served, not cultivated, not waited upon.

(ख) अज्झुपेक्खितब्बो न सेवितब्बो पुग्गलो

३५. कतमो च पुग्गलो अज्झुपेक्खितब्बो न सेवितब्बो न भजितब्बो न पयिरुपासितब्बो ?

इधेकच्चो पुग्गलो कोधनो होति उपायासबहुलो, अप्पं पि वुत्तो समानो अभिसज्जति कुप्पति ब्यापज्जति पतित्थीयति, कोपं च दोसं च अप्पच्चयं च पातुकरोति। सेय्यथापि नाम दुट्ठारुको[१] कट्ठेन वा कठलाय वा घट्टितो[२] भिय्योसो मत्ताय आसवं[३] देति,[४] एवमेवं इधेकच्चो पुग्गलो कोधनो होति उपायासबहुलो, अप्पं पि वुत्तो समानो अभिसज्जति कुप्पति ब्यापज्जति पतित्थीयति, कोपं च दोसं च अप्पच्चयं च पातुकरोति। सेय्यथापि नाम तिन्दुकालातं कट्ठेन वा कठलाय वा घट्टितं भिय्योसो मत्ताय चिच्चिटायति चिटिचिटायति, एवमेवं इधेकच्चो पुग्गलो कोधनो होति उपायासबहुलो, अप्पं पि वुत्तो समानो अभिसज्जति कुप्पति ब्यापज्जति पतित्थीयति, कोपं च दोसं च अप्पच्चयं च पातुकरोति। सेय्यथापि नाम गूथकूपो कट्ठेन वा कठलाय वा घट्टितो भिय्योसो मत्ताय दुग्गन्धो होति, एवमेवं इधेकच्चो पुग्गलो कोधनो होति उपायासबहुलो, अप्पं पि वुत्तो समानो अभिसज्जति कुप्पति ब्यापज्जति पतित्थीयति, कोपं च दोसं च अप्पच्चयं [R.37] च पातुकरोति; एवरूपो पुग्गलो अज्झुपेक्खितब्बो न सेवितब्बो न भजितब्बो न पयिरुपासितब्बो। तं किस्स हेतु? "अक्कोसेय्य पि मं परिभासेय्य पि मं [B.142] अनत्थं पि मे[५] करेय्या"ति! तस्मा एवरूपो पुग्गलो अज्झुपेक्खितब्बो न सेवितब्बो न भजितब्बो न पयिरुपासितब्बो।

(B) A person who is to be treated with indifference, not to be served

35. What sort of person is to be treated with indifference, not served, not cultivated, not waited upon?

Here a certain person who is wrathful and irascible, who, if anything, however little, is said, at once becomes displeased, angry, out of sorts, stubborn, and gives vent to anger, enmity, and discontent. Just as a gangrenous sore when poked by means of a

---

१. दुट्ठारुका — सी०।

२. घट्टिता — सी०।

३. अस्सवनो — सी०।

४. ति — सी०।

५. मं — सी०।

wooden stick or stone discharges putrid matter largely, so also there is such a person who is wrathful and irascible, who, if anything, however little, is said, at once becomes displeased, angry, out of sorts, stubborn, and gives vent to anger, enmity and discontent. Just as an ember of tiṇḍuka when poked by means of a stick or stone makes a hissing noise, so also there is such a person who is wrathful and irascible, who, if anything, however little, is said, at once becomes displeased, angry, out of sorts, stubborn, and gives vent to anger, enmity and discontent. Just as a pit full of filth when churned by means of a stick or stone gives out an exceedingly bad odour, so also there is such a person who is wrathful and irascible, who, if anything, however little, is said, at once becomes displeased, angry, out of sorts, stubborn, and gives vent to anger, enmity and discontent. Such a person is to be treated with indifference, not served, not cultivated, not waited upon; and for what reason? "Because, out of anger he may speak ill of me, ridicule me, and do me some harm." Therefore, such a person is to be treated with indifference, not to be served, not cultivated, not waited upon.

(ग) सेवितब्बो पुग्गलो

३६. [S.322] कतमो च पुग्गलो सेवितब्बो भजितब्बो पयिरुपासितब्बो ?

[N.58] इधेकच्चो पुग्गलो सीलवा होति कल्याणधम्मो। एवरूपो पुग्गलो सेवितब्बो भजितब्बो पयिरुपासितब्बो। तं किस्स हेतु? किञ्चापि एवरूपस्स पुग्गलस्स पन[१] दिट्ठानुगतिं आपज्जति, अथ खो नं कल्याणो कित्तिसद्दो अब्भुग्गच्छति— "कल्याणमित्तो पुरिसपुग्गलो कल्याणसहायो कल्याणसम्पवङ्को"ति! तस्मा एवरूपो पुग्गलो सेवितब्बो भजितब्बो पयिरुपासितब्बो।

---

१. न — ना०, म०।

(C) A person who is to be served

36. What sort of person is to be served, cultivated, waited upon?

Here a certain person happens to be virtuous and of lovely disposition. Such a person is to be served, cultivated, waited upon; and for what reason? Even if such a person happens to entertain a heretical view, still a good fame will be abroad that such a person is the friend, the associate, of lovely persons, is entangled with them. Therefore, such a person should be served, cultivated, waited upon.

(१५. क) सीलेसु परिपूरकारी पुग्गलो

३७. कतमो च पुग्गलो सीलेसु परिपूरकारी[१], समाधिस्मिं मत्तसो कारी, पञ्ञाय मत्तसो कारी ?

सोतापन्नसकदागामिनो— इमे वुच्चन्ति पुग्गला सीलेसु परिपूरकारिनो, समाधिस्मिं मत्तसो कारिनो, पञ्ञाय मत्तसो कारिनो ।

(15. A) A person who fulfils the moral laws

37. What sort of person is he who fulfils the moral laws but incompletely practises concentration and the way of insight?

The 'stream-attainer' as also the 'once-returner'—these are the persons who fulfil the moral laws, but incompletely practises concentration and the way of insight.

(ख) सीलसमाधिसु परिपूरकारी पुग्गलो

३८. कतमो च पुग्गलो सीलेसु च परिपूरकारी, समाधिस्मिं च परिपूरकारी, पञ्ञाय मत्तसो कारी ?

अनागामी— अयं वुच्चति पुग्गलो सीलेसु च परिपूरकारी, समाधिस्मिं च परिपूरकारी, पञ्ञाय मत्तसो कारी ।

---

१. परिपूरीकारी — स्या०, एवमुपरि पि ।

(B) A person who fulfils the moral laws and completes the practices of concentration

38. What sort of person is he who fulfils the moral laws and completes the practices of concentration, but incompletely practises the way of insight?

The 'never-returner'— such is the person who fulfils the moral laws and completes the practices of concentration, but incompletely practises the way of insight.

(ग) सीलसमाधिपञ्ञासु परिपूरकारी पुग्गलो

३९. कतमो च पुग्गलो सीलेसु च परिपूरकारी, समाधिस्मिं च परिपूरकारी, पञ्ञाय च परिपूरकारी ?

अरहा— अयं वुच्चति पुग्गलो सीलेसु च परिपूरकारी, समाधिस्मिं च परिपूरकारी, पञ्ञाय च परिपूरकारी।

(C) A person who fulfils the moral laws and completes the practices of concentration and also completely practises the way of insight

39. What sort of person is he who fulfils the moral laws and completes the practices of concentration and also completely practises the way of insight?

The 'Arahant'— such is the person who fulfils the moral laws and completes the practices of concentration and also completely practises the way of insight.

(१६) तयो सत्थारो

४०. तत्थ कतमे तयो सत्थारो ?

इधेकच्चो सत्था कामानं परिञ्ञं पञ्ञपेति[१], न रूपानं परिञ्ञं पञ्ञपेति, न वेदनानं परिञ्ञं पञ्ञपेति। इध पनेकच्चो सत्था कामानं च परिञ्ञं पञ्ञपेति, रूपानं च परिञ्ञं पञ्ञपेति, न वेदनानं [N.59] परिञ्ञं पञ्ञपेति। इध पनेकच्चो सत्था

१. पञ्ञापेति — सी०, स्या०, रो०, एवमुपरि पि।

कामानं च परिञ्ञं पञ्ञपेति, रूपानं च परिञ्ञं पञ्ञपेति, वेदनानं च परिञ्ञं पञ्ञपेति।

(16) Three teachers

40. Who are the three teachers?

Here a certain teacher sets out an understanding of sense-desires, but neither sets out an understanding of the objects of sense nor sets out an understanding of sense-feelings. Again, here another teacher sets out an understanding of sense-desires and sets out an understanding of the objects of sense, but not sets out an understanding of sense-feelings. And lastly here there is a teacher who sets out an understanding of sense-desires and sets out an understanding of the objects of sense and also sets out an understanding of sense-feelings.

तत्र य्वायं सत्था कामानं परिञ्ञं पञ्ञपेति, न रूपानं परिञ्ञं पञ्ञपेति, न वेदनानं परिञ्ञं पञ्ञपेति, रूपावचरसमापत्तिया लाभी सत्था तेन दट्ठब्बो।

Now, here a teacher sets out an understanding of sense-desires, but neither sets out an understanding of the objects of sense nor sets out an understanding of sense-feelings as a teacher who has attained the ecstatic state belonging to the world of form (Rūpa-loka).

[R.38] तत्र य्वायं सत्था कामानं च परिञ्ञं पञ्ञपेति, [B.143] रूपानं च परिञ्ञं पञ्ञपेति, न वेदनानं परिञ्ञं पञ्ञपेति, अरूपावचरसमापत्तिया लाभी सत्था तेन दट्ठब्बो।

Again, there is a teacher who sets out an understanding of sense-desires and sets out an understanding of the objects of sense, but not sets out an understanding of sense-feelings as a teacher who has attained ecstatic meditation belonging to the world of the formless (Arūpa-loka).

तत्र य्वायं सत्था कामानं च परिञ्ञं पञ्ञपेति, रूपानं च परिञ्ञं पञ्ञपेति, वेदनानं च परिञ्ञं पञ्ञपेति, सम्मासम्बुद्धो सत्था तेन दट्ठब्बो। इमे तयो सत्थारो।

Lastly, there is a teacher who sets out an understanding of sense-desires and sets out an understanding of the objects of sense and also sets out an understanding of sense-feelings as a teacher who is Perfectly Enlightened. These are the three teachers.

(१७) अपरे पि तयो सत्थारो

४१. [S.324] तत्थ कतमे अपरे पि तयो सत्थारो?

इधेकच्चो सत्था दिट्ठे चेव धम्मे अत्तानं सच्चतो थेततो पञ्ञपेति, अभिसम्परायं च अत्तानं सच्चतो थेततो पञ्ञपेति। इध पनेकच्चो सत्था दिट्ठे[1] चेव[1] धम्मे अत्तानं सच्चतो थेततो पञ्ञपेति, नो च खो अभिसम्परायं अत्तानं सच्चतो थेततो पञ्ञपेति। इध पनेकच्चो सत्था दिट्ठे चेव धम्मे अत्तानं सच्चतो थेततो न पञ्ञपेति, अभिसम्परायं च अत्तानं सच्चतो थेततो न पञ्ञपेति।

(17) Other three teachers

41. Who are other three teachers?

Here a certain teacher sets out soul as something real and permanent in the present life as well as in the future life. Again, another teacher sets out soul as something real and permanent as far as this world is concerned but does not say so with regard to any future existence. Lastly, a certain teacher does not set it out as a real and permanent entity either in regard to the present or to the future life.

तत्र य्वायं सत्था दिट्ठे चेव धम्मे अत्तानं सच्चतो थेततो पञ्ञपेति, अभिसम्परायं च अत्तानं सच्चतो थेततो पञ्ञपेति, सस्सतवादो सत्था तेन दट्ठब्बो।

Here the teacher sets out soul as something real and permanent in the present life as well as in the future life. This is to be understood as a teacher who upholds the doctrine of Eternalism.

तत्र य्वायं सत्था दिट्ठे चेव धम्मे अत्तानं सच्चतो थेततो पञ्ञपेति, नो च खो अभिसम्परायं अत्तानं सच्चतो थेततो पञ्ञपेति, उच्छेदवादो सत्था तेन दट्ठब्बो।

१-१. दिट्ठेव — सी०, रो०।

Again, the teacher sets out soul as somethings real and permanent as far as this world is concerned but does not say so with regard to any future existence. This is to be understood as a teacher who upholds the doctrine of Annihilationism.

तत्र ख्वायं सत्था दिट्ठे चेव धम्मे अत्तानं सच्चतो थेततो न पञ्ञपेति, अभिसम्परायं च अत्तानं सच्चतो थेततो न पञ्ञपेति, सम्मासम्बुद्धो सत्था तेन दट्ठब्बो। इमे अपरे पि तयो सत्थारो।

तिकनिद्देसो निट्ठितो।

Lastly, the teacher does not set it out as a real and permanent entity either in regard to the present or to the future life. This is to be understood as the teacher who is Perfectly Enlightened. These are the other three teachers.

Here ends the specification of grouping by three.

चतुत्थो परिच्छेदो

४. चतुक्कपुग्गलपञ्ञत्ति

(१. क) असप्पुरिसो पुग्गलो

१. [N.60; S.326] कतमो च पुग्गलो असप्पुरिसो ?

इधेकच्चो पुग्गलो पाणातिपाती होति, अदिन्नादायी होति, कामेसुमिच्छाचारी होति, मुसावादी होति, सुरामेरयमज्जपमादट्ठायी होति। अयं वुच्चति पुग्गलो "असप्पुरिसो"।

CHAPTER FOUR

4. Division of Human Types by Four

(1. A) A person who is not a good man

1. What sort of person is 'not a good man'?

Here a certain person is a destroyer of life, taker of things not given, misbehaving in sensual desires, liar, one indulging in the enjoyment of spirituous, fermented liquors and intoxicants. Such is the person who is called 'not a good man.'

(ख) असप्पुरिसेन असप्पुरिसतरो पुग्गलो

२. [R.39] कतमो च पुग्गलो असप्पुरिसेन असप्पुरिसतरो ?

इधेकच्चो पुग्गलो अत्तना च पाणातिपाती होति परं च पाणातिपाते [B.144] समादपेति, अत्तना च अदिन्नादायी होति परं च अदिन्नादाने समादपेति, अत्तना च कामेसुमिच्छाचारी होति परं च कामेसुमिच्छाचारे समादपेति, अत्तना च मुसावादी होति परं च मुसावादे समादपेति, अत्तना च सुरामेरयमज्जपमादट्ठायी

होति परं च सुरामेरयमज्जपमादट्ठाने समादपेति। अयं वुच्चति पुग्गलो "असप्पुरिसेन असप्पुरिसतरो"।

(B) A person who is more not a good man, than the not good man

2. What sort of person is more 'not a good man,' than the 'not good man'?

Here a certain person is himself a destroyer of life and instigates others to destroy life, himself takes things not given and instigates others to takes things not given, himself misbehaves in the matter of sensual desires and instigates others to misbehave in the matter of sensual desires, himself tells a lie and instigates others to tell a lie, himself indulges in the enjoyment of spirituous, fermented liquors and intoxicants and instigates others to indulges in the enjoyment of spirituous, fermented liquors and intoxicants. Such is the person who is said to be more 'not a good man' than the 'not good man.'

(ग) सप्पुरिसो पुग्गलो

३. कतमो च पुग्गलो सप्पुरिसो ?

इधेकच्चो पुग्गलो पाणातिपाता पटिविरतो होति, अदिन्नादाना पटिविरतो होति, कामेसुमिच्छाचारा पटिविरतो होति, मुसावादा[१] पटिविरतो होति[१], सुरामेरयमज्जपमादट्ठाना पटिविरतो होति। अयं वुच्चति पुग्गलो "सप्पुरिसो"।

(C) A person who is a good man

3. What sort of person is a 'good man'?

Here a certain person refrains from destruction of life, refrains from taking anything not given, refrains from misbehaviour in the matter of sensual pleasures, refrains from speaking falsehood, and refrains from indulging in the enjoyment of spirituous, fermented

१-१. रो० पोत्थके नत्थि।

liquors and intoxicants. Such is the person who is said to be a 'good man.'

(घ) सप्पुरिसेन सप्पुरिसतरो पुग्गलो

४. कतमो च पुग्गलो सप्पुरिसेन सप्पुरिसतरो ?

इधेकच्चो पुग्गलो अत्तना च पाणातिपाता पटिविरतो होति परं च पाणातिपाता वेरमणिया समादपेति, अत्तना च अदिन्नादाना पटिविरतो होति परं च अदिन्नादाना वेरमणिया समादपेति, अत्तना च कामेसुमिच्छाचारा पटिविरतो होति परं च कामेसुमिच्छाचारा वेरमणिया [N.61] समादपेति, अत्तना च मुसावादा पटिविरतो होति परं च मुसावादा वेरमणिया समादपेति, अत्तना च सुरामेरयमज्जपमादट्ठाना पटिविरतो होति परं च सुरामेरयमज्जपमादट्ठाना वेरमणिया समादपेति। अयं वुच्चति पुग्गलो "सप्पुरिसेन सप्पुरिसतरो"।

(D) A person who is a better man than the good man

4. What sort of person is a better man than the good man?

Here a certain person, while he himself refrains from the destruction of life, incites others to refrain from the destruction of life; himself refrains from taking things not given, incites others to refrain from taking things not given; himself refrains from misbehaviour in sensual pleasures, incites others to refrain, from misbehaviour in sensual pleasures; himself refrains from speaking falsehood, incites others to refrain from speaking falsehood; himself refrains from indulging in the enjoyment of spirituous, fermented liquors and intoxicants, incites others to refrain from indulging in the enjoyment of spirituous, fermented liquors and intoxicants. Such is the person who is said to be a better man than the good man.

(२. क) पापो पुग्गलो

५. [S.328] कतमो च पुग्गलो पापो ?

इधेकच्चो पुग्गलो पाणातिपाती होति, अदिन्नादायी होति, कामेसुमिच्छाचारी होति, मुसावादी होति, पिसुणवाचो[१] होति, फरुसवाचो[२] होति, सम्फप्पलापी होति, अभिज्झालु होति, ब्यापन्नचित्तो होति, मिच्छादिट्ठि होति। अयं वुच्चति पुग्गलो "पापो"।

(2. A) A person who is wicked

5. What sort of person is wicked?

Here a certain person is a destroyer of life, taker of things not given, misbehaves in sensual pleasures, is a liar, a slanderer, speaks harsh words, is a gossip, covetous, of malevolent thoughts, an upholder of false doctrines. Such a person is said to be wicked.

(ख) पापेन पापतरो पुग्गलो

६. कतमो च पुग्गलो पापेन पापतरो?

इधेकच्चो पुग्गलो अत्तना च पाणातिपाती होति परं च पाणातिपाते समादपेति, [B.145] अत्तना च अदिन्नादायी होति परं च अदिन्नादाने समादपेति, अत्तना च कामेसुमिच्छाचारी होति परं च कामेसुमिच्छाचारे समादपेति, अत्तना च मुसावादी होति परं च मुसावादे समादपेति, अत्तना च पिसुणवाचो होति परं च पिसुणाय वाचाय समादपेति, अत्तना च [R.40] फरुसवाचो होति परं च फरुसाय वाचाय समादपेति, अत्तना च सम्फप्पलापी होति परं च सम्फप्पलापे समादपेति, अत्तना च अभिज्झालु होति परं च अभिज्झाय समादपेति, अत्तना च ब्यापन्नचित्तो होति परं च ब्यापादे समादपेति, अत्तना च मिच्छादिट्ठि होति परं च मिच्छादिट्ठिया समादपेति। अयं वुच्चति पुग्गलो "पापेन पापतरो"।

(B) A person who is more wicked than the wicked

6. What sort of person is more wicked than the wicked?

Here a certain person, while he himself destroys life and instigates others to destroy life, while himself takes things not given and instigates others to take

---

१. पिसुनावाचो — सी०।

२. फरुसावाचो — सी०।

things not given, while himself misbehaves in sensual pleasures and instigates others to misbehave in sensual pleasures, while himself is a liar and instigates others to tell a lie, while himself is a slanderer and instigates others to slander, himself a harsh speaker and instigates others to use harsh language, himself a gossip and instigates others to gossip, himself covetous and instigates others towards covetousness, himself of malevolent nature and instigates others to be malevolent, himself an upholder of wrong views and instigates others to entertain such wrong views. Such a person is said to be more wicked than the wicked.

(ग) कल्याणो पुग्गलो

७. कतमो च पुग्गलो कल्याणो ?

इधेकच्चो पुग्गलो पाणातिपाता पटिविरतो होति, अदिन्नादाना पटिविरतो होति, कामेसुमिच्छाचारा पटिविरतो होति, मुसावादा पटिविरतो होति, पिसुणाय वाचाय पटिविरतो होति, फरुसाय वाचाय पटिविरतो होति, सम्फप्पलापा पटिविरतो होति, अनभिज्झालु होति, [N.62] अब्यापन्नचित्तो होति, सम्मादिट्ठि होति। अयं वुच्चति पुग्गलो "कल्याणो"।

(C) A person who is of lovely disposition

7. What sort of person is of lovely disposition?

Here a certain person refrains from killing life, refrains from taking what is not given, refrains from misbehaving in sensual pleasures, refrains from speaking falsehood, refrains from slanderous speech, refrains from using harsh language, refrains from gossip, is not covetous, is not malevolent, is an upholder of right views. Such a person is said to be of lovely disposition.

(घ) कल्याणेन कल्याणतरो पुग्गलो

८. कतमो च पुग्गलो कल्याणेन कल्याणतरो ?

इधेकच्चो पुग्गलो अत्तना च पाणातिपाता पटिविरतो होति परं च पाणातिपाता वेरमणिया समादपेति, अत्तना च अदिन्नादाना पटिविरतो होति परं च अदिन्नादाना वेरमणिया समादपेति, अत्तना च कामेसुमिच्छाचारा पटिविरतो होति परं च कामेसुमिच्छाचारा वेरमणिया समादपेति, अत्तना च मुसावादा पटिविरतो होति [S.330] परं च मुसावादा वेरमणिया समादपेति, अत्तना च पिसुणाय वाचाय पटिविरतो होति परं च पिसुणाय वाचाय वेरमणिया समादपेति, अत्तना च फरुसाय वाचाय पटिविरतो होति परं च फरुसाय वाचाय वेरमणिया समादपेति, अत्तना च सम्फप्पलापा पटिविरतो होति परं च सम्फप्पलापा वेरमणिया समादपेति, अत्तना च अनभिज्झालु होति परं च अनभिज्झाय समादपेति, अत्तना च अब्यापन्नचित्तो होति परं च अब्यापादे समादपेति, अत्तना च सम्मादिट्ठि होति [B.146] परं च सम्मादिट्ठिया समादपेति । अयं वुच्चति पुग्गलो "कल्याणेन कल्याणतरो" ।

(D) A person who is more lovely than one of lovely disposition

8. What sort of person is more lovely than one of lovely disposition?

Here a certain person himself refrains from destruction of life, and incites others as well to cease to kill; himself a refrainer from taking things not given, and incites others to abstain from taking what is not given; himself refrains from misbehaving in sensual pleasures, and incites others to refrain from misbehaving in sensual pleasures; himself refrains from speaking falsehood, and incites others to refrain from speaking falsehood; himself refrains from slanderous speech, and incites others to refrain from slanderous speech; himself refrains from using harsh language, and incites others to refrain from using harsh language; himself refrains from gossip, and incites others to refrain from gossip; himself is not covetous, and incites others to not covetous; himself is not molevolent, and incites others to not molevolent; himself is an upholder of right views, and incites others to right views. Such is the person who is more lovely than one of lovely disposition.

(३. क) पापधम्मो पुग्गलो

९. कतमो च पुग्गलो पापधम्मो ?

इधेकच्चो पुग्गलो पाणातिपाती होति, अदिन्नादायी होति ... पे० ... मिच्छादिट्ठि होति। अयं वुच्चति पुग्गलो "पापधम्मो"।

(3. A) A person who is of a wicked nature

9. What sort of person is of a 'wicked nature'?

Here a certain person is a destroyer of life, taker of things not given ....pe... an upholder of false doctrines. Such a person is said to be 'wicked nature.'

(ख) पापधम्मेन पापधम्मतरो पुग्गलो

१०. कतमो च पुग्गलो पापधम्मेन पापधम्मतरो ?

इधेकच्चो पुग्गलो अत्तना च पाणातिपाती होति परं च पाणातिपाते समादपेति, अत्तना च अदिन्नादायी होति परं च अदिन्नादाने समादपेति ...पे०... अत्तना च मिच्छादिट्ठि होति परं च मिच्छादिट्ठिया समादपेति। अयं वुच्चति पुग्गलो "पापधम्मेन पापधम्मतरो"।

(B) A person who is more wicked nature than the wicked nature

10. What sort of person is of a more wicked nature than he who is wicked nature?

Here a certain person, while he himself destroys life, instigates others to destroy life; while himself takes things not given, instigates others to take things not given ...pe... himself an upholder of wrong views, instigates others to entertain such views. Such a person is said to be 'more wicked nature than the wicked nature'.

(ग) कल्याणधम्मो पुग्गलो

११. कतमो च पुग्गलो कल्याणधम्मो ?

[N.63] इधेकच्चो पुग्गलो पाणातिपाता पटिविरतो होति, अदिन्नादाना पटिविरतो होति...पे०... सम्मादिट्ठि होति । अयं वुच्चति पुग्गलो "कल्याणधम्मो" ।

(C) A person who is of a lovely nature?

11. What sort of person is of a lovely nature?

Here a certain person refrains from killing life, refrains from taking what is not given ...pe... is an upholder of right views. Such a person is said to be of a 'lovely nature'.

(घ) कल्याणधम्मेन कल्याणधम्मतरो पुग्गलो

१२. कतमो च पुग्गलो कल्याणधम्मेन कल्याणधम्मतरो ?

इधेकच्चो पुग्गलो अत्तना च पाणातिपाता पटिविरतो होति परं च पाणातिपाता वेरमणिया समादपेति...पे०... अत्तना च सम्मादिट्ठि होति परं च सम्मादिट्ठिया समादपेति। अयं वुच्चति पुग्गलो "कल्याणधम्मेन कल्याणधम्मतरो" ।

(D) A person who is of a more lovely nature than one of lovely nature

12. What sort of person is of a more lovely nature than he who is of a lovely nature?

Here a certain person himself refrains from destruction of life, and incites others to refrain from destruction of life ...pe... himself is an upholder of right views, and incites others to right views. Such is the person who is 'more lovely than one of lovely nature'.

(४. क) सावज्जो पुग्गलो

१३. [R.41] कतमो च पुग्गलो सावज्जो ?

इधेकच्चो पुग्गलो सावज्जेन कायकम्मेन समन्नागतो होति, सावज्जेन वचीकम्मेन समन्नागतो होति, सावज्जेन मनोकम्मेन समन्नागतो होति। अयं वुच्चति पुग्गलो "सावज्जो"।

(4. A) A person who is blameworthy

13. What sort of person is blameworthy?

Here a certain person has come to have blameworthy action, has come to have blameworthy speech, and has come to have blameworthy thought. Such is the person who is said to be 'blameworthy'.

(ख) वज्जबहुलो पुग्गलो

१४. [S.332] कतमो च पुग्गलो वज्जबहुलो[१] ?

इधेकच्चो पुग्गलो सावज्जेन बहुलं कायकम्मेन समन्नागतो होति अप्पं अनवज्जेन, सावज्जेन बहुलं वचीकम्मेन समन्नागतो होति अप्पं अनवज्जेन, सावज्जेन बहुलं मनोकम्मेन समन्नागतो होति अप्पं अनवज्जेन। अयं वुच्चति पुग्गलो "वज्जबहुलो"।

(B) A person who is exceedingly blameworthy

14. What sort of person is exceedingly blameworthy?

Here a certain person has come to have more of blameworthy action and less of unblameworthy (action), has come to have more of blameworthy speech and less of unblameworthy (speech), has come to have more of blameworthy thought and less of unblameworthy (thought). Such is the person who is said to be 'exceedingly blameworthy'.

(ग) अप्पवज्जो पुग्गलो

१५. [B.147] कतमो च पुग्गलो अप्पवज्जो[२] ?

---

१. सावज्जबहुलो — सी०, एवमुपरि पि।

२. अप्पसावज्जो — सी०, रो०, एवमुपरि पि।

इधेकच्चो पुग्गलो अनवज्जेन बहुलं कायकम्मेन समन्नागतो होति अप्पं सावज्जेन, अनवज्जेन बहुलं वचीकम्मेन समन्नागतो होति अप्पं सावज्जेन, अनवज्जेन बहुलं मनोकम्मेन समन्नागतो होति अप्पं सावज्जेन। अयं वुच्चति पुग्गलो "अप्पवज्जो"।

(C) A person who is little blameworthy

15. What sort of person is little blameworthy?

Here a certain person has come to have more of unblameworthy action and less of blameworthy, has come to have more of unblameworthy speech and less of blameworthy, has come to have more of unblameworthy thought and less of blameworthy. Such is the person who is said to be 'little blameworthy.'

(घ) अनवज्जो पुग्गलो

१६. [N.64] कतमो च पुग्गलो अनवज्जो?

इधेकच्चो पुग्गलो अनवज्जेन कायकम्मेन समन्नागतो होति, अनवज्जेन वचीकम्मेन समन्नागतो होति, अनवज्जेन मनोकम्मेन समन्नागतो होति। अयं वुच्चति पुग्गलो "अनवज्जो"।

(D) A person who is blameless

16. What sort of person is blameless?

Here a certain person has come to have blameless action, has come to have blameless speech, and has come to have blameless thought. Such a person is said to be 'blameless'.

(५. क) उग्घटितञ्ञू पुग्गलो

१७. कतमो च पुग्गलो उग्घटितञ्ञू?

यस्स पुग्गलस्स सह उदाहटवेलाय धम्माभिसमयो होति— अयं वुच्चति पुग्गलो "उग्घटितञ्ञू"।

(5. A) A person who is quick in acquiring

17. What sort of person is quick in acquiring?

The person who comprehends the doctrine at the time of its pronouncement— such a person is said to be 'quick in acquiring.'

(ख) विपञ्चितञ्ञू पुग्गलो

१८. कतमो च पुग्गलो विपञ्चितञ्ञू[१]?

यस्स पुग्गलस्स सङ्खित्तेन भासितस्स वित्थारेन अत्थे विभजियमाने धम्माभिसमयो होति— अयं वुच्चति पुग्गलो "विपञ्चितञ्ञू"।

(B) A person who learns by exposition

18. What sort of person learns by exposition?

The person to whom comprehension of the doctrine comes when the meaning of what is briefly uttered is analysed in detail— such a person is said to be learn by exposition.

(ग) नेय्यो पुग्गलो

१९. कतमो च पुग्गलो नेय्यो?

यस्स पुग्गलस्स उद्देसतो परिपुच्छतो योनिसो मनसिकरोतो कल्याणमित्ते सेवतो भजतो पयिरुपासतो एवं अनुपुब्बेन धम्माभिसमयो होति— अयं वुच्चति पुग्गलो "नेय्यो"।

(C) A person who may be led

19. What sort of person is one who may be led?

The person to whom comprehension of the doctrine comes by recitation, questioning, and earnest attention and by serving, cultivating and waiting upon lovely friends— such a person is one who may be led.

(घ) पदपरमो पुग्गलो

२०. कतमो च पुग्गलो पदपरमो?

---

१. विपचितञ्ञू — सी०; विपच्चितञ्ञू — रो०।

यस्स पुग्गलस्स बहुं पि सुणतो बहुं पि भणतो बहुं पि धारयतो बहुं पि वाचयतो न ताय जातिया धम्माभिसमयो होति— अयं वुच्चति पुग्गलो "पदपरमो"।

(D) A person who is one with whom the word is the chief thing

20. What sort of person is one with whom the word is the chief thing?

The person to whom comprehension of doctrine would not come in this life, however much he may hear and much he may say and much he may bear in mind and much he may recite— such a person is said to be one with whom the word is the chief thing.

(६. क) युत्तप्पटिभानो, नो मुत्तप्पटिभानो

२१. [R.42; S.334] कतमो च पुग्गलो युत्तप्पटिभानो[१] नो मुत्तप्पटिभानो[२] ?

इधेकच्चो पुग्गलो पञ्हं पुट्ठो समानो युत्तं वदति नो सीघं। अयं वुच्चति पुग्गलो "युत्तप्पटिभानो नो मुत्तप्पटिभानो"।

(6. A) A person who makes a fit but not a prompt reply

21. What sort of person is one who makes a fit but not a prompt reply?

Here a certain person answers correctly but not quickly when a question is put to him. Such a person is said to be one who 'makes a fit but not a prompt reply.'

(ख) मुत्तप्पटिभानो, नो युत्तप्पटिभानो

२२. [N.65; B.148] कतमो च पुग्गलो मुत्तप्पटिभानो नो युत्तप्पटिभानो ?

---

१. युत्तपटिभानो — सी०, रो०; युत्तपटिभाणो — स्या०, एवमुपरि पि।

२. नो मुत्तपटिभानो — सी० रो०; नो मुत्तपटिभाणो — स्या०, एवमुपरि पि।

इधेकच्चो पुग्गलो पञ्हं पुट्ठो समानो सीघं वदति नो युत्तं। अयं वुच्चति पुग्गलो "मुत्तप्पटिभानो नो युत्तप्पटिभानो"।

(B) A person who makes a prompt but not a fit reply

22. What sort of person is one who makes a prompt but not a fit reply?

Here a certain person answers quickly but not fitly when a question is put to him. Such a person is said to be one who 'makes a prompt but not a fit reply'.

(ग) युत्तप्पटिभानो च मुत्तप्पटिभानो च

२३. कतमो च पुग्गलो युत्तप्पटिभानो च मुत्तप्पटिभानो च?

इधेकच्चो पुग्गलो पञ्हं पुट्ठो समानो युत्तं च वदति सीघं च। अयं वुच्चति पुग्गलो "युत्तप्पटिभानो च मुत्तप्पटिभानो च"।

(C) A person who makes a fit and prompt reply

23. What sort of person is one who makes a fit and prompt reply?

Here a certain person who answers quickly and says the fit thing when a question is put to him. Such a person is said to be one who 'makes both a fit and prompt reply.'

(घ) नेव युत्तप्पटिभानो नो मुत्तप्पटिभानो

२४. कतमो च पुग्गलो नेव युत्तप्पटिभानो नो मुत्तप्पटिभानो?

इधेकच्चो पुग्गलो पञ्हं पुट्ठो समानो नेव युत्तं वदति नो सीघं। अयं वुच्चति पुग्गलो "नेव युत्तप्पटिभानो नो मुत्तप्पटिभानो"।

(D) A person who makes neither a fit nor a prompt reply

24. What sort of person is one who makes neither a fit nor a prompt reply?

Here a certain person who answers neither quickly nor fitly when a question is put to him. Such a person is said to be one who 'makes neither a fit nor a prompt reply.'

(७) चत्तारो धम्मकथिका पुग्गला

२५. तत्थ कतमे चत्तारो[१] धम्मकथिका पुग्गला[१] ?

(क) इधेकच्चो धम्मकथिको अप्पं च भासति असहितं च, परिसा चस्स न[२] कुसला[२] होति सहितासहितस्स। एवरूपो धम्मकथिको एवरूपाय परिसाय धम्मकथिको त्वेव सङ्खं गच्छति।

(7) Four persons who are the preachers of Dhamma (Law)

25. Who are the four preachers of Dhamma?

(A) Here a certain religious teacher speaks but little and what is irrelevant, and the congregation may not be competent to judge what is relevant and what not. Such a teacher, in a congregation such as this, passes for a preacher of the 'Law.'

(ख) इध पनेकच्चो धम्मकथिको अप्पं च भासति सहितं च, परिसा चस्स कुसला होति सहितासहितस्स। एवरूपो धम्मकथिको एवरूपाय परिसाय धम्मकथिको त्वेव सङ्खं गच्छति।

(B) Here a certain religious teacher speaks but little and what is relevant, and the congregation is competent to judge what is relevant and what not. Such a teacher, in such a congregation, passes for a preacher of the 'Law'.

(ग) इध पनेकच्चो धम्मकथिको बहुं च भासति असहितं च, परिसा चस्स न कुसला होति सहितासहितस्स। एवरूपो धम्मकथिको एवरूपाय परिसाय धम्मकथिको त्वेव सङ्खं गच्छति।

१-१. पुग्गला चत्तारो धम्मकथिका — सी०।

२-२. अकुसला — स्या०।

(C) Here a certain religious teacher speaks much and what is irrelevant, and the congregation is incompetent to judge what is relevant and what not. Such a person in a congregation like this, passes as a preacher of the 'Law'.

(घ) इध पनेकच्चो धम्मकथिको बहुं च भासति सहितं [N.66] च, परिसा चस्स कुसला होति सहितासहितस्स। एवरूपो धम्मकथिको एवरूपाय परिसाय धम्मकथिको त्वेव सङ्खं गच्छति।

इमे चत्तारो "धम्मकथिका पुग्गला"।

(D) Here again a certain religious teacher speaks much and what is relevant, and the congregation is competent to judge what is relevant and what not. Such a teacher, in such a congregation as this, passes as a preacher of the 'Law'.

These are the four 'religious preachers of Dhamma (Law)'.

(८) चत्तारो वलाहकूपमा पुग्गला

२६. [S.336] तत्थ कतमे चत्तारो वलाहकूपमा पुग्गला?

चत्तारो वलाहका— गज्जिता नो वस्सिता, वस्सिता नो गज्जिता, गज्जिता च वस्सिता च, नेव गज्जिता नो वस्सिता। एवमेवं[१] [R.43] चत्तारोमे वलाहकूपमा पुग्गला सन्तो संविज्जमाना लोकस्मिं। कतमे [B.149] चत्तारो? गज्जिता नो वस्सिता, वस्सिता नो गज्जिता, गज्जिता च वस्सिता च, नेव गज्जिता नो वस्सिता।

(8) Four persons who are comparable to the cloud

26. What are the four types of persons comparable to the cloud?

The four kinds of clouds are— That which thunders but rains not, that which rains but thunders not, that which both thunders and rains, that which neither thunders nor rains. Thus are to be found in this world four types of persons who are comparable

---

१. एवमेव — सी०, स्या०।

to these four kinds of clouds. What are the four? One who thunders but rains not, one who rains but thunders not, one who rains and also thunders, one who neither thunders not rains.

(क) कथं च पुग्गलो गज्जिता होति नो वस्सिता ?

इधेकच्चो पुग्गलो भासिता होति, नो कत्ता। एवं पुग्गलो गज्जिता होति, नो वस्सिता। सेय्यथापि सो वलाहको गज्जिता नो वस्सिता, तथूपमो अयं पुग्गलो।

(A) What sort of person is one who thunders but rains not?

Here a certain person does not act up to what he says. Such a person is said to be one who thunders but rains not. Just as the cloud that thunders but rains not, so also is this person.

(ख) कथं च पुग्गलो वस्सिता होति नो गज्जिता ?

इधेकच्चो पुग्गलो कत्ता होति, नो भासिता। एवं पुग्गलो वस्सिता होति नो गज्जिता। सेय्यथापि सो वलाहको वस्सिता नो गज्जिता, तथूपमो अयं पुग्गलो।

(B) What sort of person is one who rains but thunders not?

Here a certain person acts but does not speak. Such a person is said to be one who rains but thunders not. Just as a cloud that rains but thunders not, so also is this person.

(ग) कथं च पुग्गलो गज्जिता च होति वस्सिता च ?

इधेकच्चो पुग्गलो भासिता च होति, कत्ता च। एवं पुग्गलो गज्जिता च होति वस्सिता च। सेय्यथापि सो वलाहको गज्जिता च वस्सिता च, तथूपमो अयं पुग्गलो।

(C) What sort of person is one who thunders as well as rains?

Here a certain person speaks and acts. Such a person is said to be one who thunders as well as rains. Just as the cloud that thunders and rains, so also is this person.

(घ) कथं च पुग्गलो नेव गज्जिता होति नो वस्सिता?

इधेकच्चो पुग्गलो नेव भासिता होति नो कत्ता। एवं पुग्गलो नेव गज्जिता होति नो वस्सिता। सेय्यथापि [N.67] सो वलाहको नेव गज्जिता नो वस्सिता, तथूपमो अयं पुग्गलो।

इमे चत्तारो वलाहकूपमा पुग्गला सन्तो संविज्जमाना लोकस्मिं।

(D) What sort of person is one who neither thunders nor rains?

Here a certain person neither speaks nor acts. Such a person is said to be one who neither thunders nor rains. Just as the cloud that neither thunders nor rains, so also is this person.

These are the four types of persons that are found in this world comparable to the cloud.

(९) चत्तारो मूसिकूपमा पुग्गला

२७. तत्थ कतमे चत्तारो मूसिकूपमा पुग्गला?

चतस्सो मूसिका— गाधं कत्ता[१] नो वसिता, वसिता नो गाधं कत्ता, गाधं कत्ता च वसिता च, नेव गाधं कत्ता नो वसिता। एवमेवं चत्तारोमे[२] मूसिकूपमा पुग्गला सन्तो संविज्जमाना लोकस्मिं। कतमे चत्तारो? गाधं कत्ता नो वसिता, वसिता नो गाधं कत्ता, गाधं कत्ता च वसिता च, नेव गाधं कत्ता नो वसिता।

(9) Four persons who are comparable to mice

27. What are the four types of persons that are comparable to mice?

Four kinds of mice— those that dig their holes but do not live therein; those that live in holes but do not (themselves) dig them; those that live in the holes that they dig; those that neither dig holes for themselves nor live therein. In the same way also there are four types of persons that are found in this world who are

१. खत्ता — रो० ,एवमुपरि पि।
२. चत्तारो — सी०।

comparable to mice. What are the four? Those that have dug holes but do not dwell, those who dwell but do not dig, those who dig and dwell, those who neither dig nor dwell.

(क) [S.338] कथं च पुग्गलो गाधं कत्ता होति नो वसिता ?

इधेकच्चो पुग्गलो धम्मं परियापुणाति— सुत्तं गेय्यं वेय्याकरणं गाथं उदानं इतिवुत्तकं जातकं अब्भुतधम्मं[१] वेदल्लं । सो "इदं दुक्खं"ति यथाभूतं नप्पजानाति, "अयं दुक्खसमुदयो"ति यथाभूतं नप्पजानाति, "अयं [B.150] दुक्खनिरोधो" ति यथाभूतं नप्पजानाति, "अयं दुक्खनिरोधगामिनी पटिपदा"ति यथाभूतं नप्पजानाति । एवं पुग्गलो गाधं कत्ता होति नो वसिता । सेय्यथापि सा मूसिका गाधं कत्ता नो वसिता, तथूपमो अयं पुग्गलो ।

(A) What sort of person is one who digs the hole but does not dwell?

Here a certain person masters the doctrine consisting of the Sutta, Geyya, Vyākaraṇa, Gāthā, Udāna, Itivuttaka, Jātaka, Abbhutadhamma, Vedalla. But all the same he does not truly realise suffering, he does not truly realise the origin of suffering, he does not truly realise the cessation of suffering, he does not truly realise the way leading to the cessation of suffering. Such is the person who is a digger but not a dweller. Just as the mouse digs a hole but does not dwell in it, so also is this person.

(ख) [R.44] कथं च पुग्गलो वसिता होति नो गाधं कत्ता ?

इधेकच्चो पुग्गलो धम्मं न परियापुणाति— सुत्तं गेय्यं वेय्याकरणं गाथं उदानं इतिवुत्तकं जातकं अब्भुतधम्मं वेदल्लं। सो "इदं दुक्खं"ति यथाभूतं पजानाति, "अयं दुक्खसमुदयो"ति यथाभूतं पजानाति, "अयं दुक्खनिरोधो"ति यथाभूतं पजानाति, "अयं दुक्खनिरोधगामिनी पटिपदा"ति यथाभूतं पजानाति । एवं पुग्गलो वसिता होति नो गाधं कत्ता । सेय्यथापि सा मूसिका वसिता नो गाधं कत्ता, तथूपमो अयं पुग्गलो ।

---

१. अब्भूतधम्मं — स्या० ।

(B) What sort of person is one who dwells in the hole but does not dig it?

Here a certain person does not master a doctrine consisting of the Sutta, Geyya, Vyākaraṇa, Gāthā, Udāna, Itivuttaka, Jātaka, Abbhutadhamma, Vedalla. But he truly realises suffering, truly realises the origin of suffering, truly realises the cessation of suffering, truly realises the path leading to the cessation of suffering. Such a person is a dweller but not a hole-digger. Just as a mouse which dwells in a hole it does not dig, so also is this person.

(ग) [N.68] कथं च पुग्गलो गाधं कत्ता च होति वसिता च ?

इधेकच्चो पुग्गलो धम्मं परियापुणाति— सुत्तं गेय्यं वेय्याकरणं गाथं उदानं इतिवुत्तकं जातकं अब्भुतधम्मं वेदल्लं । सो "इदं दुक्खं"ति यथाभूतं पजानाति, "अयं दुक्खसमुदयो"ति यथाभूतं पजानाति, "अयं दुक्खनिरोधो"ति यथाभूतं पजानाति, "अयं दुक्खनिरोधगामिनी पटिपदा"ति यथाभूतं पजानाति । एवं पुग्गलो गाधं कत्ता च होति वसिता च । सेय्यथापि सा मूसिका गाधं कत्ता च वसिता च, तथूपमो अयं पुग्गलो ।

(C) What sort of person is a digger as well as a dweller?

Here a certain person learns the doctrine consisting of Sutta, Geyya, Vyākaraṇa, Gāthā, Udāna, Itivuttaka, Jātaka, Abbhutadhamma, Vedalla. And he truly realises suffering, he truly realises the origin of suffering, truly realises the cessation of suffering, truly realises the path leading to the cessation of suffering. Such a person is a digger as well as a dweller. Just as the mouse which digs its hole and dwells in it, so also is this person.

(घ) कथं च पुग्गलो नेव गाधं कत्ता होति नो वसिता ?

इधेकच्चो पुग्गलो धम्मं न परियापुणाति— सुत्तं गेय्यं वेय्याकरणं गाथं उदानं इतिवुत्तकं जातकं अब्भुतधम्मं वेदल्लं । सो "इदं दुक्खं"ति यथाभूतं नप्पजानाति, "अयं दुक्खसमुदयो"ति यथाभूतं नप्पजानाति, "अयं दुक्खनिरोधो"ति

यथाभूतं नप्पजानाति, "अयं दुक्खनिरोधगामिनी पटिपदा"ति यथाभूतं नप्पजानाति। एवं पुग्गलो नेव गाधं कत्ता होति नो वसिता। सेय्यथापि सा मूसिका नेव गाधं कत्ता नो वसिता, तथूपमो अयं पुग्गलो।

इमे चत्तारो मूसिकूपमा पुग्गला सन्तो संविज्जमाना लोकस्मिं।

(D) What sort of person is neither a digger nor a dweller?

Here a certain person does not learn the doctrine consisting of Sutta, Geyya, Vyākaraṇa, Gāthā, Udāna, Itivuttaka, Jātaka, Abbhutadhamma, Vedalla. And he does not truly realise suffering, does not truly realise the origin of suffering, does not truly realise the cessation of suffering, does not truly realise the path leading to the cessation of suffering. Such a person is one who is neither a digger nor a dweller. Just as the mouse which neither digs its hole nor dwells in it, so also is this person.

These are the four kinds of persons that live in this world who are comparable to mice.

(१०) चत्तारो अम्बूपमा पुग्गला

२८. [B.151; S.340] तत्थ कतमे चत्तारो अम्बूपमा पुग्गला?

चत्तारि अम्बानि— आमं पक्कवण्णि,[१] पक्कं आमवण्णि,[२] आमं[३] आमवण्णि, पक्कं पक्कवण्णि। एवमेवं चत्तारोमे अम्बूपमा पुग्गला सन्तो संविज्जमाना लोकस्मिं। कतमे चत्तारो? आमो पक्कवण्णी, पक्को आमवण्णी, आमो आमवण्णी, पक्को पक्कवण्णी।

(10) Four persons who are comparable to the mango

28. What are the four types of person that are comparable to the mango?

१. पक्कवण्णी — स्या०, एवमुपरि पि।

२. पक्को आमवण्णी — स्या०, एवमुपरि पि।

३. आमो — स्या०।

Four kinds of mangoes— immature but of ripe colour; of ripe colour but immature; immature and of unripe colour; ripe as well as of ripe colour. So also there are four persons that live in this world who are comparable to the mango. What are the four? One unripe but ripe-hued; one ripe but unripe-hued; one unripe and unripe-hued; one ripe and ripe-hued.

(क) कथं च पुग्गलो आमो होति पक्कवण्णी ?

इधेकच्चस्स पुग्गलस्स पासादिकं होति अभिक्कन्तं [N.69] पटिक्कन्तं आलोकितं विलोकितं सम्मिञ्जितं[१] पसारितं सङ्घाटिपत्तचीवरधारणं। सो "इदं दुक्खं"ति यथाभूतं नप्पजानाति, "अयं दुक्खसमुदयो"ति यथाभूतं नप्पजानाति, "अयं दुक्खनिरोधो"ति यथाभूतं नप्पजानाति, "अयं दुक्खनिरोधगामिनी पटिपदा" ति यथाभूतं[२] नप्पजानाति। एवं पुग्गलो आमो होति पक्कवण्णी। सेय्यथापि तं अम्बं आमं पक्कवण्णि, तथूपमो अयं पुग्गलो।

(A) How is a person unripe but ripe-hued?

Here a certain person looks graceful when proceeding forward of backward, when looking this way of that way, while stretching out or bending in (his arms), and when wearing the uppermost robe or the ordinary dress and holding the alms-bowl. He does not truly realise suffering, does not truly realise the origin of suffering, does not truly realise the cessation of suffering, and he does not truly realise also the path leading to the cessation of suffering. Thus is a person who is unripe but ripe-hued. Just as a mango, which is unripe but ripe-hued, so also is this person.

(ख) कथं च पुग्गलो पक्को होति आमवण्णी ?

[R.45] इधेकच्चस्स पुग्गलस्स न पासादिकं होति अभिक्कन्तं पटिक्कन्तं आलोकितं विलोकितं सम्मिञ्जितं पसारितं सङ्घाटिपत्तचीवरधारणं। सो "इदं

१. समिञ्जितं — म०।

२. रो० पोत्थके नत्थि।

दुक्खं"ति यथाभूतं पजानाति, "अयं दुक्खसमुदयो"ति यथाभूतं पजानाति, "अयं दुक्खनिरोधो"ति यथाभूतं पजानाति, "अयं दुक्खनिरोधगामिनी पटिपदा" ति यथाभूतं पजानाति। एवं पुग्गलो पक्को होति आमवण्णी। सेय्यथापि तं अम्बं पक्कं आमवण्णि, तथूपमो अयं पुग्गलो।

(B) How is a person ripe but of immature hue?

Here a certain person is not graceful while proceeding forward or backward, while looking this way or that way, while stretching out or bending in (his arms), and when wearing the uppermost robe or the ordinary dress and holding the alms-bowl. But he truly realises suffering, truly realises the origin of suffering, truly realises the cessation of suffering, truly realises the path leading to the cessation of suffering. Such a person is ripe but of immature hue. Just as a mango which is ripe but of immature hue, so also is this person.

(ग) कथं च पुग्गलो आमो होति आमवण्णी?

इधेकच्चस्स पुग्गलस्स न पासादिकं होति अभिक्कन्तं पटिक्कन्तं आलोकितं विलोकितं सम्मिञ्जितं पसारितं सङ्घाटिपत्तचीवरधारणं। सो "इदं दुक्खं"ति यथाभूतं नप्पजानाति ...पे०... "अयं दुक्खनिरोधगामिनी पटिपदा"ति यथाभूतं नप्पजानाति। एवं पुग्गलो आमो होति आमवण्णी। सेय्यथापि तं अम्बं आमं आमवण्णि, तथूपमो अयं पुग्गलो।

(C) How is a person unripe and of immature hue?

Here a certain person is not graceful while proceeding forward or backward, while looking this way or that way, while stretching out or bending in (his arms), and when wearing the uppermost robe or the ordinary dress and holding the alms-bowl. And also he does not truly realise suffering ...pe... does not truly realise the path leading to the cessation of suffering. Such a person is unripe and of immature hue. Just as a mango which is unripe and of immature hue, so also is this person.

(घ) [S.342] कथं च पुग्गलो पक्को होति पक्कवण्णी ?

इधेकच्चस्स पुग्गलस्स पासादिकं होति अभिक्कन्तं पटिक्कन्तं आलोकितं विलोकितं सम्मिञ्जितं पसारितं [N.70] सङ्घाटिपत्तचीवरधारणं। सो "इदं दुक्खं"ति यथाभूतं [B.152] पजानाति ...पे०... "अयं दुक्खनिरोधगामिनी पटिपदा"ति यथाभूतं पजानाति। एवं पुग्गलो पक्को होति पक्कवण्णी। सेय्यथापि तं अम्बं पक्कं पक्कवण्णि, तथूपमो अयं पुग्गलो।

इमे चत्तारो अम्बूपमा पुग्गला सन्तो संविज्जमाना लोकस्मिं।

(D) What sort of person is ripe and ripe-hued?

Here a certain person looks graceful when proceeding forward or backward, when looking this way or that way, while stretching out or bending in (his arms), and when wearing the uppermost robe or the ordinary dress and holding the alms-bowl. He truly realises suffering ...pe... truly realises the path leading to the cessation of suffering. Thus is a person ripe and also ripe-hued. Just as a mango which is ripe and ripe-hued, so also is this person.

These are the four types of person existing in this world who are comparable to the mango.

(११) चत्तारो कुम्भूपमा पुग्गला

२९. तत्थ कतमे चत्तारो कुम्भूपमा पुग्गला ?

चत्तारो कुम्भा— तुच्छो पिहितो, पूरो विवटो,[१] तुच्छो विवटो, पूरो पिहितो। एवमेवं चत्तारोमे कुम्भूपमा पुग्गला सन्तो संविज्जमाना लोकस्मिं। कतमे चत्तारो ? तुच्छो पिहितो, पूरो विवटो, तुच्छो विवटो, पूरो पिहितो।

(11) Four person who are comparable to a jar

29. What are the four types of persons comparable to a jar?

---

१. पि वटो — रो०, एवमुपरि पि।

Four kinds of jar— that which is empty but well covered, that which is full but uncovered, that which is empty as well as uncovered, that which is full as well as covered. In the same way there are four types of persons existing in this world that are comparable to a jar. What are the four? Empty but covered, full and uncovered, empty as well as uncovered, full as well as covered.

(क) कथं च पुग्गलो तुच्छो होति पिहितो ?

इधेकच्चस्स पुग्गलस्स पासादिकं होति अभिक्कन्तं पटिक्कन्तं आलोकितं विलोकितं सम्मिञ्जितं पसारितं सङ्घाटिपत्तचीवरधारणं। सो "इदं दुक्खं"ति यथाभूतं नप्पजानाति ...पे०... "अयं दुक्खनिरोधगामिनी पटिपदा"ति यथाभूतं नप्पजानाति। एवं पुग्गलो तुच्छो होति पिहितो। सेय्यथापि सो कुम्भो तुच्छो पिहितो, तथूपमो अयं पुग्गलो।

(A) How is a person empty but covered?

Here a certain person looks graceful when proceeding forward or backward, when looking this way or that way, while stretching out or bending in (his arms), and when wearing the uppermost robe or the ordinary dress and holding the alms-bowl. He does not truly realise suffering ...pe... does not truly realise the path leading to the cessation of suffering. Such a person is empty but well covered. Just as the jar is empty but covered, so also is this person.

(ख) कथं च पुग्गलो पूरो होति विवटो ?

इधेकच्चस्स पुग्गलस्स न पासादिकं होति अभिक्कन्तं पटिक्कन्तं आलोकितं विलोकितं सम्मिञ्जितं पसारितं सङ्घाटिपत्तचीवरधारणं। सो "इदं दुक्खं"ति यथाभूतं पजानाति ...पे०... "अयं दुक्खनिरोधगामिनी पटिपदा"ति यथाभूतं पजानाति। एवं पुग्गलो पूरो होति विवटो। सेय्यथापि सो कुम्भो पूरो विवटो, तथूपमो अयं पुग्गलो।

(B) What sort of person is full and uncovered?

Here a certain person is not graceful while proceeding forward or backward, while looking this way or that way, while stretching out or bending in (his arms), and when wearing the uppermost robe or the ordinary dress and holding the alms-bowl. But he truly realises suffering ...pe... truly realises the path leading to the cessation of suffering. Such a person is full and uncovered. Just as the jar is full and uncovered, so also is this person.

(ग) [N.71; R.46] कथं च पुग्गलो तुच्छो होति विवटो?

इधेकच्चस्स पुग्गलस्स न पासादिकं होति अभिक्कन्तं पटिक्कन्तं आलोकितं विलोकितं सम्मिञ्जितं पसारितं सङ्घाटिपत्तचीवरधारणं। सो "इदं दुक्खं"ति यथाभूतं नप्पजानाति ... पे० ... "अयं दुक्खनिरोधगामिनी पटिपदा"ति यथाभूतं नप्पजानाति। एवं पुग्गलो तुच्छो होति विवटो। सेय्यथापि सो कुम्भो तुच्छो विवटो, तथूपमो अयं पुग्गलो।

(C) What sort of person is empty as well as uncovered?

Here a certain person is not graceful while proceeding forward or backward, while looking this way or that way, while stretching out or bending in (his arms), and when wearing the uppermost robe or the ordinary dress and holding the alms-bowl. And also he does not truly realise suffering ...pe... does not truly realise the path leading to the cessation of suffering. Such is the person who is empty as well as uncovered. Just as the jar is empty and uncovered, so also is this person.

(घ) [S.344] कथं च पुग्गलो पूरो होति पिहितो?

इधेकच्चस्स पुग्गलस्स पासादिकं होति अभिक्कन्तं पटिक्कन्तं आलोकितं विलोकितं [B.153] सम्मिञ्जितं पसारितं सङ्घाटिपत्तचीवरधारणं। सो "इदं दुक्खं"ति यथाभूतं पजानाति ...पे०... "अयं दुक्खनिरोधगामिनी पटिपदा"ति यथाभूतं पजानाति। एवं पुग्गलो पूरो होति पिहितो। सेय्यथापि सो कुम्भो पूरो पिहितो, तथूपमो अयं पुग्गलो।

इमे चत्तारो कुम्भूपमा पुग्गला सन्तो संविज्जमाना लोकस्मिं।

(D) What sort of person is full as well as covered?

Here a certain person looks graceful when proceeding forward or backward, when looking this way or that way, while stretching out or bending in (his arms), and when wearing the uppermost robe or the ordinary dress and holding the alms-bowl. He truly realises suffering ...pe... truly realises the path leading to the cessation of suffering. Thus is a person full as well as covered. Just as a jar is full as well as covered, so also is this person.

These are the four types of persons existing in this world who are comparable to a jar.

(१२) चत्तारो उदकरहदूपमा पुग्गला

३०. तत्थ कतमे चत्तारो उदकरहदूपमा पुग्गला?

चत्तारो उदकरहदा— उत्तानो गम्भीरोभासो, गम्भीरो उत्तानोभासो, उत्तानो उत्तानोभासो, गम्भीरो गम्भीरोभासो। एवमेवं चत्तारोमे उदकरहदूपमा पुग्गला सन्तो संविज्जमाना लोकस्मिं। कतमे चत्तारो? उत्तानो गम्भीरोभासो, गम्भीरो उत्तानोभासो, उत्तानो उत्तानोभासो, गम्भीरो गम्भीरोभासो।

(12) Four persons who are comparable to a pool of water

30. What are the four types of persons who are comparable to a pool of water?

Four kinds of pools— shallow but seeming to be deep, deep but seeming to be shallow, shallow and appearing to be shallow, lastly, deep and appearing to be deep. In the same manner there are four types of persons existing in this world who are comparable to pools What are the four? Shallow but seeming to be deep, deep but seeming to be shallow, shallow and seeming to be shallow, lastly, deep and seeming to be deep.

(क) कथं च पुग्गलो उत्तानो होति गम्भीरोभासो ?

इधेकच्चस्स पुग्गलस्स पासादिकं होति अभिक्कन्तं पटिक्कन्तं आलोकितं विलोकितं सम्मिञ्जितं पसारितं सङ्घाटिपत्तचीवरधारणं। सो "इदं दुक्खं"ति यथाभूतं नप्पजानाति ...पे०... "अयं दुक्खनिरोधगामिनी [N.72] पटिपदा"ति यथाभूतं नप्पजानाति। एवं पुग्गलो उत्तानो होति गम्भीरोभासो। सेय्यथापि सो उदकरहदो उत्तानो गम्भीरोभासो, तथूपमो अयं पुग्गलो।

(A) What sort of person is one who is shallow but seems to be deep?

Here a certain person looks graceful when proceeding forward or backward, when looking this way or that way, while stretching out or bending in (his arms), and when wearing the uppermost robe or the ordinary dress and holding the alms-bowl. He does not truly realise suffering ...pe... does not truly realise the path leading to the cessation of suffering. Such a person is shallow but seems to be deep. Just as the pool is shallow but seems to be deep, so also is this person.

(ख) कथं च पुग्गलो गम्भीरो होति उत्तानोभासो ?

इधेकच्चस्स पुग्गलस्स न पासादिकं होति अभिक्कन्तं पटिक्कन्तं आलोकितं विलोकितं सम्मिञ्जितं पसारितं सङ्घाटिपत्तचीवरधारणं। सो "इदं दुक्खं"ति यथाभूतं पजानाति ...पे०... "अयं दुक्खनिरोधगामिनी पटिपदा"ति यथाभूतं पजानाति। एवं पुग्गलो गम्भीरो होति उत्तानोभासो। सेय्यथापि सो उदकरहदो गम्भीरो उत्तानोभासो, तथूपमो अयं पुग्गलो।

(B) What sort of person is deep but seems to be shallow?

Here a certain person is not graceful while proceeding forward or backward, while looking this way or that way, while stretching out or bending in (his arms), and when wearing the uppermost robe or the ordinary dress and holding the alms-bowl. But he truly realises suffering ...pe... truly realises the path leading to the cessation of suffering. Such a person is deep but seems to be shallow. Just as the pool is deep but seems to be shallow, so also is this person.

(ग) कथं च पुग्गलो उत्तानो होति उत्तानोभासो ?

इधेकच्चस्स पुग्गलस्स न पासादिकं होति अभिक्कन्तं पटिक्कन्तं आलोकितं विलोकितं सम्मिञ्जितं पसारितं सङ्घाटिपत्तचीवरधारणं। सो "इदं दुक्खं"ति यथाभूतं नप्पजानाति ...पे०... "अयं दुक्खनिरोधगामिनी पटिपदा"ति [B.154] यथाभूतं नप्पजानाति। एवं पुग्गलो उत्तानो होति उत्तानोभासो। सेय्यथापि सो उदकरहदो उत्तानो उत्तानोभासो, तथूपमो अयं पुग्गलो।

(C) What sort of person is shallow and seems to be shallow?

Here a certain person is not graceful while proceeding forward or backward, while looking this way or that way, while stretching out or bending in (his arms), and when wearing the uppermost robe or the odinary dress and holding the alms-bowl. And also he does not truly realise suffering ...pe... does not truly realise the path leading to the cessation of suffering. Thus is a person shallow and seems to be shallow. Just as a pool is shallow and seems to be shallow, so also is this person.

(घ) [S.346] कथं च पुग्गलो गम्भीरो होति गम्भीरोभासो ?

[R.47] इधेकच्चस्स पुग्गलस्स पासादिकं होति अभिक्कन्तं पटिक्कन्तं आलोकितं विलोकितं सम्मिञ्जितं पसारितं सङ्घाटिपत्तचीवरधारणं। सो "इदं दुक्खं"ति यथाभूतं पजानाति ...पे०..."अयं दुक्खनिरोधगामिनी पटिपदा"ति यथाभूतं पजानाति। एवं पुग्गलो गम्भीरो होति गम्भीरोभासो। सेय्यथापि सो उदकरहदो गम्भीरो गम्भीरोभासो, तथूपमो अयं पुग्गलो।

इमे चत्तारो उदकरहदूपमा पुग्गला सन्तो संविज्जमाना लोकस्मिं।

(D) What sort of person is deep and seems to be deep?

Here a certain person looks graceful when proceeding forward or backward, when looking this way or that way, while stretching out or bending in (his arms), and when wearing the uppermost robe or the ordinary dress and holding the alms-bowl. And he truly realises suffering ...pe... truly realises the path leading to the cessation of suffering. Such a person is one who is deep and seems to be deep. Just as the pool is deep and seems to be deep, so also is this person.

These are the four types of persons existing in this world who are comparable to a pool of water.

(१३) चत्तारो बलीबद्दूपमा पुग्गला

३१. [N.73] तत्थ कतमे चत्तारो बलीबद्दूपमा[1] पुग्गला ?

चत्तारो बलीबद्दा— सकगवचण्डो नो परगवचण्डो, परगवचण्डो नो सकगवचण्डो, सकगवचण्डो च परगवचण्डो च, नेव सकगवचण्डो नो परगवचण्डो। एवमेवं चत्तारोमे[2] बलीबद्दूपमा पुग्गला सन्तो संविज्जमाना लोकस्मिं। कतमे चत्तारो ? सकगवचण्डो नो परगवचण्डो, परगवचण्डो नो सकगवचण्डो, सकगवचण्डो च परगवचण्डो च, नेव सकगवचण्डो नो परगवचण्डो।

(13) Four persons who are comparable to the ox

31. What are the four persons that are comparable to the ox?

There are four kinds of oxen— pest to its own herd but not to another herd, pest to another herd but not to its own herd, pest to its own as well as to another herd, pest neither to its own herd nor to another herd. In the same manner there are four types of persons existing in the world comparable to the ox. What are the four? A pest in the congregation but not outside it, a pest outside the congregation but not in it, a pest in as well as outside the congregation, a pest neither in his won nor in another congregation.

---

१. बलिबद्दूपमा — सी०, रो०; बलिबद्धूपमा — स्या०, एवमुपरि पि।
२. चत्तारो — सी०, रो०।

(क) कथं च पुग्गलो सकगवचण्डो होति नो परगवचण्डो ?

इधेकच्चो पुग्गलो सकपरिसं उब्बेजिता होति, नो परपरिसं । एवं पुग्गलो सकगवचण्डो होति नो परगवचण्डो । सेय्यथापि सो बलीबद्दो सकगवचण्डो नो परगवचण्डो, तथूपमो अयं पुग्गलो ।

(A) How is a person a pest in his own congregation but not outside it?

Here a certain person creates trouble in his own congregation but not in another congregation. Such a person is a pest in his own congregation but not in another. Just as that ox is a pest in its own herd but not in another herd, so also is this person.

(ख) कथं च पुग्गलो परगवचण्डो होति नो सकगवचण्डो ?

इधेकच्चो पुग्गलो परपरिसं उब्बेजिता होति, नो सकपरिसं । एवं पुग्गलो परगवचण्डो होति नो सकगवचण्डो । सेय्यथापि सो बलीबद्दो परगवचण्डो नो सकगवचण्डो, तथूपमो अयं पुग्गलो ।

(B) How is a person a pest outside but not in his own congregation?

Here a certain person creates trouble in another congregation but not in his own. Such a person is a pest outside but not in his congregation. Just as that ox is a pest outside, but not in its own herd, so also is this person.

(ग) कथं च पुग्गलो सकगवचण्डो च होति परगवचण्डो च ?

इधेकच्चो पुग्गलो सकपरिसं च उब्बेजिता होति, परपरिसं च। एवं [B.155] पुग्गलो सकगवचण्डो च होति परगवचण्डो च । सेय्यथापि सो बलीबद्दो सकगवचण्डो च परगवचण्डो च, तथूपमो अयं पुग्गलो ।

(C) How is a person a pest in as well as outside his own congregation?

Here a certain person creates trouble in as well as outside his own congregation. Such a person is one who is a pest in as well as outside his own congregation.

Just as that ox is a pest in as well as outside its own herd, so also is this person.

(घ) कथं च पुग्गलो नेव सकगवचण्डो होति नो परगवचण्डो ?

इधेकच्चो पुग्गलो नेव सकपरिसं उब्बेजिता होति नो परपरिसं । एवं पुग्गलो नेव सकगवचण्डो होति नो परगवचण्डो। सेय्यथापि सो बलीबद्दो नेव सकगवचण्डो नो परगवचण्डो, तथूपमो अयं पुग्गलो ।

[N.74] इमे चत्तारो बलीबद्दूपमा पुग्गला सन्तो संविज्जमाना लोकस्मिं ।

(D) How is a person a pest neither of his own congregation nor of another congregation?

Here a certain person creates trouble neither in his own congregation nor in another congregation. Such a person is said to be a pest neither to his own congregation nor to another congregation. Just as that ox is neither a pest to his own herd nor to another herd, so also is this person.

These are the four types of persons, who live and have their being in this world, comparable to the ox.

(१४) चत्तारो आसीविसूपमा पुग्गला

३२. [R.48; S.348] तत्थ कतमे चत्तारो आसीविसूपमा[१] पुग्गला ?

चत्तारो आसीविसा— आगतविसो नो घोरविसो, घोरविसो नो आगतविसो, आगतविसो च घोरविसो च, नेव आगतविसो नो घोरविसो। एवमेवं चत्तारोमे आसीविसूपमा पुग्गला सन्तो संविज्जमाना लोकस्मिं । कतमे चत्तारो ? आगतविसो नो घोरविसो, घोरविसो नो आगतविसो, आगतविसो च घोरविसो च, नेव आगतविसो नो घोरविसो ।

(14) Four persons who are comparable to a serpent

32. What are the four types of persons comparable to a serpent?

१. आसिविसूपमा — सी०, स्या०, एवमुपरि पि ।

Four kinds of snake— the quick but not strong poisoning, strong but not quick poisoning, quick as well as strong poisoning, neither quick nor strong poisoning. In the same manner, there are four types of persons existing in this world, who are comparable to a serpent. What are the four? Persons of quick but strong poison, of strong but not quick poison, of quick as well as strong poison, of neither quick nor strong poison.

(क) कथं च पुग्गलो आगतविसो होति नो घोरविसो ?

इधेकच्चो पुग्गलो अभिण्हं कुज्झति। सो च ख्वस्स कोधो न चिरं दीघरत्तं अनुसेति। एवं पुग्गलो आगतविसो होति, नो घोरविसो। सेय्यथापि सो आसीविसो आगतविसो नो घोरविसो, तथूपमो अयं पुग्गलो।

(A) What sort of person is of quick but not strong poison?

Here a certain person gets angry repeatedly but the anger does not linger for a very long time. Thus is a person of quick but not of strong poison. Just as that serpent has a quick but has not a strong poison, so also is this person.

(ख) कथं च पुग्गलो घोरविसो होति नो आगतविसो ?

इधेकच्चो पुग्गलो नहेव[१] खो अभिण्हं कुज्झति। सो च ख्वस्स कोधो चिरं दीघरत्तं अनुसेति। एवं पुग्गलो घोरविसो होति, नो आगतविसो। सेय्यथापि सो आसीविसो घोरविसो नो आगतविसो, तथूपमो अयं पुग्गलो।

(B) What sort of person is of strong but not of quick poison?

Here a certain person does not get angry repeatedly, but when he is angry, his anger endures for a pretty long time. Thus is a person of strong but not of quick poison. Just as that serpent has a strong but not quick poison, so also is this person.

(ग) कथं च पुग्गलो आगतविसो च होति घोरविसो च ?

---

१. नेव—सी०।

इधेकच्चो पुग्गलो अभिण्हं कुज्झति। सो च ख्वस्स कोधो चिरं दीघरत्तं अनुसेति। एवं पुग्गलो आगतविसो च होति घोरविसो च। [B.156] सेय्यथापि सो आसीविसो आगतविसो च घोरविसो च, तथूपमो अयं पुग्गलो।

(C) What sort of person is of quick as well as of strong poison?

Here a certain person gets angry repeatedly, but when he is angry his anger endures for a pretty long time. Such a person is of quick as well as of strong poison. Just as that serpent has quick as well as strong poison, so also is this person.

(घ) कथं च पुग्गलो नेव आगतविसो होति नो घोरविसो?

इधेकच्चो पुग्गलो नहेव खो अभिण्हं कुज्झति। सो च ख्वस्स कोधो न चिरं दीघरत्तं अनुसेति। एवं [N.75] पुग्गलो नेव आगतविसो होति नो घोरविसो। सेय्यथापि सो आसीविसो नेव आगतविसो नो घोरविसो, तथूपमो अयं पुग्गलो।

इमे चत्तारो आसीविसूपमा पुग्गला सन्तो संविज्जमाना लोकस्मिं।

(D) What sort of a person is of neither quick nor strong poison?

Here a certain person does not get angry repeatedly, and the anger does not linger for a very long time. Such a person is neither of quick nor of strong poison. Just as the serpent has neither quick nor strong poison, so also is this person.

These are the four types of persons existing in this world, who are comparable to a serpent.

(१५. क) अवण्णारहस्स वण्णं भासति

३३. [S.350] कथं च पुग्गलो अननुविच्च अपरियोगाहेत्वा अवण्णारहस्स वण्णं भासिता होति?

इधेकच्चो पुग्गलो दुप्पटिपन्नानं मिच्छापटिपन्नानं तित्थियानं तित्थियसावकानं वण्णं भासति—"सुप्पटिपन्ना[१]" इति पि, "सम्मापटिपन्ना" इति

१. सुपटिपन्ना — स्या०।

पी ति। एवं पुग्गलो अननुविच्च अपरियोगाहेत्वा अवण्णारहस्स वण्णं भासिता होति।

(15. A) A person who speaks in praise of an unworthy of praise

33. How is a person one who speaks in praise of one unworthy of praise without inquiring into and scrutinising (his nature)?

Here a certain person speaks in praise of the heretics or their disciples who are badly or wrongly regulated in conduct, that they are both well conducted and properly conducted. Such a person is one who speaks in praise of one unworthy of praise without inquiring into and scrutinising (his nature).

(ख) वण्णारहस्स अवण्णं भासति

३४. कथं च पुग्गलो अननुविच्च अपरियोगाहेत्वा वण्णारहस्स अवण्णं भासिता होति?

[R.49] इधेकच्चो पुग्गलो सुप्पटिपन्नानं सम्मापटिपन्नानं बुद्धानं बुद्धसावकानं अवण्णं भासति— "दुप्पटिपन्ना" इति पि, "मिच्छापटिपन्ना" इति पी ति। एवं पुग्गलो अननुविच्च अपरियोगाहेत्वा वण्णारहस्स अवण्णं भासिता होति।

(B) A person who speaks in dispraise of a person worthy of praise

34. How is a person one who speaks in dispraise of a person worthy of praise without inquiring into and scrutinising (his nature)?

Here a certain person speaks ill of Buddhas and their disciples who are really well and properly regulated as to their conduct, saying that they are wrongly and badly regulated in conduct. Such a person is one who speaks ill of a person worthy of praise without inquiring into and scrutinising (his nature).

(ग) अप्पसादनीये ठाने पसादं उपदंसेति

३५. कथं च पुग्गलो अननुविच्च अपरियोगाहेत्वा अप्पसादनीये ठाने पसादं उपदंसिता होति ?

इधेकच्चो पुग्गलो दुप्पटिपदाय मिच्छापटिपदाय पसादं जनेति— "सुप्पटिपदा" इति पि, "सम्मापटिपदा" इति पी ति। एवं पुग्गलो अननुविच्च अपरियोगाहेत्वा अप्पसादनीये ठाने पसादं उपदंसिता होति।

(C) A person who shows satisfaction in an unsatisfactory thing

35. How is a person one who shows satisfaction in an unsatisfactory thing without inquiring into and scrutinising it?

Here a certain person finds satisfaction in a bad and wrong course, saying that this is the good path, this is the right path. Such a person is one who finds satisfaction in an unsatisfactory thing without inquiring into and scrutinising it.

(घ) पसादनीये ठाने अप्पसादं उपदंसेति

३६. कथं च पुग्गलो अननुविच्च अपरियोगाहेत्वा पसादनीये ठाने अप्पसादं उपदंसिता होति ?

[N.76] इधेकच्चो पुग्गलो सुप्पटिपदाय सम्मापटिपदाय अप्पसादं जनेति— "दुप्पटिपदा" इति पि, "मिच्छापटिपदा" इति पी ति। एवं पुग्गलो अननुविच्च अपरियोगाहेत्वा पसादनीये ठाने अप्पसादं उपदंसिता होति।

(D) A person who shows dissatisfaction in a satisfactory thing

36. How is a person one who shows dissatisfaction in a satisfactory thing without inquiring into and scrutinising it?

Here a certain person finds dissatisfaction in a good and right course, saying that this is a bad path, this is a wrong path. Such a person is one who finds dissatisfaction in a satisfactory thing without inquiring into and scrutinising it.

(१६. क) अवण्णारहस्स अवण्णं भासति

३७. [B.157] कथं च पुग्गलो अनुविच्च परियोगाहेत्वा अवण्णारहस्स अवण्णं भासिता होति ?

इधेकच्चो पुग्गलो दुप्पटिपन्नानं मिच्छापटिपन्नानं तित्थियानं तित्थियसावकानं अवण्णं भासति— "दुप्पटिपन्ना" इति पि, "मिच्छापटिपन्ना" इति पी ति। एवं पुग्गलो अनुविच्च परियोगाहेत्वा अवण्णारहस्स अवण्णं भासिता होति।

(16. A) A person who speaks in dispraise of a person unworthy of praise

37. How is a person a speaker in dispraise of a person unworthy of praise after inquiring into and scrutinising (his nature)?

Here a certain person rightly speaks in dispraise of the heretics or their disciples, who are wrongly and badly regulated as to conduct, saying that they are badly as well as wrongly conducted. Thus is a person a speaker in dispraise of an unworthy person after inquiring into and scrutinising (his nature).

(ख) वण्णारहस्स वण्णं भासति

३८. कथं च पुग्गलो अनुविच्च परियोगाहेत्वा वण्णारहस्स वण्णं भासिता होति ?

इधेकच्चो पुग्गलो सुप्पटिपन्नानं सम्मापटिपन्नानं बुद्धानं बुद्धसावकानं वण्णं भासति— "सुप्पटिपन्ना" इति पि, "सम्मापटिपन्ना" इति पी ति। एवं पुग्गलो अनुविच्च परियोगाहेत्वा वण्णारहस्स वण्णं भासिता होति।

(B) A person who speaks in praise of a praiseworthy person

38. How is a person a speaker in praise of a praiseworthy person after inquiring into and scrutinising (his nature)?

Here a certain person speaks rightly in praise of the Buddhas and their disciples, who are well and perfectly regulated in conduct, saying that they are well and perfectly conducted. Such a person is a speaker in praise of a praiseworthy person after inquiring into and scrutinising (his nature).

(ग) अप्पसादनीये ठाने अप्पसादं उपदंसेति

३९. [S.352] कथं च पुग्गलो अनुविच्च परियोगाहेत्वा अप्पसादनीयं ठाने अप्पसादं उपदंसिता होति ?

इधेकच्चो पुग्गलो दुप्पटिपदाय मिच्छापटिपदाय अप्पसादं जनेति— "दुप्पटिपदा" इति पि, "मिच्छापटिपदा" इति पी ति। एवं पुग्गलो अनुविच्च परियोगाहेत्वा अप्पसादनीये ठाने अप्पसादं उपदंसिता होति।

(C) A person who finds dissatisfaction in an unsatisfactory thing

39. How is a person one who finds dissatisfaction in an unsatisfactory thing after inquiring into and scrutinising it?

Here a certain person finds dissatisfaction in a bad and wrong course, saying that this is a bad path, this is a wrong path. Such a person is one who finds dissatisfaction in an unsatisfactory thing after inquiring into and scrutinising it.

(घ) पसादनीये ठानं पसादं उपदंसेति

४०. कथं च पुग्गलो अनुविच्च परियोगाहेत्वा पसादनीये ठाने पसादं उपदंसिता होति ?

[R.50] इधेकच्चो पुग्गलो सुप्पटिपदाय सम्मापटिपदाय पसादं जनेति— "सुप्पटिपदा" इति पि, "सम्मापटिपदा" इति पी ति। एवं पुग्गलो अनुविच्च परियोगाहेत्वा पसादनीये ठाने पसादं उपदंसिता होति।

(D) A person who finds satisfaction in a satisfactory thing

40. How is a person one who finds satisfaction in a satisfactory thing after inquiring into and scrutinising it?

Here a certain person finds satisfaction in a good and right course, saying that this is the good path, this is the right path. Such a person is one who finds satisfaction in a satisfactory thing after inquiring into and scrutinising it.

(१७. क) अवण्णारहस्स अवण्णं भासति, नो च वण्णारहस्स वण्णं

४१. [N.77] कथं च पुग्गलो अवण्णारहस्स अवण्णं भासिता होति भूतं तच्छं कालेन, नो च खो वण्णारहस्स वण्णं भासिता होति भूतं तच्छं कालेन?

इधेकच्चो पुग्गलो वण्णो पि संविज्जति अवण्णो पि संविज्जति। यो तत्थ अवण्णो तं भणति भूतं तच्छं कालेन, यो तत्थ वण्णो तं न भणति भूतं तच्छं कालेन। एवं पुग्गलो अवण्णारहस्स अवण्णं भासिता होति भूतं तच्छं कालेन, नो च खो वण्णारहस्स वण्णं भासिता होति भूतं तच्छं कालेन।

(17. A) A person who speaks in dispraise of a person unworthy of praise, but does not speak in praise of the praiseworthy

41. How is a person one who speaks in dispraise of a person unworthy of praise, expressing what is true and right at the right time about him, but does not in the same way speak in praise of what is praiseworthy?

Here a person, when there is something creditable as well as something discreditable (in regard to a person), speaks about the latter, expressing what is true and right at the right time, but does not speak in the same way about the something creditable. It is thus that a person speaks in dispraise of a person unworthy of praise, expressing what is true and right at the right time about him, but does not in the same way speak in praise of what is praiseworthy.

(ख) वण्णारहस्स वण्णं भासति, नो च अवण्णारहस्स अवण्णं

४२. कथं च पुग्गलो वण्णारहस्स वण्णं भासिता होति भूतं तच्छं कालेन, नो च खो अवण्णारहस्स अवण्णं भासिता होति भूतं तच्छं कालेन ?

इधेकच्चो पुग्गलो वण्णो पि संविज्जति अवण्णो पि [B.158] संविज्जति। यो तत्थ वण्णो तं भणति भूतं तच्छं कालेन, यो तत्थ अवण्णो तं न भणति भूतं तच्छं कालेन। एवं पुग्गलो वण्णारहस्स वण्णं भासिता होति भूतं तच्छं कालेन, नो च खो अवण्णारहस्स अवण्णं भासिता होति भूतं तच्छं कालेन।

(B) A person who speaks in praise of a person worthy of praise, but does not speak in dispraise of the unwothy

42. How does a person speak in praise of a person worthy of praise, expressing what is true and right at the right time about him, but does not in the same way speak in dispraise of what is unworthy of praise?

Here a person, when there is something creditable as well as something discreditable (in regard to a person), speaks about the former, expressing what is true and right at the right time but does not in the same way speak about the latter. It is thus that a person speaks in praise of a person worthy of praise, expressing what is true and right at the right time about him, but does not in the same way speak in dispraise of what is unworthy of praise.

(ग) अवण्णारहस्स च अवण्णं वण्णारहस्स च वण्णं भासति

४३. कथं च पुग्गलो अवण्णारहस्स च अवण्णं भासिता होति भूतं तच्छं कालेन, वण्णारहस्स च वण्णं भासिता होति भूतं तच्छं कालेन ?

इधेकच्चो[१] पुग्गलो[२] वण्णो पि संविज्जति अवण्णो पि संविज्जति। यो तत्थ अवण्णो तं भणति भूतं तच्छं कालेन, यो पि[३] तत्थ वण्णो तं पि भणति भूतं तच्छं कालेन। तत्र[४] कालञ्ञू होति तस्स पञ्हस्स वेय्याकरणाय। एवं पुग्गलो अवण्णारहस्स च अवण्णं भासिता होति भूतं तच्छं कालेन, वण्णारहस्स च वण्णं भासिता होति भूतं तच्छं कालेन।

(C) A person who speaks in dispraise of a person unworthy of praise and in praise of the praiseworthy

43. How does a person speak in dispraise of a person unworthy of praise and in praise of the praiseworthy, expressing what is true and right at the right time?

Here a person, when there is something creditable as well as something discreditable (in regard to a person), speaks about the latter and also about the former, expressing what is true and right at the right time, being aware of the proper time for answering the question put to him. It is thus that a person speaks in dispraise of a person unworthy of praise and in praise of the praiseworthy, expressing what is true and right at the right time.

(घ) नेव अवण्णारहस्स अवण्णं न वण्णारहस्स वण्णं भासति

४४. [S.354] कथं च पुग्गलो नेव अवण्णारहस्स अवण्णं भासिता होति भूतं तच्छं कालेन, नो च वण्णारहस्स वण्णं भासिता होति भूतं [N.78] तच्छं कालेन?

इधेकच्चो पुग्गलो वण्णो पि संविज्जति अवण्णो पि संविज्जति। यो तत्थ अवण्णो तं न भणति भूतं तच्छं कालेन, यो पि तत्थ वण्णो तं पि न भणति भूतं

---

१. इधेकच्चे — सी०।

२. पुग्गले — सी०।

३. स्या०, रो० पोत्थकेसु नत्थि।

४. तत्थ — स्या०।

[R.51] तच्छं कालेन। उपेक्खको विहरति सतो सम्पजानो। एवं पुग्गलो नेव अवण्णारहस्स अवण्णं भासिता होति भूतं तच्छं कालेन, नो पि वण्णारहस्स वण्णं भासिता होति भूतं तच्छं कालेन।

(D) A person who neither speak in dispraise of a person unworthy of praise nor speak in praise of a person worthy of praise

44. How does a person neither speak in dispraise of a person unworthy of praise nor speak in praise of a person worthy of praise, expressing what is true and right at the right time?

Here a person, when there is something creditable as well as something discreditable (in regard to a person), speaks neither about the former nor about the latter, expressing what is true and right at the right time, but keeps up an indifferent attitude, being mindful and thoughtful. It is thus that a person neither speaks in dispraise of a person unworthy of praise nor speaks in praise of a person worthy of praise, expressing the right thing at the right time.

(१८. क) उट्ठानफलूपजीवी नो पुञ्ञफलूपजीवी

४५. कतमो च पुग्गलो उट्ठानफलूपजीवी नो पुञ्ञफलूपजीवी?

यस्स पुग्गलस्स उट्ठहतो घटतो वायमतो आजीवो अभिनिब्बत्तति, नो पुञ्ञतो— अयं वुच्चति पुग्गलो "उट्ठानफलूपजीवी, नो पुञ्ञफलूपजीवी"।

(18. A) A person who lives on the fruit of his exertions but not on the fruit of his merit

45. What sort of person is he who lives on the fruit of his exertions but not on the fruit of his previous merit?

Here a person whose living springs from his present exertions (lit. uprising), endeavours, and efforts, not as a result of his previous merit, is said to be a person who lives on the fruit of his exertions but not on the fruit of his previous merit.

(ख) पुञ्ञफलूपजीवी नो उट्ठानफलूपजीवी

४६. कतमो च पुग्गलो पुञ्ञफलूपजीवी नो उट्ठानफलूपजीवी ?

परनिम्मितवसवत्ती[1] देवे[1] उपादाय ततूपरि[2] देवा पुञ्ञफलूपजीविनो न उट्ठानफलूपजीविनो।

(B) A person who lives on the fruit of his merit but not on the fruit of his exertions

46. What sort of person lives on the fruit of his merit but not on the fruit of his exertions?

The devas commencing from Paranimmitavasavattī and those above them— these live on the fruit of merits and not on the fruit of their exertions.

(ग) उट्ठानफलूपजीवी च पुञ्ञफलूपजीवी च

४७. [B.159] कतमो च पुग्गलो उट्ठानफलूपजीवी च पुञ्ञफलूपजीवी च ?

यस्स पुग्गलस्स उट्ठहतो घटतो वायमतो आजीवो अभिनिब्बत्तति पुञ्ञतो च— अयं वुच्चति पुग्गलो "उट्ठानफलूपजीवी च पुञ्ञफलूपजीवी च"।

(C) A person who lives on the fruit of his exertions and on the fruit of his merits

47. What sort of person is he who lives on the fruit of his exertions as well as on the fruit of his merits?

The person whose living springs from his own exertions, endeavours, and efforts, as also from merits, is the person who lives on the fruit of his own exertions as well as on the fruit of his merits.

१-१. परनिम्मितवसवत्तिदेवे — सी०, स्या०, रो०।

२. तत्थुपरि — स्या०।

(घ) नेव उट्ठानफलूपजीवी नो पुञ्ञफलूपजीवी

४८. कतमो च पुग्गलो नेव उट्ठानफलूपजीवी नो पुञ्ञफलूपजीवी ?

नेरयिका नेव उट्ठानफलूपजीविनो नो पुञ्ञफलूपजीविनो ।

(D) A person who lives neither on the fruit of his exertions nor on the fruit of his merits

48. What sort of person lives neither on the fruit of his own exertions nor on the fruit of his own merits?

Persons (suffering) in purgatory are persons who live neither on the fruit of their own exertions nor on the fruit of merits.

(१९. क) तमो तमपरायनो पुग्गलो

४९. कथं च पुग्गलो तमो होति तमपरायनो[१] ?

[N.79] इधेकच्चो पुग्गलो नीचे कुले पच्चाजातो होति— चण्डालकुले वा नेसादकुले वा वेनकुले[२] वा रथकारकुले वा पुक्कुसकुले वा दलिद्दे[३] अप्पन्नपानभोजने कसिरवुत्तिके, यत्थ कसिरेन घासच्छादो लब्भति । सो च होति दुब्बण्णो दुद्दसिको ओकोटिमको बव्हाबाधो काणो वा कुणी वा खञ्जो वा पक्खहतो वा, न लाभी अन्नस्स पानस्स वत्थस्स यानस्स मालागन्धविलेपनस्स सेय्यावसथपदीपेय्यस्स । सो कायेन दुच्चरितं चरति, वाचाय दुच्चरितं चरति, मनसा दुच्चरितं चरति । सो कायेन दुच्चरितं चरित्वा वाचाय दुच्चरितं चरित्वा मनसा दुच्चरितं चरित्वा कायस्स भेदा परं मरणा अपायं दुग्गतिं विनिपातं निरयं उपपज्जति । एवं पुग्गलो तमो होति तमपरायनो ।

(19. A) A person who does remain in the dark and tend towards darkness

49. How does a person remain in the dark and tend towards darkness?

---

१. तमपरायणो — सी० ।

२. वेणकुले — सी०, स्या०, रो० ।

३. दळिद्दे — सी० ।

Here a person born in a family of low degree, be it of Caṇḍālas, or of Nesādas, or of basket-weavers, or of chariot makers, or of Pukkusas, poor, ill-fed, in straitened circumstances, where victuals are obtained with difficulty. He is swarthy, ill-featured, hunch-backed, a prey to many diseases, purblind, or with a crooked hand, lame or paralysed, one who receives neither food nor drink, nor raiment, nor conveyances, nor wreaths, perfumes and unguents, nor bed, dwelling, and light. He is an evil-doer in deed, evil-doer in word and evil-doer in thought. He having been an evil-doer in deed, evil-doer in word and evil-doer in thought, is reborn at the disintegration of the body after death in misery, to woeful doom, to disaster. Thus does a person remain in the dark and tend towards darkness.

(ख) तमो जोतिपरायनो पुग्गलो

५०. [S.356] कथं च पुग्गलो तमो होति जोतिपरायनो ?

इधेकच्चो पुग्गलो नीचे कुले पच्चाजातो होति— चण्डालकुले वा नेसादकुले वा वेनकुले वा रथकारकुले वा पुक्कुसकुले वा दलिद्दे अप्पन्नपानभोजने कसिरवुत्तिके, यत्थ कसिरेन घासच्छादो लब्भति। सो च होति दुब्बण्णो दुद्दसिको ओकोटिमको बव्हाबाधो काणो वा कुणी वा खञ्जो वा पक्खहतो वा, न लाभी अन्नस्स पानस्स वत्थस्स यानस्स मालागन्धविलेपनस्स सेय्यावसथपदीपेय्यस्स। सो कायेन सुचरितं चरति, वाचाय सुचरितं [R.52] चरति, मनसा सुचरितं चरति। सो कायेन सुचरितं चरित्वा वाचाय सुचरितं चरित्वा मनसा सुचरितं चरित्वा कायस्स भेदा परं मरणा सुगतिं सग्गं लोकं उपपज्जति। एवं पुग्गलो तमो होति जोतिपरायनो।

(B) A person who is in the dark and tend towards light

50. How does a person who is in the dark and tend towards light?

Here a person born in a family of low degree, be it of Caṇḍālas, or of Nesādas, or of basket-weavers, or of chariot makers, or of Pukkusas, poor, ill-fed, in straitened circumstances, where victuals are obtained with difficulty. He is swarthy, ill-featured, hunch-backed, a prey to many diseases, purblind, or with a crooked hand, lame or paralysed, one who receives neither food nor drink, nor raiment, nor conveyances, nor wreaths, perfumes and unguents, nor bed, dwelling, and light. He is a well-doer in deed, well-doer in word and well-doer in thought. He having been a well-doer in deed, well-doer in word and well-doer in thought, is reborn at the disintegration of the body after death to a happy destiny in the bright worlds. Thus does a person who is in the dark and tend towards light.

(ग) जोति तमपरायनो पुग्गलो

५१. कथं च पुग्गलो जोति होति तमपरायनो ?

इधेकच्चो पुग्गलो उच्चे कुले पच्चाजातो होति— खत्तियमहासालकुले वा [B.160] ब्राह्मणमहासालकुले[१] वा गहपतिमहासालकुले वा अड्ढे महद्धने महाभोगे पहूतजातरूपरजते पहूतवित्तूपकरणे पहूतधनधञ्ञे। सो च होति अभिरूपो दस्सनीयो पासादिको परमाय वण्णपोक्खरताय समन्नागतो, लाभी [N.80] अन्नस्स पानस्स वत्थस्स यानस्स मालागन्धविलेपनस्स सेय्यावसथपदीपेय्यस्स। सो कायेन दुच्चरितं चरति, वाचाय दुच्चरितं चरति, मनसा दुच्चरितं चरति। सो कायेन दुच्चरितं चरित्वा वाचाय दुच्चरितं चरित्वा मनसा दुच्चरितं चरित्वा कायस्स भेदा परं मरणा अपायं दुग्गतिं विनिपातं निरयं उपपज्जति। एवं पुग्गलो जोति होति तमपरायनो।

(C) A person who is in the light and tend towards darkness

51. How does a person who is in the light and tend towards darkness?

---

१. ब्राह्मणमहासाळकुले — सी०, एवमुपरि पि।

Here a person who is reborn into a family of high degree, be it eminently noble or of a brahmin magnate, or of a house-holder of high position, rich, of enormous wealth, owner of abundant objects of enjoyment, having ample hoards of gold and silver, having ample aids to enjoyment, ample stores of money and corn. He is handsome, fair-looking, charming, endowed with the most exquisite complexion, the recipient of food, drink, raiment, means of transport, wreaths, perfumes and unguents, bed, dwelling, and light. He is an evil-doer in deed, evil-doer in word and evil-doer in thought. He having been an evil-doer in deed, evil-doer in word and evil-doer in thought, is reborn at the disintegration of the body after death, in misery, to woeful doom, to disaster. Thus does a person who is in the light and tend towards darkness.

(घ) जोति जोतिपरायनो पुग्गलो

५२. कथं च पुग्गलो जोति होति जोतिपरायनो ?

इधेकच्चो पुग्गलो उच्चे कुले पच्चाजातो होति— खत्तियमहासालकुले वा ब्राह्मणमहासालकुले वा गहपतिमहासालकुले वा अड्ढे महद्धने महाभोगे पहूतजातरूपरजते पहूतवित्तूपकरणे पहूतधनधञ्ञे। सो च होति अभिरूपो दस्सनीयो पासादिको परमाय वण्णपोक्खरताय समन्नागतो, लाभी अन्नस्स पानस्स वत्थस्स यानस्स मालागन्धविलेपनस्स सेय्यावसथपदीपेय्यस्स। सो कायेन सुचरितं चरति, वाचाय सुचरितं चरति, मनसा सुचरितं चरति। सो कायेन सुचरितं चरित्वा वाचाय सुचरितं चरित्वा मनसा सुचरितं चरित्वा कायस्स भेदा परं मरणा सुगतिं सग्गं लोकं उपपज्जति। एवं पुग्गलो जोति होति जोतिपरायनो।

(D) A person who is in the light tend towards light

52. How does a person who is in the light tend towards light?

Here a person who is reborn into a family of high degree, be it eminently noble or of a brahmin magnate, or of a householder of high position, rich, of enormous wealth, owner of abundant objects of enjoyment, having ample hoards of gold and silver, having ample aids to enjoyment, ample stores of money and corn. He is handsome, fair-looking, charming, endowed with the most exquisite complexion, the recipient of food, drink, raiment, means of transport, wreaths, perfumes, unguents, bed, dwelling, and light. He is a well-doer in deed, well-doer in word and well-doer in thought. He having been a well-doer in deed, well-doer in word and well-doer in thought, is reborn at the disintegration of the body after death to a happy destiny in the bright worlds. Thus does a person who is in the light proceed towards light.

(२०. क) ओणतोणतो पुग्गलो

५३. [S.358] कथं च पुग्गलो ओणतोणतो[१] होति ... पे०... एवं पुग्गलो ओणतोणतो होति।

(20. A) A person who is depressed and the unprogressive

53. How is a person depressed and the unprogressive ...pe... Thus is a person depressed and the unprogressive.

(ख) ओणतुण्णतो पुग्गलो

५४. कथं च पुग्गलो ओणतुण्णतो होति ...पे०... एवं पुग्गलो ओणतुण्णतो होति।

(B) A person who is depressed but the progressive

54. How is a person depressed but the progressive ...pe... Thus is a person depressed but the progressive.

१. ओनतोनतो — सी०, एवमुपरि पि।

(ग) उण्णतोणतो पुग्गलो

५५. कथं च पुग्गलो उण्णतोणतो होति ...पे०... एवं पुग्गलो उण्णतोणतो होति।

(C) A person who is prosperous but the unprogressive

55. How is a person prosperous but the unprogressive ...pe... Thus is a person prosperous but the unprogressive.

(घ) उण्णतुण्णतो पुग्गलो

५६. कथं च पुग्गलो उण्णतुण्णतो होति ...पे०... एवं पुग्गलो उण्णतुण्णतो होति।

(D) A person who is prosperous as well as the progressive

56. How is a person prosperous as well as the progressive ...pe... Thus is a person prosperous as well as the progressive.

(These four types correspond respectively to the above four. It means as 'tamo tamaparāyano, tamo jotiparāyano, joti tamaparāyano, joti jotiparāyano puggalo.')

(२१) चत्तारो रुक्खूपमा पुग्गला

५७. [N.81; B.161] तत्थ कतमे चत्तारो रुक्खूपमा पुग्गला?

चत्तारो रुक्खा— फेग्गु सारपरिवारो, सारो फेग्गुपरिवारो, फेग्गु फेग्गुपरिवारो, सारो सारपरिवारो। एवमेवं चत्तारोमे रुक्खूपमा पुग्गला सन्तो संविज्जमाना लोकस्मिं। कतमे चत्तारो? फेग्गु सारपरिवारो, सारो फेग्गुपरिवारो, फेग्गु फेग्गुपरिवारो, सारो सारपरिवारो।

(21) Four persons who are comparable to trees

57. Who are the four persons comparable to tree?

The four kinds of trees— one itself weak but surrounded by strong ones, one itself strong but surrounded by weak ones, one itself weak and surrounded by weak ones, one itself strong and surrounded by strong ones. In the same way the four types of person likened repectively unto these four classes of trees exist in this world. And what are the four? A person himself weak but surrounded by the strong, a person himself strong but surrounded by the weak, a person himself weak and surrounded by the weak, a person himself strong and surrounded by the strong.

(क) [R.53] कथं च पुग्गलो फेग्गु होति सारपरिवारो ?

इधेकच्चो पुग्गलो दुस्सीलो होति पापधम्मो, परिसा च ख्वस्स होति सीलवती कल्याणधम्मा। एवं पुग्गलो फेग्गु होति सारपरिवारो। सेय्यथापि सो रुक्खो फेग्गु सारपरिवारो, तथूपमो अयं पुग्गलो।

(A) How is a person who himself is weak surrounded by the strong?

Here a certain person who is immorals, wicked, while his associates are moral men of lovely nature. Thus is a person who himself is weak surrounded by the strong. Just in the same way as a weak tree is surrounded by strong ones, so also is this person.

(ख) कथं च पुग्गलो सारो होति फेग्गुपरिवारो ?

इधेकच्चो पुग्गलो सीलवा होति कल्याणधम्मो, परिसा च ख्वस्स होति दुस्सीला[१] पापधम्मा[२]। एवं पुग्गलो सारो होति फेग्गुपरिवारो। सेय्यथापि सो रुक्खो सारो फेग्गुपरिवारो, तथूपमो अयं पुग्गलो।

(B) How is a person who is strong surrounded by the weak?

१. दुस्सीलो — रो०।

२. पापधम्मो — रो०।

Here a certain person who is moral, of lovely nature, having associates who are immoral, wicked. Thus is a person who is strong surrounded by the weak. Just in the same way as a strong tree is surrounded by weak ones, so also is this person.

(ग) कथं च पुग्गलो फेग्गु होति फेग्गुपरिवारो ?

इधेकच्चो पुग्गलो दुस्सीलो होति पापधम्मो, परिसा पिस्स होति दुस्सीला पापधम्मा। एवं पुग्गलो फेग्गु होति फेग्गुपरिवारो। सेय्यथापि सो रुक्खो फेग्गु फेग्गुपरिवारो, तथूपमो अयं पुग्गलो।

(C) How is a person who himself is weak surrounded by the weak?

Here a certain person who is immoral, wicked, and his associates are also immoral, wicked. Thus is a person who himself is weak surrounded by the weak. Just in the same way as a weak tree is surrounded by weak ones, so also is this person.

(घ) कथं च पुग्गलो सारो होति सारपरिवारो ?

इधेकच्चो पुग्गलो सीलवा होति कल्याणधम्मो, परिसा पिस्स होति सीलवती कल्याणधम्मा। एवं पुग्गलो सारो होति सारपरिवारो। सेय्यथापि सो रुक्खो सारो[१] सारपरिवारो, तथूपमो अयं पुग्गलो।

इमे चत्तारो रुक्खूपमा पुग्गला सन्तो संविज्जमाना लोकस्मिं।

(D) How is a person who is strong surrounded by the strong?

Here a certain person who himself is moral and of lovely nature, and his associates are also moral and of lovely nature. Thus is a person who is strong surrounded by the strong. Just in the same way as a

१. सारो होति — रो॰।

strong tree is surrounded by strong ones, so also is this person.

These are the four persons comparable to trees existing in this world.

(२२. क) रूपप्पमाणो रूपप्पसन्नो पुग्गलो

५८. [S.360] कतमो च पुग्गलो रूपप्पमाणो रूपप्पसन्नो ?

इधेकच्चो [N.82] पुग्गलो आरोहं वा पस्सित्वा परिणाहं वा पस्सित्वा सण्ठानं वा पस्सित्वा पारिपूरिं[१] वा पस्सित्वा तत्थ पमाणं गहेत्वा पसादं जनेति। अयं वुच्चति पुग्गलो रूपप्पमाणो रूपप्पसन्नो।

(22. A) A person who is one estimating by and satisfied with the outward form

58. What sort of person is one estimating by and satisfied with the outward form?

Here a person having observed the height, the compass, the shape, and the finish of a material object, finds satisfaction in it. Such a person is one estimating by and satisfied with the outward form.

(ख) घोसप्पमाणो घोसप्पसन्नो पुग्गलो

५९. [B.162] कतमो च पुग्गलो घोसप्पमाणो घोसप्पसन्नो ?

इधेकच्चो पुग्गलो परवण्णनाय परथोमनाय परपसंसनाय परवण्णहारिकाय[२] तत्थ पमाणं गहेत्वा पसादं जनेति। अयं वुच्चति पुग्गलो घोसप्पमाणो घोसप्पसन्नो।

(B) A person who is one estimating by and satisfied with others' words

59. What sort of person is one estimating by and satisfied with others' words?

१. परिपूरं — रो०।

२. परवण्णहारिया — सी०; परवण्णभारिताय — रो०।

Here a person engenders faith on the basis of the praise, the adulation, the admiration, the encomiums of others, treating them as a standard of judgement. Such a person is one estimating by and satisfied with others' words.

(ग) लूखप्पमाणो लूखप्पसन्नो पुग्गलो

६०. कतमो च पुग्गलो लूखप्पमाणो लूखप्पसन्नो ?

इधेकच्चो पुग्गलो चीवरलूखं वा पस्सित्वा पत्तलूखं[१] वा पस्सित्वा[२] सेनासनलूखं वा पस्सित्वा विविधं वा दुक्करकारिकं पस्सित्वा तत्थ पमाणं गहेत्वा पसादं जनेति । अयं वुच्चति पुग्गलो लूखप्पमाणो लूखप्पसन्नो ।

(C) A person who is one estimating by and esteeming outward austerity

60. What sort of person is one estimating by and esteeming outward austerity?

Here a person having noticed the austere nature of the garments, or of begging bowls, or of beds and sheets, or having observed manifold austerities, finds satisfaction in them, taking these austerities as a standard of judgement. Such a person is one estimating by and esteeming outward austerity.

(घ) धम्मप्पमाणो धम्मप्पसन्नो पुग्गलो

६१. कतमो च पुग्गलो धम्मप्पमाणो धम्मप्पसन्नो ?

इधेकच्चो पुग्गलो सीलं वा पस्सित्वा समाधिं वा पस्सित्वा [R.54] पञ्ञं वा पस्सित्वा तत्थ पमाणं गहेत्वा पसादं जनेति । अयं वुच्चति पुग्गलो धम्मप्पमाणो धम्मप्पसन्नो ।

---

१. सी० पोत्थके नत्थि ।

२. सी० पोत्थके नत्थि ।

(D) A person who is one estimating by and esteeming the Law

61. What sort of person is one estimating by and esteeming the Law?

Here a person having noticed the practice of morality, or the practice of concentration, or the practice of insight, finds satisfaction therein, taking these practices as a standard of judgement. Such a person is one estimating by and esteeming the Law.

(२३. क) अत्तहिताय पटिपन्नो नो परहिताय

६२. कथं च पुग्गलो अत्तहिताय पटिपन्नो होति नो परहिताय?

इधेकच्चो पुग्गलो अत्तना सीलसम्पन्नो होति, नो परं सीलसम्पदाय समादपेति; अत्तना समाधिसम्पन्नो होति, नो परं समाधिसम्पदाय समादपेति; अत्तना पञ्ञासम्पन्नो होति, नो परं पञ्ञासम्पदाय समादपेति; अत्तना विमुत्तिसम्पन्नो होति, नो परं विमुत्तिसम्पदाय समादपेति; अत्तना विमुत्तिञाणदस्सनसम्पन्नो होति, नो परं विमुत्तिञाणदस्सनसम्पदाय समादपेति। एवं पुग्गलो अत्तहिताय पटिपन्नो होति नो परहिताय।

(23. A) A person who strive after his own welfare but not after that of others' welfare

62. How does a person strive after his own welfare but not after that of others' welfare?

Here a certain person attains to the moral life but does not encourage others to attain the moral life, himself attains to the practice of concentration but does not encourage others to attain the practice of concentration, himself attains to insight but does not encourage others to attain insight, himself attains to the practice of emancipation but does not encourage others to attain the practice of emancipation, himself attains to the perception of a consciousness of emancipation but does not encourage others to attain the perception of a consciousness of emancipation. Such a person is one who strives after his own welfare but not after that of others' welfare.

(ख) परहिताय पटिपन्नो नो अत्तहिताय

६३. [N.83; S.362] कथं च पुग्गलो परहिताय पटिपन्नो होति नो अत्तहिताय ?

इधेकच्चो पुग्गलो अत्तना न सीलसम्पन्नो होति, परं सीलसम्पदाय समादपेति; अत्तना न समाधिसम्पन्नो होति, परं समाधिसम्पदाय समादपेति; अत्तना न पञ्ञासम्पन्नो होति, परं पञ्ञासम्पदाय समादपेति; अत्तना न विमुत्तिसम्पन्नो होति, परं विमुत्तिसम्पदाय समादपेति; अत्तना न विमुत्तिञाणदस्सनसम्पन्नो होति, परं विमुत्तिञाणदस्सनसम्पदाय समादपेति । एवं पुग्गलो परहिताय पटिपन्नो होति नो अत्तहिताय ।

(B) A person who strive after others' welfare but not after his own welfare

63. How does a person strive after others' welfare but not after his own welfare?

Here a certain person does not himself attain to the moral life but encourages others to attain the moral life, does not himself attain to the practice of concentration but encourages others to attain the practice of concentration, does not himself attain to insight but encourages others to attain insight, does not himself attain to the practice of emancipation but encourages others to attain the practice of emancipation, does not himself attain to the perception of a consciousness of emancipation but encourages others to attain the perception of a consciousness of emancipation. Thus does a person strive after others' welfare but not after his own welfare.

(ग) अत्तहिताय चेव पटिपन्नो परहिताय च

६४. [B.163] कथं च पुग्गलो अत्तहिताय चेव पटिपन्नो होति परहिताय च ?

इधेकच्चो पुग्गलो अत्तना च सीलसम्पन्नो होति, परं च सीलसम्पदाय समादपेति; अत्तना च समाधिसम्पन्नो होति, परं च समाधिसम्पदाय समादपेति; अत्तना च पञ्ञासम्पन्नो होति, परं च पञ्ञासम्पदाय समादपेति; अत्तना च विमुत्तिसम्पन्नो होति, परं च विमुत्तिसम्पदाय समादपेति; अत्तना च विमुत्तिञाणदस्सनसम्पन्नो होति, परं च विमुत्तिञाणदस्सनसम्पदाय समादपेति। एवं[१] पुग्गलो अत्तहिताय चेव पटिपन्नो होति परहिताय च।

(C) A person who strive after his own welfare as well as after that of others' welfare

64. How does a person strive after his own welfare as well as after that of others' welfare?

Here a certain person himself attains to the moral life and also encourages others to attain the moral life, himself attains to the practice of concentration and also encourages others to attain the practice of concentration, himself attains to insight and also encourages others to attain insight, himself attains to the practice of emancipation and also encourages others to attain the practice of emancipation, himself attains to the perception of a consciousness of emancipation and also encourages others to attain the perception of a consciousness of emancipation. Such a person is one who strives after his own welfare as well as after that of thers' welfare.

(घ) नेव अत्तहिताय पटिपन्नो नो परहिताय

६५. कथं च पुग्गलो नेव अत्तहिताय पटिपन्नो होति नो परहिताय?

इधेकच्चो पुग्गलो अत्तना न सीलसम्पन्नो होति, नो परं सीलसम्पदाय समादपेति; अत्तना न समाधिसम्पन्नो होति, नो परं समाधिसम्पदाय समादपेति; अत्तना न पञ्ञासम्पन्नो होति, नो परं पञ्ञासम्पदाय समादपेति; अत्तना न विमुत्तिसम्पन्नो होति, नो परं विमुत्तिसम्पदाय समादपेति; अत्तना [R.55] न

१. रो० पोत्थके नत्थि।

विमुत्तिञाणदस्सनसम्पन्नो होति, नो परं विमुत्तिञाणदस्सनसम्पदाय समादपेति। एवं पुग्गलो नेव अत्तहिताय पटिपन्नो होति नो परहिताय।

(D) A person who strive neither after his own welfare nor after that of others' welfare

65. How does a person strive neither after his own welfare nor after that of others' welfare?

Here a certain person neither himself attains to the moral life nor encourages others to attain the moral life, neither himself attains to the practice of concentration nor encourages others to attain the practice of concentration, neither himself attains to the practice of insight nor encourages others to attain the practice of insight, neither himself attains to the practice of emancipation nor encourages others to attain the practice of emancipation, neither himself attains to perception of a consciousness of emancipation nor encourages others to attain the perception of a consciousness of emancipation. Such a person is one who strives neither after his own welfare nor after that of others' welfare.

(२४. क) अत्तन्तपो पुग्गलो

६६. [S.364] कथं च पुग्गलो अत्तन्तपो होति अत्तपरितापनानु-योगमनुयुत्तो ?

[N.84] इधेकच्चो पुग्गलो अचेलको होति मुत्ताचारो हत्थापलेखनो[१] नएहिभद्दन्तिको[२] नतिट्ठभद्दन्तिको नाभिहटं न उद्दिस्सकतं न निमन्तनं सादियति, सो न कुम्भिमुखा[३] पटिग्गण्हाति[४] न कळोपिमुखा[५] पटिग्गण्हाति न एळकमन्तरं[६] न

१. हत्थावलेखनो — स्या०।

२. न एहिभदन्तिको — सी०, स्या०, रो०, एवमुपरि पि।

३. कुम्भीमुखा — स्या०।

४. पतिगण्हाति — सी०; पटिगण्हाति — रो०।

५. कलोपिमुखा — सी०, स्या०; खळोपिमुखा — रो०।

६. एलकमन्तरं — सी०।

दण्डमन्तरं न मुसलमन्तरं[1] न द्विन्नं भुञ्जमानानं न गब्भिनिया न पायमानाय न पुरिसन्तरगताय न सङ्कित्तीसु न यत्थ सा उपट्ठितो होति न यत्थ मक्खिका सण्डसण्डचारिनी, न मच्छं न मंसं न सुरं न मेरयं न थुसोदकं पिवति। सो एकागारिको वा होति एकालोपिको, द्वागारिको वा होति द्वालोपिको ...पे०... सत्तागारिको वा होति सत्तालोपिको; एकिस्सा पि दत्तिया यापेति, द्वीहि पि दत्तीहि यापेति ...पे०... सत्तहि पि दत्तीहि यापेति; एकाहिकं पि आहारं आहारेति, द्वीहिकं[2] पि आहारं आहारेति ...पे०... सत्ताहिकं पि आहारं आहारेति। इति [B.164] एवरूपं अड्ढमासिकं पि परियायभत्तभोजनानुयोगमनुयुत्तो विहरति। सो साकभक्खो वा होति सामाकभक्खो वा होति नीवारभक्खो वा होति दद्दुलभक्खो वा होति हटभक्खो वा होति कणभक्खो वा होति आचामभक्खो वा होति पिञ्ञाकभक्खो वा होति तिणभक्खो वा होति गोमयभक्खो वा होति, वनमूलफलाहारो[3] यापेति पवत्तफलभोजी। सो साणानि पि धारेति मसाणानि पि धारेति छवदुस्सानि पि धारेति पंसुकूलानि पि धारेति तिरीटानि पि धारेति अजिनं[4] पि धारेति अजिनक्खिपं पि धारेति कुसचीरं पि धारेति वाकचीरं पि धारेति फलकचीरं पि धारेति केसकम्बलं पि धारेति वाळकम्बलं[5] पि धारेति उलूकपक्खं[6] पि धारेति, केसमस्सुलोचको[7] पि होति केसमस्सुलोचनानुयोगमनुयुत्तो, उब्भट्ठको पि होति आसनपटिक्खित्तो, उक्कुटिको पि होति उक्कुटिकप्पधानमनुयुत्तो, कण्टकापस्सयिको पि होति कण्टकापस्सये सेय्यं कप्पेति, सायततियकं[8] पि उदकोरोहनानुयोगमनुयुत्तो विहरति। इति एवरूपं अनेकविहितं कायस्स आतापनपरितापनानुयोगमनुयुत्तो [N.85; R.56] विहरति। एवं पुग्गलो अत्तन्तपो होति अत्तपरितापनानुयोगमनुयुत्तो।

---

१. मूसलमन्तरं — स्या०।

२. द्वाहिकं — सी०।

३. वनमूलफलाहारे — रो०।

४. अजिनानि — सी०, रो०।

५. वालकम्बलं — सी०, स्या०, रो०।

६. उलुकपक्खं — स्या०; उलूकपक्खिकं — रो०।

७. केसमस्सुलोचनो — रो०।

८. सायंततियकं — स्या०, रो०।

(24. A) A person who is self-mortifying

66. How does a person become self-mortifying and addicted to practices tending to self-mortification?

Here a person goes naked, is of loose habits, licks his hand clean, does not stop nearer or wait a moment if politely requested to do so, refuses to accept food brought to him, refuses to accept food especially prepared for him, does not accept any invitation, does not accept food from a cooking-pot or a pan, does not accept food placed within the threshold, does not accept food placed among the pestles, does not accept food when two persons are eating together, does not accept from a pregnant woman, from a woman giving suck, from a woman living as a wife, does not accept food offered at consecrated places, does not accept food when a dog is standing by, nor where flies are swarming down, does not accept fish, or flesh, or strong drink, or intoxicant, or sour gruel, begs from one house, eats just one morsel, or begs from two houses, eats just two morsels ...pe... begs from seven houses, eats just seven morsels, keeps himself going on only one alms or only two ...pe... seven alms, takes only once a day or once every two days ...pe... once every seven days, conforming in this way to the practice of taking food according to rule, at regular intervals, up to even half a month. He feeds on pot-herbs, feeds on wild rice, feeds on Nīvāra rice, feeds on Daddūla rice, feeds on unhusked grain, feeds on grains of rice or scum of rice, feeds on oil cakes, feeds on grasses, feeds on cowdung, feeds on fruits and roots from the woods, feeds on fruits that have fallen of themselves. He wears coarse hempen cloth, coarse cloth of mixed fibres, wears cloth taken from a dead body, clothing made of dust-heap rags, clothing made of bark, the skin of a black antelope, dress made of a black antelope's hide, dress made of Kusa grass, garments made of bark, garments made of pieces of wood, hair-garments, garments made up of horses' tails, garments made up of feathers of owls; he is a plucker-out of hair and beard, addicted to the practice of plucking out both hair and beard; he is a stander-up rejecting the use of a seat, he is a squatter addicted to the effort of squatting, he is a bed-of-thorns-man, lying on a bed of thorns, he is addicted to the practice of going down into water thrice a day up to the evening. Thus he dwells addicted to many such tortures of the body. Thus does a person become a self-mortifier and addicted to practices tending to self-mortification.

(ख) परन्तपो पुग्गलो

६७. [S.366] कथं च पुग्गलो परन्तपो होति परपरितापनानुयोगमनुयुत्तो ?

इधेकच्चो पुग्गलो ओरब्भिको होति सूकरिको साकुणिको मागविको लुद्दो मच्छघातको चोरो चोरघातको गोघातको[१] बन्धनागारिको, ये वा पनञ्ञे पि केचि कुरूरकम्मन्ता । एवं पुग्गलो परन्तपो होति परपरितापनानुयोगमनुयुत्तो ।

(B) A person who is tormentor of others

67. How does a person become tormentor of others and remain addicted to practices tending to oppression?

Here a person is a sheep-butcher, a boar-hunter, a bird-catcher, a deer-stalker, a snarer, a fish-killer, a thief, a public executor, a butcher, a jailer, or a committer of other such cruel acts. Thus does a person become tormentor of others and remain addicted to practices tending to oppress others.

(ग) अत्तन्तपो च परन्तपो च पुग्गलो

68. कथं च पुग्गलो अत्तन्तपो च होति अत्तपरितापनानुयोगमनुयुत्तो, परन्तपो च[२] परपरितापनानुयोगमनुयुत्तो ?

---

१. सी०, रो० पोत्थकेसु नत्थि ।

२. च होति — सी० ।

इधेकच्चो पुग्गलो राजा वा होति खत्तियो मुद्धावसित्तो[१] ब्राह्मणो वा महासालो। सो पुरत्थिमेन नरस्स नवं[२] सन्धागारं[३] कारापेत्वा केसमस्सुं ओहारेत्वा खराजिनं[४] निवासेत्वा सप्पितेलेन कायं [B.165] अब्भञ्जित्वा मिगविसाणेन[५] पिट्ठिं कण्डुवमानो[६] सन्धागारं पविसति सद्धिं महेसिया ब्राह्मणेन च पुरोहितेन। सो तत्थ अनन्तरहिताय भूमिया हरितुपलित्ताय[७] सेय्यं कप्पेति। एकिस्सा[८] गाविया सरूपवच्छाय यं एकस्मिं थने खीरं होति तेन[९] राजा यापेति, यं दुतियस्मिं थने खीरं होति[९] तेन महेसी यापेति, यं ततियस्मिं थने खीरं होति तेन ब्राह्मणो पुरोहितो यापेति, यं चतुत्थस्मिं थने खीरं होति तेन अग्गिं जुहति, अवसेसेन वच्छको यापेति। सो एवमाह— "एत्तका उसभा हञ्ञन्तु यञ्ञत्थाय, एत्तका वच्छतरा हञ्ञन्तु यञ्ञत्थाय, एत्तका वच्छतरियो हञ्ञन्तु यञ्ञत्थाय, एत्तका अजा हञ्ञन्तु यञ्ञत्थाय, एत्तका उरब्भा हञ्ञन्तु यञ्ञत्थाय, एत्तका[१०] अस्सा हञ्ञन्तु यञ्ञत्थाय,[१०] एत्तका रुक्खा छिज्जन्तु यूपत्थाय, एत्तका दब्भा लूयन्तु[११] बरिहिसत्थाया[१२]"ति। ये पिस्स ते होन्ति दासा ति वा पेस्सा ति वा कम्मकरा[१३] [N.86] ति वा, ते पि दण्डतज्जिता भयतज्जिता अस्सुमुखा रुदमाना परिकम्मानि करोन्ति। एवं पुग्गलो अत्तन्तपो च होति अत्तपरितापनानुयोगमनुयुत्तो, परन्तपो च परपरितापनानुयोगमनुयुत्तो।

---

१. मुद्धाभिसित्तो — स्या०।

२. नवं यञ्ञागारं — सी०; नवं सन्थागारं — स्या०; नवयञ्ञागारं — रो०।

३. नवं यञ्ञागारं — सी०; नवं सन्थागारं — स्या०; नवयञ्ञागारं — रो०।

४. खुराजिनं — स्या०।

५. मगविसाणेन — सी०।

६. कण्डूयमानो — सी०।

७. हरितुपत्ताय — सी०।

८. एतिस्सा — स्या०।

९-९. सी० पोत्थके न दिस्सति।

१०-१०. सी०, रो० पोत्थकेसु नत्थि।

११. लुयन्तु — स्या०।

१२. परहिंसत्थाया — सी०; परिहिंसत्थाया — स्या०।

१३. कम्मकारा — रो०।

(C) A person who is self-mortifying and tormentor of others

68. How does a person become self-mortifying and addicted to practices tending to self-mortification, and become tormentor of others and remain addicted to practices tending to oppression?

Here a person is a king, a crowned monarch, or a brahmin of great wealth and influence. He having a new sacrificial house built to the east of the capital city, having his hair and beard shaven, having put on a black antelope's skin, anointed his body with clarified butter and oil, scratching the back with the horn of an antelope, he enters the sacrificial house together with his queen-consort and brahmin priest. There he lies down in a narrow space on the yellow painted ground. The king lives on the quantity of milk that can be drawn from one udder of a cow with a calf resembling her (in colour), the queen-consort lives upon the quantity of milk that can be drawn from the second udder, the brahmin priest lives upon the quantity of milk that can be drawn from the third, the fire-sacrifices are performed with the quantity of milk that can be drawn from the fourth, and the calf lives upon the quantity that is left. Thus he commands— "that so many bullocks be slain for the sacrifice, that so many bull-calves be slain for the sacrifice, so many cow-calves be slain for the sacrifice, so many goats be slain for the sacrifice, so many rams be slain for the sacrifice, and so many horses be slain for the sacrifice, so many trees be cut down to make posts, so much Kusa grass be mown to be strewn around the sacrificial spot." The slaves or the messengers or the workmen that are employed carry out his orders impelled by the whip, impelled by fear, weeping with tears upon their faces. Thus does a person become a self-mortifying and addicted to practices tending to self-mortification, and become tormentor of others and remain addicted to practices tending to oppression.

(घ) नेव अत्तन्तपो च न परन्तपो च पुग्गलो

६९. कथं च पुग्गलो नेव अत्तन्तपो च होति न अत्तपरितापनानुयोगमनुयुत्तो, न परन्तपो न परपरितापनानुयोगमनुयुत्तो?

सो अनत्तन्तपो अपरन्तपो दिट्ठेव धम्मे निच्छातो निब्बुतो सीतिभूतो[१] सुखप्पटिसंवेदी[२] ब्रह्मभूतेन अत्तना विहरति।

(D) A person who tortures neither himself nor the self of others

69. How does a person neither become self-mortifying nor addicted to practices tending to self-mortification, and nor become tormentor of others nor remain addicted to practices tending to oppression?

He tortures neither himself nor others, and in this world he without any hankering, at peace, cool, enjoying bliss, lives with a self become godlike.

७०. इध तथागतो लोके उप्पज्जति अरहं सम्मासम्बुद्धो [R.57] विज्जाचरणसम्पन्नो सुगतो लोकविदू अनुत्तरो पुरिसदम्मसारथि सत्था देवमनुस्सानं बुद्धो भगवा। सो इमं लोकं सदेवकं समारकं सब्रह्मकं सस्समणब्राह्मणिं पजं सदेवमनुस्सं सयं अभिञ्ञा सच्छिकत्वा पवेदेति। सो धम्मं देसेति आदिकल्याणं मज्झेकल्याणं परियोसानकल्याणं सात्थं सब्यञ्जनं, केवलपरिपुण्णं परिसुद्धं ब्रह्मचरियं पकासेति। तं धम्मं सुणाति गहपति वा गहपतिपुत्तो वा अञ्ञतरस्मिं वा कुले [B.166] पच्चाजातो। [S.368] सो तं धम्मं सुत्वा तथागते सद्धं पटिलभति। सो तेन सद्धापटिलाभेन समन्नागतो इति पटिसञ्चिक्खति— "सम्बाधो घरावासो रजापथो, अब्भोकासो पब्बज्जा। नयिदं सुकरं अगारं अज्झावसता एकन्तपरिपुण्णं एकन्तपरिसुद्धं सङ्खलिखितं[३] ब्रह्मचरियं चरितुं। यन्नूनाहं केसमस्सुं ओहारेत्वा कासायानि वत्थानि अच्छादेत्वा अगारस्मा अनगारियं पब्बजेय्यं"ति!

---

१. सीतिभूतो — सी०, रो०।

२. सुखपटिसंवेदी — सी०, स्या०, रो०।

३. सङ्खलिक्खितं — स्या०, रो०।

सो अपरेन समयेन अप्पं वा भोगक्खन्धं पहाय महन्तं वा भोगक्खन्धं पहाय अप्पं वा ञातिपरिवट्टं पहाय महन्तं वा ञातिपरिवट्टं पहाय केसमस्सुं ओहारेत्वा कासायानि वत्थानि अच्छादेत्वा अगारस्मा अनगारियं पब्बजति।

70. Here it happens that a Tathāgata is born in this world, an exalted, Perfectly Enlightened Buddha, enriched with insight, and virtuous deportment, walking in the right path, the knower of the world, the unsurpassed, the guide to persons amenable to discipline, the teacher of devas and men, Buddha, the Blessed One, he having come to know and realise by himself, this world together with those of the Devas, the Māras, the Brahmās, together with the recluses and brahmins, dwellers together with devas and men, instructs others about it. He imparts instruction beneficial in its inception, beneficial in its continuation, beneficial in its conclusion, full of meaning, couched in appropriate terms, couched in suitable language. He expresses, sets forth the higher life in its purity and entire fulness. To this instruction does a householder listen or his offspring or one who is born in another family. He listening to this instruction gains faith in the Tathāgata. Endowed with this acquisition of faith, he ponders thus— "Cramping is household life, a dusty path! Open and wide is the way of renunciation! Not easy is it while living the household life to practise the higher life, full and entire, supremely pure, pure like well-wrought conchshell, I must therfore depart from home into a homeless life, having my hair and beard shaven, covering my body with yellow garments". So it happens that at a subsequent date, he abandoning his entire store of wealth, whether this be large or small, abandoning his circle of relations, whether this be few or numerous, wanders away from home into the homeless state, having his hair and beard shaven, covering his body with yellow garments.

७१. सो एवं पब्बजितो समानो भिक्खूनं सिक्खासाजीवसमापन्नो पाणातिपातं पहाय पाणातिपाता पटिविरतो होति निहितदण्डो निहितसत्थो लज्जी दयापन्नो सब्बपाणभूतहितानुकम्पी विहरति। [N.87] अदिन्नादानं पहाय अदिन्नादाना पटिविरतो होति दिन्नादायी दिन्नपाटिकङ्खी, अथेनेन सुचिभूतेन अत्तना विहरति। अब्रह्मचरियं पहाय ब्रह्मचारी होति आराचारी पटिविरतो मेथुना गामधम्मा। मुसावादं पहाय मुसावादा पटिविरतो होति सच्चवादी सच्चसन्धो थेतो पच्चयिको अविसंवादको लोकस्स। पिसुणं वाचं पहाय पिसुणाय वाचाय पटिविरतो होति, इतो सुत्वा न अमुत्र अक्खाता इमेसं भेदाय, अमुत्र वा सुत्वा न इमेसं अक्खाता अमूसं भेदाय। इति भिन्नानं वा सन्धाता सहितानं[१] वा अनुप्पदाता समग्गारामो समग्गरतो समग्गनन्दी समग्गकरणिं वाचं भासिता होति। फरुसं[२] वाचं पहाय फरुसाय वाचाय पटिविरतो होति। या सा वाचा नेला कण्णसुखा पेमनीया हदयङ्गमा पोरी बहुजनकन्ता बहुजनमनापा तथारूपिं वाचं भासिता होति। [R.58; B.167] सम्फप्पलापं पहाय सम्फप्पलापा पटिविरतो होति, कालवादी भूतवादी अत्थवादी धम्मवादी विनयवादी निधानवतिं वाचं भासिता[३] कालेन सापदेसं परियन्तवतिं अत्थसंहितं।

71. Thus he initiated into the religious order, while adopting the mode of training and living followed by the bhikkhus, he putting away the (intentional) killing of living beings, abstains from the (intentional) slaughter of life, putting aside the rod, putting aside the sword, ashamed of cruelty, merciful, compassionate, and kind to all living beings. Putting away the taking of what has not been given him, he abstains from accepting what is not given; he takes what is given expecting only what is given, he passes his life in honesty, with a self become pure. Putting away the unchaste life, he is chaste, not unchaste, refraining from sexual life, from village nature. Putting away lying words, he refrains from telling a lie, speaks the truth, always aiming at the truth, is trustworthy, never betraying his

१. समाहितानं — स्या॰।

२. फरुसा — सी॰।

३. भासिता होति — सी॰।

trust to the world. Putting away slanderous speech, he refrains from calumny, hearing something at one place, he does not relate the same at another place with a view to foment quarrel against the former party, hearing something elsewhere, he does not relate it here with a view to foment a quarrel against the people there. Thus as a reconciliator of those that have separated, as an augmentor of the unity of those who are already united, rejoicing in union, jubilant over unity, he is in the habit of uttering words tending to reunion. Putting away rough words, he refrains from offensive language, he speaks those words that are blameless, pleasing to the ear, affectionate, appealing to the heart, refined, gladdening the people, captivating the heart of many. Putting away silly talk, he refrains from idle talk, speaks at the right time, speaks what is true, speaks according to the good, according to religion, according to self-control, utters speech worthy of being treasured up, sometimes with illustrations, clearly defined, pregnant with meaning.

७२. [S.370] सो बीजगामभूतगामसमारम्भा पटिविरतो होति, एकभत्तिको होति रत्तूपरतो विरतो विकालभोजना, नच्चगीतवादितविसूकदस्सना पटिविरतो होति, मालागन्धविलेपनधारणमण्डनविभूसनट्ठानापटिविरतो होति, उच्चासयनमहासयना पटिविरतो होति, जातरूपरजतपटिग्गहणा पटिविरतो होति, आमकधञ्ञपटिग्गहणा पटिविरतो होति, आमकमंसपटिग्गहणा पटिविरतो होति, इत्थिकुमारिकापटिग्गहणा[१] पटिविरतो होति, दासिदासपटिग्गहणा[२] पटिविरतो होति, अजेळकपटिग्गहणा[३] पटिविरतो होति, कुक्कुटसूकरपटिग्गहणा पटिविरतो होति, हत्थिगवास्सवळवपटिग्गहणा[४] पटिविरतो होति, खेत्तवत्थुपटिग्गहणा पटिविरतो होति, दूतेय्यपहिणगमनानुयोगा[५] पटिविरतो होति, [N.88]

---

१. इत्थीकुमारीपटिग्गहणा — स्या०; इत्थिकुमारिपटिग्गहणा — रो० ।

२. दासीदास० — स्या० ।

३. अजेलक० — सी० ।

४. हत्थिगवास्सवलवा० — सी०; हत्थिगवस्सवळव० — स्या० ।

५. दूतेय्यपहीनगमनानुयोगा — स्या०; दूतेय्यपहीण० — रो० ।

कयविक्कया पटिविरतो होति, तुलाकूटकंसकूटमानकूटा[१] पटिविरतो होति, उक्कोटनवञ्चननिकतिसाचियोगा[२] पटिविरतो होति, छेदनवधबन्धनविपरामोस-आलोपसहसाकारा[३] पटिविरतो होति।

72. He refrains from doing injury to the forms of life whether in the germinal or grown-up state; he takes but one meal a day, not eating at night, refraining from an untimely meal; he abstains from being a spectator at dances, songs, music, and (such other) amusements; he abstains from wearing garlands, besmearing and adorning his body with scents and unguents, and using (such other) articles for beautifying; he abstains from using high and fine couches; he abstains from taking (all that is included under) gold and silver; he abstains from accepting uncooked rice, uncooked meat, women and girls, male and female slaves, goat and sheep, fowls and pigs, elephants, cows, horses and mules, fields and residences, as gifts; he refrains from the practice of acting as a go-between or a messenger, he abstains from buying and selling; he abstains from cheating with scales or coins or measures; he abstains from the crooked way of bribery, cheating, and fraud; he abstains from mutilating, killing, putting in bonds, highway robbery, dacoity, and acts of violence.

७३. सो सन्तुट्ठो होति कायपरिहारिकेन चीवरेन कुच्छिपरिहारिकेन पिण्डपातेन। सो येन येनेव पक्कमति समादायेव पक्कमति, सेय्यथापि नाम[४] पक्खी सकुणो येन येनेव डेति सपत्तभारो व डेति। एवमेवं भिक्खु सन्तुट्ठो होति कायपरिहारिकेन चीवरेन कुच्छिपरिहारिकेन पिण्डपातेन। सो[५] येन येनेव पक्कमति

१. तुलाकूटमानकूटा — सी०।

२. उक्कोटन वञ्चन निकतिसावियोगा — सी०, स्या०।

३. छेदन वध बन्ध विपरामोसआलोप सहसाकारा — स्या०।

४. सी० पोत्थके नत्थि।

५. सी० पोत्थके नत्थि।

समादायेव पक्कमति। सो इमिना अरियेन सीलक्खन्धेन समन्नागतो अज्झत्तं अनवज्जसुखं पटिसंवेदेति।

73. He is satisfied with robes just enough to protect his body, with alms just enough to feed his stomach, wherever he goes taking these with him. Just as a winged bird wherever it flies, flies with just the load of its wings, in the same way the bhikkhu is satisfied with robes just enough to protect his body, with alms just enough to feed his stomach, wherever he goes he goes taking these with him. Endowed with these Ariyan moral precepts, he experiences within himself the happiness which is blameless.

७४. सो चक्खुना रूपं दिस्वा न निमित्तग्गाही होति नानुब्यञ्जनग्गाही। यत्वाधिकरणमेनं चक्खुन्द्रियं असंवुतं विहरन्तं अभिज्झादोमनस्सा पापका अकुसला धम्मा अन्वास्सवेय्युं, तस्स संवराय पटिपज्जति, रक्खति चक्खुन्द्रियं, चक्खुन्द्रिये संवरं आपज्जति; सोतेन सद्दं सुत्वा ... पे० ... [B.168] घानेन गन्धं घायित्वा ...पे०... जिव्हाय रसं सायित्वा ... पे० ... कायेन फोट्ठब्बं फुसित्वा ... पे० ... मनसा[१] धम्मं विञ्ञाय न निमित्तग्गाही होति नानुब्यञ्जनग्गाही। यत्वाधिकरणमेनं मनिन्द्रियं असंवुतं विहरन्तं अभिज्झादोमनस्सा पापका अकुसला धम्मा अन्वास्सवेय्युं, तस्स संवराय पटिपज्जति, रक्खति मनिन्द्रियं, [R.59] मनिन्द्रियं संवरं आपज्जति। सो इमिना अरियेन इन्द्रियसंवरेन समन्नागतो अज्झत्तं अब्यासेकसुखं पटिसंवेदेति।

74. He having seen an object with his eye does not fasten his mind upon the general form of details thereof, but sets himself to restrain that which gives occasion for the sinful immoral tendencies, covetousness, and dejection to flow in over him while he was dwelling unrestrained as to the sense of sight, he guards the faculty of sight, he attains to control over the sense of sight. Similarly having heard sound with his ear ...pe... having smelt an odour with his nose ...pe... having tasted a savour with his tongue

१. मानसा — सी०।

...pe... having touched a tangible thing with his body ...pe... having cognised a mental object with his mind, he does not fasten his mind upon the general form of details thereof but sets himself to restrain that which gives an occasion for the sight and immoral tendencies, covetousness, and dejection to flow in over him while he was dwelling unrestrained as to his mind, his faculty of thought; he guards his mind, he attains to control over the faculty of thought. Endowed with this Ariyan mastery over the senses, he experiences within himself the happiness which is blameless.

७५. [S.372] सो अभिक्कन्ते पटिक्कन्ते सम्पजानकारी होति, आलोकिते विलोकिते सम्पजानकारी होति, सम्मिञ्जिते पसारिते सम्पजानकारी होति, सङ्घाटिपत्तचीवरधारणे सम्पजानकारी होति, असिते पीते खायिते सायिते सम्पजानकारी होति, उच्चारपस्सावकम्मे सम्पजानकारी होति, गते ठिते निसिन्ने सुत्ते जागरिते भासिते तुण्हीभावे सम्पजानकारी होति।

75. In going forth and in coming back, he acts deliberately, and as also in looking at or around, in stretching forth his arm, or in drawing it in again, in putting on the Saṅghāṭī and other robes, or in carrying the alms-bowl, in eating or drinking, in masticating or swallowing, in obeying the calls of nature, in going or standing or sitting, in sleeping or waking, in speaking or in remaining in a state of silence.

७६. [N.89] सो इमिना च[१] अरियेन सीलक्खन्धेन समन्नागतो इमिना च अरियेन इन्द्रियसंवरेन समन्नागतो इमिना च अरियेन सतिसम्पजञ्ञेन समन्नागतो इमाय च अरियाय सन्तुट्ठिया समन्नागतो विवित्तं सेनासनं भजति अरञ्ञं रुक्खमूलं पब्बतं कन्दरं गिरिगुहं सुसानं वनपत्थं अब्भोकासं पलालपुञ्जं। सो पच्छाभत्तं पिण्डपातपटिक्कन्तो निसीदति पल्लङ्कं आभुजित्वा उजुं कायं पणिधाय परिमुखं सतिं उपट्ठपेत्वा। सो अभिज्झं लोके पहाय विगताभिज्झेन चेतसा विहरति, अभिज्झाय चित्तं परिसोधेति; ब्यापादपदोसं पहाय अब्यापन्नचित्तो विहरति सब्बपाणभूतहितानुकम्पी, ब्यापादपदोसा चित्तं परिसोधेति; थीनमिद्धं[२] पहाय

१. सी० पोत्थके नत्थि।

२. थिनमिद्धं — म०, एवमुपरि पि।

विगतथीनमिद्धो विहरति आलोकसञ्ञी सतो सम्पजानो, थीनमिद्धा चित्तं परिसोधेति; उद्धच्चकुक्कुच्चं पहाय अनुद्धतो विहरति अज्झत्तं वूपसन्तचित्तो, उद्धच्चकुक्कुच्चा चित्तं परिसोधेति; विचिकिच्छं पहाय तिण्णविचिकिच्छो विहरति अकथङ्कथी कुसलेसु धम्मेसु, विचिकिच्छाय चित्तं परिसोधेति।

76. He endowed with this Ariyan moral behaviour and endowed also with this excellent practice of mindfulness and awareness, endowed also with this Ariyan way of contentment, he takes shelter in a lonely spot, whether it be forest, or the foot of a tree, or a hill side, or a grotto, or a rocky cave, or a cemetery, or a forest tract, or an open field, or a heap of straw. He returning thither after his round for alms, seats himself cross-legged when his meal is done, keeping his body erect, setting mindfulness ahead. He putting away the hankering after the world he dwells with his mind free from covetousness, he purifies his mind of greed; putting away the evil propensities to injure he dwells with a heart free from ill-will; compassionate and kind to all living beings he purifies his mind of malevolence; putting away laziness and drowsiness he dwells being free therefrom; conscious of the presence of light, mindful and aware of experiences he purifies his mind of sloth and torpor; putting away worry and flurry he dwells free from fretfulness; with his heart tranquil within he purifies his mind of worry and flurry; putting away perplexity he dwells free from doubt; no longer doubting as to what is good he purifies his mind of scepticism.

७७. सो इमे पञ्च नीवरणे पहाय चेतसो उपक्किलेसे पञ्ञाय दुब्बलीकरणे विविच्चेव कामेहि विविच्च[१] अकुसलेहि धम्मेहि [B.169] सवितक्कं सविचारं विवेकजं पीतिसुखं पठमं झानं उपसम्पज्ज विहरति; वितक्कविचारानं वूपसमा अज्झत्तं सम्पसादनं चेतसो एकोदिभावं अवितक्कं अविचारं समाधिजं पीतिसुखं दुतियं झानं उपसम्पज्ज विहरति; पीतिया च विरागा उपेक्खको च विहरति, सतो च

---

१. विविच्चेव — सी०।

सम्पजानो सुखं च कायेन पटिसंवेदेति, यं तं अरिया आचिक्खन्ति— "उपेक्खको सतिमा सुखविहारी"ति ततियं झानं उपसम्पज्ज विहरति; सुखस्स च पहाना[१] दुक्खस्स च पहाना पुब्बेव सोमनस्सदोमनस्सानं अत्थङ्गमा अदुक्खमसुखं उपेक्खासतिपारिसुद्धिं चतुत्थं झानं उपसम्पज्ज विहरति।

77. He putting away these five hindrances which trouble the heart and weaken insight, he eschewing sensual desires, eschewing evil states enters upon and dwells in the first stage of ecstatic meditation, attended with applied and sustained thought, joy and bliss born of mental isolation. With the cessation of applied and sustained thought he enters upon and dwells in the second stage of ecstatic meditation, a state of joy and bliss boon of concentration free from applied and sustained thought— a state of concentration of mind, and inner tranquillisation of heart. By absence of passionate longing for joy he remains in equanimity, and aware of his mental states and experiences, he enjoys bliss through his body, which the Ariyas describe when they say— "the man serene and mindful dwells at ease." And thus he dwells entering upon the third stage of ecstatic meditation. Then putting away both ease and pain, and with the previous dying away of joys and griefs he dwells entering upon the fourth stage of meditation void of ease and pain, a state made pure by equanimity and thoughtfulness.

७८. [R.60; S.374] सो एवं समाहिते चित्ते परिसुद्धे परियोदाते अनङ्गणे विगतूपक्किलेसे मुदुभूते कम्मनिये[२] ठिते आनेञ्जप्पत्ते पुब्बेनिवासानुस्सतिञाणाय चित्तं अभिनिन्नामेति। सो अनेकविहितं पुब्बेनिवासं अनुस्सरति, सेय्यथीदं[३]— एकम्पि जातिं द्वेपि जातियो तिस्सोपि जातियो [N.90] चतस्सोपि जातियो पञ्चपि जातियो दसपि जातियो वीसम्पि[४] जातियो तिंसम्पि

१. पहाणा — सी०, एवमुपरि पि।

२. कम्मनीये — स्या०, रो०।

३. सेय्यथिदं — म०, एवमुपरि पि।

४. वीसतिं — सी०।

जातियो चत्तालीसम्पि[१] जातियो पञ्ञासम्पि जातियो जातिसतम्पि जातिसहस्सम्पि जातिसतसहस्सम्पि अनेकेपि संवट्टकप्पे अनेकेपि विवट्टकप्पे अनेकेपि संवट्टविवट्टकप्पे— "अमुत्रासिं एवंनामो एवंगोत्तो एवंवण्णो एवमाहारो एवंसुखदुक्खपटिसंवेदी एवमायुपरियन्तो, सो ततो चुतो अमुत्र उदपादिं[२]; तत्रापासिं एवंनामो एवंगोत्तो एवंवण्णो एवमाहारो एवंसुखदुक्खपटिसंवेदी एवमायुपरियन्तो, सो ततो चुतो इधूपपन्नो"ति। इति साकारं सउद्देसं अनेकविहितं पुब्बेनिवासं अनुस्सरति।

78. Now he with his mind thus concentrated, rendered supremely pure and bright, freed from contamination, with disturbing factors cleared off, rendered soft and pliant, fixed, and unperturbed, he bends forth his mind to acquire the knowledge enabling him to remember his previous births. He calls to mind previous existences in various shapes, as it may be one birth, two births, three births, four births, five births, ten births, twenty births, thirty births, forty births fifty births, one hundred births, one thousand births or one hundred thousand births in many periods of cosmic revolution, in many periods of envelopment and development taken together to the effect— "there I have been born under such and such a name, in such and such a family, of such and such a caste, lived on such and such kinds of food, experienced such and such pleasure and pain, and had such and such an end of (that) life; when I had deceased from that state I was reborn in another state, where I was of such and such a name, of such and such a family, of such and such a caste, lived upon such and such kinds of food experienced such and such pleasure and pain, such was the end of (that) life, having again deceased from that state I was reborn here." Thus does he recall in manifold ways his previous dwelling-places with forms of destinies in details.

---

१. चत्तारीसं — सी०।

२. उप्पादिं — सी०।

७९. सो एवं समाहिते चित्ते परिसुद्धे परियोदाते अनङ्गणे विगतूपक्किलेसे मुदुभूते कम्मनिये ठिते आनेञ्जप्पत्ते सत्तानं चुतूपपातञाणाय चित्तं अभिनिन्नामेति। सो दिब्बेन चक्खुना विसुद्धेन अतिक्कन्तमानुसकेन सत्ते पस्सति चवमाने उपपज्जमाने हीने[1] पणीते सुवण्णे दुब्बण्णे, सुगते दुग्गते यथाकम्मूपगे सत्ते पजानाति— "इमे वत भोन्तो सत्ता कायदुच्चरितेन समन्नागता, वचीदुच्चरितेन समन्नागता, मनोदुच्चरितेन समन्नागता, अरियानं उपवादका, मिच्छादिट्ठिका मिच्छादिट्ठिकम्मसमादाना। ते कायस्स भेदा परं मरणा अपायं दुग्गतिं विनिपातं निरयं उपपन्ना[2]। इमे वा पन[3] भोन्तो सत्ता [B.170] कायसुचरितेन समन्नागता वचीसुचरितेन समन्नागता मनोसुचरितेन समन्नागता अरियानं अनुपवादका सम्मादिट्ठिका सम्मादिट्ठिकम्मसमादाना। ते कायस्स भेदा परं मरणा सुगतिं सग्गं लोकं उपपन्ना"ति। सो इति दिब्बेन चक्खुना विसुद्धेन अतिक्कन्तमानुसकेन सत्ते पस्सति चवमाने उपपज्जमाने हीने पणीते सुवण्णे दुब्बण्णे, सुगते दुग्गते यथाकम्मूपगे सत्ते पजानाति।

79. He again with his mind thus concentrated, rendered supremely pure and bright, freed from contamination, with disturbing factors cleared off, rendered soft and pliant, fixed and unperturbed, he bends forth his mind to acquire the perception of appearance and disappearance of other beings. He sees with deva-vision clarified, surpassing that of ordinary human beings, living beings deceasing from one state and being reborn into another; he perceives beings of inferior or superior order, good-looking and ugly, well-situated or ill-fated, faring according to their own karma. "He recognises that these are verily beings guilty of evil deeds, of offences committed by way of words and thoughts, calumniators of the Ariyas, upholders of erroneous views, adhering to practices associated with erroneous judgement, they on the dissolution of the body after death, are reborn in hell, in a condition

---

१. हीणे — सी०।

२. उप्पन्ना — सी०।

३. रो० पोत्थके नत्थि।

of utter ruin, a woeful state of pain; that those (others) are, on the other hand, beings who came into full possession of good deeds, of merits earned by them on account of words and thoughts; not reviling the Ariyas, upholders of right views, adhering to practices associated with sound judgement, they on the dissolution of the body after death are reborn in the heavenly world, to a happy destination." Thus does he see with deva-vision clarified, surpassing that of ordinary human beings, living beings deceasing from one state and being reborn into another; he perceives beings of inferior or superior order, good-looking and ugly, well-situated or ill-fated, faring according to their own karma.

८०. [S.376] सो एवं समाहिते चित्ते परिसुद्धे परियोदाते अनङ्गणे विगतूपक्किलेसे मुदुभूते कम्मनिये ठिते आनेञ्जप्पत्ते आसवानं खयञाणाय चित्तं अभिनिन्नामेति। सो "इदं दुक्खं"ति यथाभूतं पजानाति, "अयं दुक्खसमुदयो"ति यथाभूतं पजानाति, "अयं दुक्खनिरोधो"ति यथाभूतं पजानाति, "अयं दुक्खनिरोधगामिनी पटिपदा"ति यथाभूतं पजानाति, [R.61] "इमे आसवा"ति यथाभूतं पजानाति, "अयं आसवसमुदयो"ति [N.91] यथाभूतं पजानाति, "अयं आसवनिरोधो"ति यथाभूतं पजानाति, "अयं आसवनिरोधगामिनी पटिपदा"ति यथाभूतं पजानाति। तस्स एवं जानतो एवं पस्सतो कामासवापि चित्तं विमुच्चति भवासवापि चित्तं विमुच्चति अविज्जासवापि चित्तं विमुच्चति। विमुत्तस्मिं विमुत्तमिति ञाणं होति। "खीणा जाति, वुसितं ब्रह्मचरियं, कतं करणीयं, नापरं इत्थत्ताया"ति पजानाति। एवं पुग्गलो नेव अत्तन्तपो च[१] होति न अत्तपरितापनानुयोगमनुयुत्तो, न परन्तपो न परपरितापनानुयोगमनुयुत्तो। सो अनत्तन्तपो अपरन्तपो दिट्ठेव धम्मे निच्छातो निब्बुतो सीतीभूतो सुखप्पटिसंवेदी ब्रह्मभूतेन अत्तना विहरति।

80. He again with his mind thus concentrated, rendered supremely pure and bright, freed from contamination, with disturbing factors cleared off, rendered soft and pliant, fixed and unperturbed, he

---

१. सी०, स्या०, रो० पोत्थकेसु नत्थि।

bends forth his mind to acquire the knowledge of the process of the destruction of sinful tendencies (Āsavas). He truly understands that "this is suffering", truly understands that "this is the origin of suffering", truly understands that "this is the cessation of suffering", truly understands that "this is the path leading to the cessation of suffering", he truly knows that "these are the sinful tendencies", truly knows that "this is the origin of sinful tendencies", truly knows that "this is the cessation of sinful tendencies", truly knows that "this is the path leading to the cessation of sinful tendencies." When he knows and sees thus, his mind becomes free from the tendency to sensual pleasures, from the tendency to be reborn, and from the tendency to ignorance. And when (the mind) is emancipated, there is the knowledge that it is emancipated and he knows that "birth is destroyed, the holy life has been led, duties have been accomplished, and there is no more of these conditions." Thus a man does not become a self-mortifier, nor become addicted to practices leading to self-mortification, and is not a mortifier of others, and is not devoted to practices leading to mortification of others. He tortures neither himself nor the self of others, and in this world he, without any hankering, at peace, cool, enjoying bliss, lives with a self become godlike.

(२५. क) सरागो पुग्गलो

८१. कतमो च पुग्गलो सरागो ?

यस्स पुग्गलस्स रागो अप्पहीनो, अयं वुच्चति पुग्गलो "सरागो"।

(25. A) A person who is possessed of passion

81. What person is said to be possessed of passion?

One whose passion has not been put away, this person is said to be one possessed of passion.

(ख) सदोसो पुग्गलो

८२. कतमो च पुग्गलो सदोसो ?

यस्स पुग्गलस्स दोसो अप्पहीनो, अयं वुच्चति पुग्गलो "सदोसो"।

(B) A person who is possessed of hatred

82. What person is said to be one possessed of hatred?

One whose hatred has not been put away, this person is said to be one possessed of hatred.

(ग) समोहो पुग्गलो

८३. कतमो च पुग्गलो समोहो ?

यस्स पुग्गलस्स मोहो अप्पहीनो, अयं वुच्चति पुग्गलो "समोहो"।

(C) A person who is possessed of delusion

83. What person is said to be one possessed of delusion?

One whose delusion has not been put away, this person is said to be one possessed of delusion.

(घ) समानो पुग्गलो

८४. कतमो च पुग्गलो समानो ?

यस्स पुग्गलस्स मानो अप्पहीनो, अयं वुच्चति पुग्गलो "समानो"।

(D) A person who is possessed of pride

84. What person is said to be one possessed of pride?

One whose pride has not been put away, this person is said to be one possessed of pride.

(२६. क) चेतोसमथस्स लाभी अधिपञ्ञाधम्मविपस्सनाय न लाभी

८५. [B.171] कथं च पुग्गलो लाभी होति अज्झत्तं चेतोसमथस्स, न लाभी अधिपञ्ञाधम्मविपस्सनाय ?

इधेकच्चो पुग्गलो लाभी होति रूपसहगतानं वा अरूपसहगतानं वा समापत्तीनं, न लाभी लोकुत्तरमग्गस्स वा फलस्स वा। एवं पुग्गलो लाभी होति अज्झत्तं चेतोसमथस्स, न लाभी अधिपञ्ञाधम्मविपस्सनाय।

(26. A) A person who attains the inner tranquillity of mind but not the higher wisdom of insight into things

85. How does a person attain the inner tranquillity of mind but not the higher wisdom of insight into things?

Here a certain person who attains ecstatic meditation accompanied by an idea of form or the idea of formlessness but does not attain the supramundane path or the fruition. In this way a person attains the inner tranquillity of mind but not the higher wisdom of insight into things.

(ख) अधिपञ्ञाधम्मविपस्सनाय लाभी चेतोसमथस्स न लाभी

८६. [N92; S.378] कथं च पुग्गलो लाभी होति अधिपञ्ञाधम्मविपस्सनाय, न लाभी अज्झत्तं चेतोसमथस्स ?

इधेकच्चो पुग्गलो लाभी होति लोकुत्तरमग्गस्स वा फलस्स वा, न लाभी रूपसहगतानं वा अरूपसहगतानं वा समापत्तीनं। एवं पुग्गलो लाभी होति अधिपञ्ञाधम्मविपस्सनाय, न लाभी अज्झत्तं चेतोसमथस्स।

(B) A person who attains the higher wisdom of insight into things but not the inner tranquillity of mind

86. How does a person attain the higher wisdom of insight into things but not the inner tranquillity of mind?

Here a certain person is an attainer of the supramundane path or the fruition, but not of ecstatic meditaion accompanied by an idea of form or the idea of formlessness. In this way a person attains the higher wisdom of insight into things but not the inner tranquillity of mind.

(ग) चेतोसमथस्स लाभी च अधिपञ्ञाधम्मविपस्सनाय लाभी

८७. [R.62] कथं च पुग्गलो लाभी चेव होति अज्झत्तं चेतोसमथस्स, लाभी च अधिपञ्ञाधम्मविपस्सनाय ?

इधेकच्चो पुग्गलो लाभी होति रूपसहगतानं वा अरूपसहगतानं वा समापत्तीनं, लाभी लोकुत्तरमग्गस्स वा फलस्स वा। एवं पुग्गलो लाभी चेव होति अज्झत्तं चेतोसमथस्स, लाभी च अधिपञ्ञाधम्मविपस्सनाय।

(C) A person who attains the inner tranquillity of mind and the higher wisdom of insight into things

87. How does a person attain the inner tranquillity of mind and the higher wisdom of insight into things?

Here a certain person attains ecstatic meditation accompanied by an idea of form or by an idea of formlessness as well as the supramundane path or the fruition. In this way a person attains the inner tranquillity of mind and the higher wisdom of insight into things.

(घ) नेव चेतोसमथस्स लाभी च न अधिपञ्ञाधम्मविपस्सनाय लाभी

८८. कथं च पुग्गलो नेव लाभी होति अज्झत्तं चेतोसमथस्स, न लाभी अधिपञ्ञाधम्मविपस्सनाय ?

इधेकच्चो पुग्गलो नेव लाभी होति रूपसहगतानं वा अरूपसहगतानं वा समापत्तीनं, न लाभी लोकुत्तरमग्गस्स वा फलस्स वा। एवं पुग्गलो नेव लाभी होति अज्झत्तं चेतोसमथस्स, न लाभी अधिपञ्ञाधम्मविपस्सनाय।

(D) A person who attains neither the inner tranquillity of mind nor the higher wisdom of insight into things

88. How does a person attain neither the inner tranquillity of mind nor the higher wisdom of insight into things?

Here a certain person attains neither ecstatic meditation accompanied by an idea of form or by an idea of formlessness nor supramundane path or the fruition. In this way a person attains neither the inner tranquillity of mind nor the higher wisdom of insight into things.

(२७. क) अनुसोतगामी पुग्गलो

८९. कतमो च पुग्गलो अनुसोतगामी ?

इधेकच्चो पुग्गलो कामे च पटिसेवति पापं च कम्मं करोति । अयं वुच्चति पुग्गलो "अनुसोतगामी" ।

(27. A) A person who is going with the stream

89. How is a person said to be going with the stream?

Here a certain person enjoys sensual pleasures and commits sinful deeds. This person is said to be going with the stream.

(ख) पटिसोतगामी पुग्गलो

९०. कतमो च पुग्गलो पटिसोतगामी ?

इधेकच्चो पुग्गलो कामे च न पटिसेवति[१] पापं च कम्मं न करोति । सो सहा[२] पि दुक्खेन सहा[३] पि दोमनस्सेन अस्सुमुखेन[४] पि[४] रुदमानो परिपुण्णं परिसुद्धं ब्रह्मचरियं चरति । अयं वुच्चति पुग्गलो "पटिसोतगामी" ।

(B) A person who is going against the stream

90. How is a person said to be going against the stream?

---

१. सेवति — सी० ।

२. सह — सी० ।

३. सह — सी० ।

४-४. अस्सुमुखो — सी० ।

Here a certain person neither enjoys sensual pleasures nor commits sinful deeds. He with suffering and with sorrow, with tears on the face and lamenting, practises purity, full and unspotted. This person is said to be one going against the stream.

(ग) ठितत्तो पुग्गलो

९१. [N.93; B.172] कतमो च पुग्गलो ठितत्तो ?

इधेकच्चो पुग्गलो पञ्चन्नं ओरम्भागियानं संयोजनानं[१] परिक्खया ओपपातिको होति तत्थ परिनिब्बायी अनावत्तिधम्मो तस्मा लोका। अयं वुच्चति पुग्गलो "ठितत्तो"।

(C) A person who is established

91. How is a person said to be established?

Here a certain person on account of the destruction of the five lower fetters causing rebirth in lower regions becomes a being of apparitional rebirth, attaining there the final release, not liable to return from that world. This person is said to be one who is established.

(घ) पारङ्गतो पुग्गलो

९२. [S.380] कतमो च पुग्गलो तिण्णो पारङ्गतो[२] थले[३] तिट्ठति ब्राह्मणो ?

इधेकच्चो पुग्गलो आसवानं खया अनासवं चेतोविमुत्तिं पञ्ञाविमुत्तिं दिट्ठेव धम्मे सयं अभिञ्ञा सच्छिकत्वा उपसम्पज्ज विहरति। अयं वुच्चति पुग्गलो तिण्णो पारङ्गतो थले[४] तिट्ठति ब्राह्मणो।

---

१. सञ्ञोजनानं — स्या०।

२. पारगतो — सी०, स्या०।

३. फले — रो०, एवमुपरि पि।

४. फले — रो०, एवमुपरि पि।

(D) A person who has gone to the other shore

92. How is a person 'a brahmin, who has crossed the stream, has gone to the other shore, and is established in safe place (fruition)'?

Here a certain person because of the destruction of his sinful tendencies lives having known and realised in this very existence, emancipation of mind and emancipation of insight, free from sinful tendencies. This person is said to be 'a brahmin, who has crossed the stream, gone to the other shore, and is established in the safe place (fruition).'

(२८. क) अप्पस्सुतो सुतेन अनुपपन्नो

९३. कथं च पुग्गलो अप्पस्सुतो होति, सुतेन अनुपपन्नो ?

इधेकच्चस्स पुग्गलस्स अप्पकं सुतं होति सुत्तं गेय्यं वेय्याकरणं गाथं उदानं इतिवुत्तकं जातकं अब्भुतधम्मं वेदल्लं । सो तस्स अप्पकस्स सुतस्स न अत्थमञ्ञाय धम्ममञ्ञाय[१] [R.63] धम्मानुधम्मप्पटिपन्नो[२] होति । एवं पुग्गलो अप्पस्सुतो होति सुतेन अनुपपन्नो[३] ।

(28. A) A person who knows little and does not act up to what he has learnt

93. How is a person one who knows little and does not act up to what he has learnt?

Here a certain person possesses little knowledge of Sutta, Geyya, Vyākaraṇa, Gāthā, Udāna, Itivuttaka, Jātaka, Abbhutadhamma and Vedalla; but knows neither the meaning nor the truth, does not follow the Dhamma either in its entirety and in its details. Such a person is said to be one who knows little and does not act up to what he has learnt.

---

१. न धम्ममञ्ञाय — स्या०, रो० ।

२. धम्मानुधम्मपटिपन्नो — सी०; न धम्मानुधम्मपटिपन्नो — स्या०, रो० ।

३. अनुप्पन्नो — सी० ।

(ख) अप्पस्सुतो सुतेन उपपन्नो

९४. कथं च पुग्गलो अप्पस्सुतो होति सुतेन उपपन्नो ?

इधेकच्चस्स पुग्गलस्स अप्पकं सुतं होति सुत्तं गेय्यं वेय्याकरणं गाथं उदानं इतिवुत्तकं जातकं अब्भुतधम्मं वेदल्लं। सो तस्स अप्पकस्स सुतस्स अत्थमञ्ञाय धम्ममञ्ञाय धम्मानुधम्मप्पटिपन्नो होति। एवं पुग्गलो अप्पस्सुतो होति सुतेन उपपन्नो।

(B) A person who knows little and acts up to what he has learnt

94. How is a person one who knows little and acts up to what he has learnt?

Here a certain person possesses little knowledge of Sutta, Geyya, Vyākaraṇa, Gāthā, Udāna, Itivuttaka, Jātaka, Abbhutadhamma and Vedalla; he, knowing the meaning and the truth of that little knowledge, practises the Dhamma in its entirety and in its details. In this way a person is said to be one who knows little and acts up to what he has learnt.

(ग) बहुस्सुतो सुतेन अनुपपन्नो

९५. कथं च पुग्गलो बहुस्सुतो होति सुतेन अनुपपन्नो ?

इधेकच्चस्स पुग्गलस्स बहुकं सुतं होति सुत्तं गेय्यं वेय्याकरणं गाथं उदानं इतिवुत्तकं जातकं अब्भुतधम्मं वेदल्लं। सो तस्स बहुकस्स सुतस्स न [N.94] अत्थमञ्ञाय धम्ममञ्ञाय धम्मानुधम्मप्पटिपन्नो होति। एवं पुग्गलो बहुस्सुतो होति सुतेन अनुपपन्नो।

(C) A person who though much learned but does not act up to his learning

95. How is a person one who though much learned but does not act up to his learning?

Here a certain person has much learning of Sutta, Geyya, Vyākaraṇa, Gāthā, Udāna, Itivuttaka, Jātaka, Abbhutadhamma and Vedalla; but he not knowing the meaning and the truth of that great learning, does not follow the Dhamma in its entirety and in its details. In this way a person is said to be one who though much learned but does not act up to his learning.

(घ) बहुस्सुतो सुतेन उपपन्नो

९६. कथं च पुग्गलो बहुस्सुतो होति सुतेन उपपन्नो ?

इधेकच्चस्स पुग्गलस्स बहुकं सुतं होति सुत्तं गेय्यं वेय्याकरणं गाथं उदानं इतिवुत्तकं जातकं अब्भुतधम्मं वेदल्लं। सो तस्स बहुकस्स सुतस्स अत्थमञ्ञाय धम्ममञ्ञाय धम्मानुधम्मप्पटिपन्नो होति। एवं पुग्गलो बहुस्सुतो होति सुतेन उपपन्नो।

(D) A person who is much learned and acts up to his learning

96. How is a person one who is much learned and acts up to his learning?

Here a certain person has great learning of Sutta, Geyya, Vyākaraṇa, Gāthā, Udāna, Itivuttaka, Jātaka, Abbhutadhamma and Vedalla; he knowing the meaning and the truth of that great learning, follows the Dhamma in its entirety and in its details. In this way a person is said to be one who is much learned and acts up to his learning.

(२९. क) समणमचलो पुग्गलो

९७. [B.173; S.382] कतमो च पुग्गलो समणमचलो ?

इधेकच्चो पुग्गलो तिण्णं संयोजनानं परिक्खया सोतापन्नो होति अविनिपातधम्मो नियतो सम्बोधिपरायनो। अयं वुच्चति पुग्गलो "समणमचलो"।

(29. A) A person who is a recluse with a firm footing

97. How is a person a recluse with a firm footing?

Here a certain person through the complete destruction of three fetters becomes a 'stream attainer', no more liable to fall into a woeful state, but is destined to succeed and has enlightenment for his end and aim. This person is said to be a recluse with a firm footing.

(ख) समणपदुमो पुग्गलो

९८. कतमो च पुग्गलो समणपदुमो ?

इधेकच्चो पुग्गलो तिण्णं संयोजनानं परिक्खया रागदोसमोहानं तनुत्ता सकदागामी होति, सकिदेव इमं लोकं आगन्त्वा दुक्खस्सन्तं करोति । अयं वुच्चति पुग्गलो "समणपदुमो" ।

(B) A person who is a red-lotus-like recluse

98. How is a person said to be a red-lotus-like recluse?

Here a certain person through the complete destruction of three fetters and having made passion, hatred and delusion attenuated, becomes a 'once-returner'; coming only once back to this world, he makes an end of suffering. This person is said to be a red-lotus-like recluse.

(ग) समणपुण्डरीको पुग्गलो

९९. कतमो च पुग्गलो समणपुण्डरीको ?

इधेकच्चो पुग्गलो पञ्चन्नं ओरम्भागियानं संयोजनानं परिक्खया ओपपातिको होति तत्थ परिनिब्बायी अनावत्तिधम्मो तस्मा लोका । अयं वुच्चति पुग्गलो "समणपुण्डरीको" ।

(C) A person who is a white-lotus-like recluse

99. How is a person a white-lotus-like recluse?

Here a person through the complete destruction of the five lower fetters causing rebirth in the lower worlds, becomes a being of apparitional rebirth, attaining there the final release, not liable to return from that world. This person is said to be a white-lotus-like recluse.

(घ) समणेसु समणसुखुमालो पुग्गलो

१००. कतमो च पुग्गलो समणेसु समणसुखुमालो ?

इधेकच्चो पुग्गलो आसवानं खया अनासवं चेतोविमुत्तिं पञ्ञाविमुत्तिं दिट्ठेव धम्मे सयं अभिञ्ञा सच्छिकत्वा उपसम्पज्ज विहरति । अयं वुच्चति पुग्गलो "समणेसु समणसुखुमालो"ति ।

चतुक्कनिद्देसो निट्ठितो ।

(D) A person who is a delicate recluse

100. How is a person said to be a delicate recluse?

Here a certain person because of the destruction of his sinful tendencies lives having known and realised in this very existence the emancipation of mind and the emancipation of insight, free from sinful tendencies. This person is said to be a delicate (tender) recluse.

Here ends the grouping of human types by four.

पञ्चमो परिच्छेदो

५. पञ्चकपुग्गलपञ्ञत्ति[१]

(१. क) आरभति च विप्पटिसारी होति

१. [N.95; R.64; S.384] तत्र य्वायं पुग्गलो आरभति[२] च विप्पटिसारी च होति तं च चेतोविमुत्तिं पञ्ञाविमुत्तिं यथाभूतं नप्पजानाति यत्थस्स ते उप्पन्ना पापका अकुसला धम्मा अपरिसेसा निरुज्झन्ति, सो एवमस्स वचनीयो— "आयस्मतो खो आरम्भजा आसवा संविज्जन्ति, विप्पटिसारजा[३] आसवा पवड्ढन्ति। साधु वतायस्मा आरम्भजे आसवे पहाय विप्पटिसारजे आसवे पटिविनोदेत्वा चित्तं पञ्ञं च भावेतु। एवमायस्मा अमुना पञ्चमेन पुग्गलेन समसमो भविस्सती"ति।

CHAPTER FIVE

5. Division of Human Types by Five

(1. A) A person who acts and becomes remorseful

1. There a certain person who acts and becomes remorseful, who does not know emancipation of mind and emancipation of insight as it really is, wherein his sinful and bad qualities which have arisen are totally destroyed, he should be told thus— "of the revered one the sinful tendencies which are due to actions exist, and the sinful tendencies which are due to remorsefulness increase. It were well if the revered one gave up sinful tendencies due to his actions and

---

१. पञ्चकनिद्देसो — सी०, स्या०; पञ्च पुग्गला — रो०।

२. आरम्भति — सी०, स्या०।

३. विप्पटिसारजा च — सी०।

suppressed sinful tendencies due to remorse, and practised thought, and insight. Thus the revered one will beocme equal to the fifth person in this group."

(ख) आरभति न विप्पटिसारी होति

२. तत्र य्वायं पुग्गलो आरभति न विप्पटिसारी च होति तं च चेतोविमुत्तिं पञ्ञाविमुत्तिं यथाभूतं नप्पजानाति यत्थस्स ते उप्पन्ना [B.174] पापका अकुसला धम्मा अपरिसेसा निरुज्झन्ति, सो एवमस्स वचनीयो— "आयस्मतो खो आरम्भजा आसवा संविज्जन्ति, विप्पटिसारजा आसवा नप्पवड्ढन्ति । साधु वतायस्मा आरम्भजे आसवे पहाय चित्तं पञ्ञं च भावेतु । एवमायस्मा अमुना पञ्चमेन पुग्गलेन समसमो भविस्सती"ति ।

(B) A person who acts and does not become remorseful

2. There a certain person who acts and does not become remorseful, who does not know emancipation of mind and emancipation of insight as it really is, wherein his sinful and bad qualities which have arisen are destroyed, he should be told thus— "of the revered one the sinful tendencies due to actions exist and the sinful tendencies due to remorse do not increase. It were well if the revered one gave up sinful tendencies due to his actions, and practised thought and insight. Thus the revered one will become equal to the fifth person in this group."

(ग) नारभति विप्पटिसारी होति

३. तत्र य्वायं पुग्गलो न आरभति विप्पटिसारी च होति तं च चेतोविमुत्तिं पञ्ञाविमुत्तिं यथाभूतं नप्पजानाति यत्थस्स ते उप्पन्ना पापका अकुसला धम्मा अपरिसेसा निरुज्झन्ति, सो एवमस्स वचनीयो— "आयस्मतो खो आरम्भजा आसवा न संविज्जन्ति, विप्पटिसारजा आसवा पवड्ढन्ति । साधु वतायस्मा विप्पटिसारजे आसवे पटिविनोदेत्वा चित्तं पञ्ञं च भावेतु । एवमायस्मा अमुना पञ्चमेन पुग्गलेन समसमो भविस्सती"ति ।

(C) A person who does not act and becomes remorseful

3. There a certain person who does not act, and yet becomes remorseful, who does not know emancipation of mind and emancipation of insight as it really is, wherein his sinful and bad qualities which have arisen are totally destroyed, he should be told thus— "of the revered one the sinful tendencies due to actions do not exist and the sinful tendencies due to remorsefulness increase. It were well if the revered one removed the sinful tendencies due to remorsefulness, and practised thought and insight. Thus the revered one will become equal to the fifth person in this group."

(घ) नारभति न विप्पटिसारी होति

४. तत्र य्वायं पुग्गलो न आरभति न विप्पटिसारी होति तं च चेतोविमुत्तिं पञ्ञाविमुत्तिं यथाभूतं नप्पजानाति यत्थस्स ते उप्पन्ना[१] पापका अकुसला धम्मा अपरिसेसा निरुज्झन्ति, सो एवमस्स वचनीयो— [N.96] "आयस्मतो खो आरम्भजा आसवा न संविज्जन्ति, विप्पटिसारजा आसवा नप्पवड्ढन्ति। साधु वतायस्मा चित्तं पञ्ञं च भावेतु। एवमायस्मा अमुना पञ्चमेन पुग्गलेन समसमो भविस्सती"ति।

(D) A person who does not act and does not become remorseful

4. There a person does not act and does not become remorseful, who does not know the emancipation of mind and emancipation of insight as it really is, whereby his sinful and bad qualities are totally destroyed, he should be told thus— "of the revered one the sinful tendencies due to actions do not exist and the sinful tendencies due to remorsefulness do not increase. It were well if the revered one practised thought and insight. Thus the

१. म० पोत्थके नत्थि।

revered one will become equal to the fifth person in this group."

(ङ) पञ्चमो पुग्गलो

५. इमे चत्तारो पुग्गला[१] अमुना पञ्चमेन पुग्गलेन एवं ओवदियमाना एवं अनुसासियमाना अनुपुब्बेन आसवानं खयं पापुणन्ति।

(E) A person who is fifth

5. These four persons being thus admonished, thus instructed by such a fifth man, gradually attain to the destruction of sinful tendencies.

(२. क) दत्वा अवजानाति

६. [R.65; S.386] कथं च पुग्गलो दत्वा अवजानाति?

इधेकच्चो पुग्गलो यस्स[२] पुग्गलस्स देति चीवरपिण्डपातसेनासनगिलानप्पच्चयभेसज्जपरिक्खारं, तस्स एवं होति— "अहं[३] दम्मि, अयं[४] पटिग्गण्हाती"ति, तमेनं दत्वा अवजानाति। एवं पुग्गलो दत्वा अवजानाति।

(2. A) A person who despises after giving

6. How does a person who has given despise?

Here is a certain person to whom a person gives garment, food, alms-bowl, bed, seat, things necessary for the sick and medicine and requisites; to the latter it occurs thus— "I give, this person, on the other hand, accepts", giving this to him, he despises him. Thus a person despises after giving.

---

१. पुग्गलो — सी०।

२. सी० पोत्थके नत्थि।

३. अयं — रो०।

४. अयं पन — सी०, स्या०, रो०।

(ख) संवासेन अवजानाति

७. कथं च पुग्गलो संवासेन अवजानाति ?

इधेकच्चो पुग्गलो येन[१] पुग्गलेन सद्धिं संवसति द्वे वा तीणि वा वस्सानि, तमेनं संवासेन अवजानाति । एवं पुग्गलो संवासेन अवजानाति ।

(B) A person who despises after living together

7. How does a person despise after living together?

Here a certain person dwells with a person for two or three years, after living together with him he despises him. Thus a person despises after living together.

(ग) आधेय्यमुखो होति

८. [B.175] कथं च पुग्गलो आधेय्यमुखो होति ?

इधेकच्चो पुग्गलो परस्स वण्णे वा अवण्णे वा भासियमाने खिप्पञ्ञेव अधिमुच्चिता होति । एवं पुग्गलो आधेय्यमुखो होति ।

(C) A person who is with gape-mouth

8. How is a person a gape-mouth?

Here a certain person, while the praise or dispraise of a person is being uttered, becomes quickly infatuated about him. Thus is a person a gape-mouth.

(घ) लोलो होति

९. कथं च पुग्गलो लोलो होति ?

इधेकच्चो पुग्गलो इत्तरसद्धो होति इत्तरभत्ती[२] इत्तरपेमो इत्तरप्पसादो । एवं पुग्गलो लोलो होति ।

(D) A person who becomes a wobbler

9. How does a person become a wobbler?

---

१. सी०, रो० पोत्थकेसु नत्थि ।

२. इत्तरभत्ति — स्या०, रो० ।

Here a certain person is of little faith, is of little devotion, is of little love, is of little contentment. Thus a person becomes a wobbler.

(ङ) मन्दो मोमूहो होति

१०. कथं च पुग्गलो मन्दो मोमूहो होति?

इधेकच्चो पुग्गलो कुसलाकुसले धम्मे न जानाति, सावज्जानवज्जे धम्मे न जानाति, हीनप्पणीते धम्मे न जानाति, कण्हसुक्कसप्पटिभागे धम्मे न जानाति। एवं पुग्गलो मन्दो मोमूहो होति।

(E) A person who becomes dull and stupid

10. How does a person become dull and stupid?

Here a certain person does not know good and bad qualities, does not know blameworthy and blameless qualities, does not know low and excellent qualities, does not know dark and bright qualities. Thus a person becomes dull and stupid.

(३) पञ्च योधाजीवूपमा पुग्गला

११. [N.97] तत्थ कतमे पञ्च योधाजीवूपमा पुग्गला?

पञ्च योधाजीवा— इधेकच्चो योधाजीवो रजग्गञ्ञेव दिस्वा संसीदति विसीदति न सन्थम्भति[१] न सक्कोति सङ्गामं ओतरितुं। एवरूपो पि इधेकच्चो योधाजीवो होति। अयं पठमो योधाजीवो सन्तो संविज्जमानो लोकस्मिं।

(3) Five persons who are comparable to professional warriors

11. Who are the five persons comparable to professional warriors?

There are five professional warriors— Here a certain professional warrior seeing the cloud of dust (raised by the march of the ememy) sinks down, becomes dejected, cannot control himself, is unable to go forward to fight. There is such a professional

१. सत्थम्भति — सी०।

warrior. This is the first professional warrior existing in the world.

पुन च परं इधेकच्चो योधाजीवो सहति रजग्गं, अपि च खो धजग्गञ्ञेव दिस्वा संसीदति विसीदति न सन्थम्भति न सक्कोति सङ्गामं ओतरितुं। एवरूपो पि इधेकच्चो योधाजीवो होति। अयं दुतियो योधाजीवो सन्तो संविज्जमानो लोकस्मिं।

Again another— Here certain professional warrior endures the cloud of dust, but seeing the top of the flag he sinks down, becomes dejected, cannot control himself, is unable to go forward to fight. There is such a professional warrior too. This is the second professional warrior existing in the world.

[S.388] पुन च परं इधेकच्चो योधाजीवो सहति रजग्गं सहति धजग्गं, अपि च खो उस्सारणञ्ञेव[1] सुत्वा संसीदति विसीदति न सन्थम्भति न सक्कोति सङ्गामं ओतरितुं। एवरूपो पि इधेकच्चो योधाजीवो होति। अयं ततियो योधाजीवो सन्तो संविज्जमानो लोकस्मिं।

Again another— Here a certain professional warrior endures the cloud of dust, endures the top of the flag, but hearing the war cries he sinks down, becomes dejected, cannot control himself, is unable to go forward to fight. There is such a professional warrior. This is the third professional warrior existing in the world.

पुन च परं इधेकच्चो योधाजीवो सहति रजग्गं [R.66] सहति धजग्गं सहति उस्सारणं[2], अपि च खो सम्पहारे हञ्ञति ब्यापज्जति[3]। एवरूपो पि इधेकच्चो योधाजीवो होति। अयं चतुत्थो योधाजीवो सन्तो संविज्जमानो लोकस्मिं।

Again another— Here a certain professional warrior endures the cloud of dust, endures the top of

---

१. उस्सादनंयेव — सी०, रो०; उस्सादनञ्ञेव — स्या०।

२. उस्सादनं — सी०, स्या०, रो०, एवमुपरि पि।

३. व्यापज्जति — सी०, रो०।

the flag, endures the war cries, but in the melee is killed and done for. There is such a professional warrior. This is the fourth professional warrior existing in the world.

[B.176] पुन च परं इधेकच्चो योधाजीवो सहति रजग्गं सहति धजग्गं सहति उस्सारणं सहति सम्पहारं। सो तं सङ्गामं अभिविजिनित्वा विजितसङ्गामो तमेव सङ्गामसीसं अज्झावसति। एवरूपो पि इधेकच्चो योधाजीवो होति। अयं पञ्चमो योधाजीवो सन्तो संविज्जमानो लोकस्मिं।

इमे पञ्च योधाजीवा सन्तो संविज्जमाना लोकस्मिं।

Again another— Here a certain professional warrior endures the cloud of dust, endures the top of the flag, endures war cries, endures the melee; winning the battle and victorious in the battle, he survives on the scene of the battle; there is such a professional warrior. This is the fifth professional warrior existing in the world.

These are the five professional warriors existing in the world.

१२. एवमेवं[१] पञ्चिमे[२] योधाजीवूपमा पुग्गला सन्तो संविज्जमाना भिक्खूसु। कतमे पञ्च?

(क) इधेकच्चो भिक्खु रजग्गञ्ञेव दिस्वा संसीदति विसीदति न सन्थम्भति न सक्कोति ब्रह्मचरियं [N.98] सन्धारितुं,[३] सिक्खादुब्बल्यं आविकत्वा[४] सिक्खं पच्चक्खाय हीनायावत्तति। किमस्स रजग्गस्मिं? इध भिक्खु सुणाति— "असुकस्मिं[५] नाम गामे वा निगमे वा इत्थी वा कुमारी वा अभिरूपा दस्सनीया पासादिका परमाय वण्णपोक्खरताय समन्नागता"ति। सो तं सुत्वा संसीदति

१. एवमेव — सी०, स्या०।
२. पञ्च — सी०।
३. सन्तानेतुं — सी०, स्या०, रो०, एवमुपरि पि।
४. आवीकत्वा — सी०।
५. अमुकस्मिं — सी०, स्या०।

विसीदति न सन्थम्भति न सक्कोति ब्रह्मचरियं सन्धारेतुं, सिक्खादुब्बल्यं आविकत्वा सिक्खं पच्चक्खाय हीनायावत्तति। इदमस्स रजग्गस्मिं।

सेय्यथापि सो योधाजीवो रजग्गञ्ञेव दिस्वा संसीदति विसीदति न सन्थम्भति न सक्कोति सङ्गामं ओतरितुं, तथूपमो अयं पुग्गलो। एवरूपो पि इधेकच्चो पुग्गलो होति। अयं पठमो योधाजीवूपमो पुग्गलो सन्तो संविज्जमानो भिक्खूसु[१]।

12. In the same manner these are the five persons who live and have their being among the monks comparable to professional warriors. Who are the five?

(A) Here a certain monk seeing the cloud of dust, sinks down, becomes remorseful, cannot control himself, is unable to develop the holy life, showing weakness in learning, giving up the precepts, he comes back to low household life. What does dust mean for him? Here a monk hears— "in such village or town lives a woman or a girl who is beautiful, charming to look at, delightful and endowed with great beauty." He listening to that sinks down, becomes remorseful, does not control himself, is unable to develop the holy life, showing weakness in learning, giving up the precepts, he comes back to low household life. This is what dust means for him.

Just as a professional warrior seeing the dust sinks down, becomes remorseful, cannot control himself, is unable to go forward to fight, so is this person. There is such a person here. This is the first person existing among the monks comparable to a professional warrior.

(ख) पुन च परं इधेकच्चो भिक्खु सहति रजग्गं, अपि च खो धजग्गञ्ञेव दिस्वा संसीदति विसीदति न सन्थम्भति न सक्कोति ब्रह्मचरियं सन्धारेतुं, सिक्खादुब्बल्यं आविकत्वा सिक्खं पच्चक्खाय हीनायावत्तति। किमस्स

१. लोकस्मिं — रो०।

धजग्गस्मिं ? इध भिक्खु न हेव खो सुणाति— "असुकस्मिं नाम गामे वा निगमे वा इत्थी वा कुमारी वा अभिरूपा दस्सनीया पासादिका परमाय वण्णपोक्खरताय समन्नागता"ति; [S.390] अपि च खो सामं[१] पस्सति इत्थिं वा कुमारिं वा अभिरूपं दस्सनीयं पासादिकं परमाय वण्णपोक्खरताय समन्नागतं । सो तं दिस्वा संसीदति विसीदति न सन्थम्भति न सक्कोति ब्रह्मचरियं सन्धारेतुं, सिक्खादुब्बल्यं आविकत्वा सिक्खं पच्चक्खाय हीनायावत्तति । इदमस्स धजग्गस्मिं ।

[R.67; B.177] सेय्यथापि सो योधाजीवो सहति रजग्गं, अपि च खो धजग्गञ्ञेव दिस्वा संसीदति विसीदति न [N.99] सन्थम्भति न सक्कोति सङ्गामं ओतरितुं, तथूपमो अयं पुग्गलो । एवरूपो पि इधेकच्चो पुग्गलो होति । अयं दुतियो योधाजीवूपमो पुग्गलो सन्तो संविज्जमानो भिक्खूसु ।

(B) Again another— Here a certain monk endures the cloud of dust, but seeing the top of the flag sinks down, becomes remorseful, does not control himself, is unable to develop the holy life, showing weakness in learning, giving up precepts, he comes back to low household life. What does the top of the flag mean for him? Here a monk does not only hear— "in such a village or town lives a woman or a girl who is beautiful, charming to look at, delightful and endowed with great beauty"; he himself sees the woman or the girl, who is beautiful, charming to look at, delightful, and endowed with great beauty. He seeing to that sinks down, becomes remorseful, does not control himself, is unable to develop a holy life, showing weakness in learning, giving up the precepts, he comes back to low household life. This is what the top of the flag means for him.

Just as the professional warrior endures the dust but seeing the top of the flag, sinks down, becomes remorseful, does not control himself, is unable to go forward to fight so is this person. There is such a person here. This is the second person existing among the monks comparable to a professional warrior.

---

१. सामंयेव — सी० ।

(ग) पुन च परं इधेकच्चो भिक्खु सहति रजग्गं सहति धजग्गं, अपि च खो उस्सारणञ्ञेव सुत्वा संसीदति विसीदति न सन्थम्भति न सक्कोति ब्रह्मचरियं सन्धारेतुं, सिक्खादुब्बल्यं आविकत्वा सिक्खं पच्चक्खाय हीनायावत्तति। किमस्स उस्सारणाय? इध भिक्खुं अरञ्ञगतं वा रुक्खमूलगतं वा सुञ्ञागारगतं वा मातुगामो उपसङ्कमित्वा ऊहसति उल्लपति उज्जग्घति[१] उप्पण्डेति[२]। सो मातुगामेन ऊहसियमानो उल्लपियमानो उज्जग्घियमानो उप्पण्डियमानो संसीदति विसीदति न सन्थम्भति न सक्कोति ब्रह्मचरियं सन्धारेतुं, सिक्खादुब्बल्यं आविकत्वा सिक्खं पच्चक्खाय हीनायावत्तति। इदमस्स उस्सारणाय।

सेय्यथापि सो योधाजीवो सहति रजग्गं सहति धजग्गं, अपि च खो उस्सारणञ्ञेव सुत्वा संसीदति विसीदति न सन्थम्भति न सक्कोति सङ्गामं ओतरितुं, तथूपमो अयं पुग्गलो। एवरूपो पि इधेकच्चो पुग्गलो होति। अयं ततियो योधाजीवूपमो पुग्गलो सन्तो संविज्जमानो भिक्खूसु।

(C) Again another— Here a certain monk endures the cloud of dust, endures the top of the flag, but hearing the war cries he sinks down, becomes remorseful, does not control himself, is unable to develop the life of purity, showing weakness is learning, giving up the precepts, he comes back to low household life. What do war cries mean for him? Here a woman approaching a monk, who has gone to the forest or to the foot of a tree or to an empty room, speaks lightly, converses, laughs and jests. He being spoken lightly to, or being conversed or jested with, or being ridiculed by the woman, sinks down, becomes remorseful, does not control himself, is unable to develop a holy life, showing weakness is learning, giving up the precepts, he comes back to low household life. This is what war cries mean for him.

Just as the professional warrior withstands dust, withstands the top of the flag, hearing the war cries, sinks down, becomes remorseful, does not control

१. उज्झग्घति — सी०; उज्जग्घेति — रो०।

२. उप्फण्डेति — स्या०, एवमुपरि पि।

himself, is unable to go forward to fight, so is this person. There is such a person here. This is the third person existing among the monks comparable to a professional warrior.

(घ) पुन च परं इधेकच्चो भिक्खु सहति रजग्गं सहति धजग्गं सहति उस्सारणं, अपि च खो सम्पहारे हञ्ञति ब्यापज्जति। किमस्स सम्पहारस्मिं? इध भिक्खुं अरञ्ञगतं वा रुक्खमूलगतं वा सुञ्ञागारगतं वा मातुगामो उपसङ्कमित्वा अभिनिसीदति अभिनिपज्जति अज्झोत्थरति। सो मातुगामेन अभिनिसीदियमानो अभिनिपज्जियमानो अज्झोत्थरियमानो [N.100] सिक्खं अप्पच्चक्खाय दुब्बल्यं अनाविकत्वा मेथुनं धम्मं पटिसेवति। इदमस्स सम्पहारस्मिं।

सेय्यथापि सो योधाजीवो सहति रजग्गं सहति धजग्गं सहति उस्सारणं, अपि च खो सम्पहारे हञ्ञति ब्यापज्जति, [B.178] तथूपमो अयं पुग्गलो। एवरूपो पि इधेकच्चो पुग्गलो होति। अयं चतुत्थो योधाजीवूपमो पुग्गलो सन्तो संविज्जमानो भिक्खूसु।

(D) Again another— Here a certain monk endures the cloud of dust, endures the top of the flag, endures war cries, but is killed in the melee and is done for. What does the melee mean for him? Here a woman approaching a monk who has gone to the forest or to the foot of a tree or to an empty room sits near, lies down near, stretches her limbs fully. He having the woman sitting near him, having her lying down near him, having her stretching her limbs near him, gives up the precepts, and showing weakness, he misconducts himself. This is what the melee means for him.

Just as the professional warrior endures dust, endures the top of the flag, endures war cries, but he is smitten and is done for, so is this person. There is such a person here. This is the fourth person existing among the monks comparable to a professional warrior.

(ङ) [S.392] पुन च परं इधेकच्चो भिक्खु सहति रजग्गं सहति धजग्गं सहति उस्सारणं सहति सम्पहारं। सो तं सङ्गामं अभिविजिनित्वा विजितसङ्गामो तमेव सङ्गामसीसं अज्झावसति। किमस्स सङ्गामविजयस्मिं? इध [R.68]

भिक्खुं अरञ्ञगतं वा रुक्खमूलगतं वा सुञ्ञागारगतं वा मातुगामो उपसङ्कमित्वा अभिनिसीदति अभिनिपज्जति अज्झोत्थरति। सो मातुगामेन अभिनिसीदियमानो अभिनिपज्जियमानो अज्झोत्थरियमानो विनिवेठेत्वा विनिमोचेत्वा येन कामं पक्कमति।

(E) Again another— Here a certain monk endures the cloud of dust, endures the top of the flag, endures war cries, and endures the melee. He winning the battle, being victorious, survives on the scene of battle. What does the winning of battle mean for him? Here a woman approaching the monk, who has gone to the forest or to the foot of a tree or to an empty room sits near, lies down near, stretches her limbs fully. He having the woman sitting near him, lying down near him, stretching her limbs fully near him, having extricated and having released himself goes away where he likes.

सो विवित्तं सेनासनं भजति अरञ्ञं रुक्खमूलं पब्बतं कन्दरं गिरिगुहं सुसानं वनपत्थं अब्भोकासं पलालपुञ्जं। सो अरञ्ञगतो वा रुक्खमूलगतो वा सुञ्ञागारगतो वा निसीदति पल्लङ्कं आभुजित्वा उजुं कायं पणिधाय परिमुखं सतिं उपट्ठपेत्वा। सो अभिज्झं लोके पहाय विगताभिज्झेन चेतसा विहरति, अभिज्झाय चित्तं परिसोधेति; ब्यापादपदोसं पहाय अब्यापन्नचित्तो विहरति, सब्बपाणभूतहितानुकम्पी ब्यापादपदोसा चित्तं परिसोधेति; थीनमिद्धं[१] पहाय विगतथीनमिद्धो विहरति आलोकसञ्ञी सतो सम्पजानो, थीनमिद्धा चित्तं परिसोधेति; उद्धच्चकुक्कुच्चं पहाय अनुद्धतो विहरति अज्झत्तं वूपसन्तचित्तो, उद्धच्चकुक्कुच्चा चित्तं परिसोधेति; [N.101] विचिकिच्छं पहाय तिण्णविचिकिच्छो विहरति अकथङ्कथी कुसलेसु धम्मेसु, विचिकिच्छाय चित्तं परिसोधेति।

He lives in a solitary place, in a forest, at the foot of a tree, in a mountain, in a cave, in a mountain grotto, in a cemetery, in a forest tract, in the open air or on a heap of straw. He having gone to the forest

१. थिनमिद्धं — म०, एवमुपरि पि।

or at the foot of a tree or in an empty room sits cross-legged, placing the body erect and making recollection ready. He giving up covetousness in the world, lives with a mind free from covetousness, he purifies the mind of covetousness; giving up malice, he lives with a mind free from malice; being compassionate to all living beings, he purifies the mind of malice; giving up sloth and drowsiness, being conscious of light, mindful and possessed of knowledge, he purifies the mind of sloth and drowsiness; giving up distraction and restlessness, he purifies the mind of these, having his mind calm internally; giving up doubt, he lives having gone beyond doubt; being free from misgivings so far as good qualities are concerned, he purifies the mind of doubt.

सो इमे पञ्च नीवरणे पहाय चेतसो उपक्किलेसे पञ्ञाय दुब्बलीकरणे विविच्चेव कामेहि विविच्च अकुसलेहि धम्मेहि सवितक्कं सविचारं विवेकजं पीतिसुखं पठमं झानं उपसम्पज्ज विहरति; वितक्कविचारानं वूपसमा[१] दुतियं झानं उपसम्पज्ज विहरति ...पे०... ततियं झानं ...पे०... चतुत्थं झानं उपसम्पज्ज विहरति।

So he giving up these five hindrances, which are the corrupters of mind, which weaken the intellect, free from sensual pleasures and bad qualities he lives in attainment of the first Jhāna (ecstatic meditation) which is with applied and sustained thought, and which has joy and happiness due to solitude; he, putting an end to applied and sustained thought, lives in attainment of the second ...pe... third ...pe... lives in attainment of fourth stages of ecstatic meditation.

सो एवं समाहिते चित्ते परिसुद्धे परियोदाते अनङ्गणे विगतूपक्किलेसे मुदुभूते कम्मनिये ठिते आनेञ्जप्पत्ते आसवानं खयञाणाय चित्तं अभिनिन्नामेति। सो "इदं दुक्खं"ति यथाभूतं पजानाति, "अयं दुक्खसमुदयो"ति यथाभूतं पजानाति, "अयं दुक्खनिरोधो"ति यथाभूतं पजानाति; "अयं दुक्खनिरोधगामिनी पटिपदा"ति यथाभूतं पजानाति; [S.394] "इमे आसवा"ति यथाभूतं पजानाति,

१. वूपसमाय — स्या०।

"अयं [B.179] आसवसमुदयो"ति यथाभूतं पजानाति, "अयं आसवनिरोधो"ति यथाभूतं पजानाति, "अयं आसवनिरोधगामिनी पटिपदा"ति यथाभूतं पजानाति।

So he with such a concentrated mind, which is pure, which is clean, which is free from impurities, which is free from sins, which is soft, which can be acted upon, which is steadfast and which is immovable, by the knowledge of the destruction of sinful tendencies bends forth his mind. He knows truly that "this is suffering", he knows truly that "this is the origin of suffering", he knows truly that "this is the cessation of suffering", he knows truly that "this is the path leading to the cessation of suffering; he knows truly that "these are sinful tendencies", he knows truly that "this is the origin of sinful tendencies", he knows truly that "this is the cessation of sinful tendencies", he knows truly that "this is the path leading to the cessation of sinful tendencies."

तस्स एवं जानतो एवं पस्सतो कामासवा पि चित्तं विमुच्चति, भवासवा पि चित्तं विमुच्चति, अविज्जासवा पि चित्तं विमुच्चति। विमुत्तस्मिं विमुत्तमिति ञाणं होति। "खीणा जाति, वुसितं ब्रह्मचरियं, कतं करणीयं, नापरं इत्थत्ताया"ति पजानाति। इदमस्स सङ्गामविजयस्मिं।

सेय्यथापि सो योधाजीवो सहति रजग्गं सहति धजग्गं सहति उस्सारणं सहति सम्पहारं, सो तं सङ्गामं अभिविजिनित्वा [R.69] विजितसङ्गामो तमेव सङ्गामसीसं अज्झावसति, तथूपमो अयं पुग्गलो। [N.102] एवरूपो पि इधेकच्चो पुग्गलो होति। अयं पञ्चमो योधाजीवूपमो पुग्गलो सन्तो संविज्जमानो भिक्खूसु।

इमे पञ्च योधाजीवूपमा पुग्गला सन्तो संविज्जमाना भिक्खूसु।

Thus that knowing and seeing, his mind becomes emancipated from the tendency towards sensual pleasures, his mind becomes freed from the tendency towards rebirth, his mind becomes emancipated from the tendency towards ignorance. When it is free, he has the knowledge that it is free. He knows that "birth is exhausted, the holy life is led, what is to be done is done, and there is nothing further of these conditions." It is this that victory in battle means for him.

Just as that professional warrior endures dust, endures the top of the flag, endures war cries, endures fight from a distance, he winning the battle, being victorious in the battle, survives on the scene of battle, so is this person. There is such a person here. This is the fifth person existing among the monks comparable to a professional warrior.

These are the five persons who live and have their being among the monks comparable to professional warrior.

(४) पञ्च पिण्डपातिका

१३. तत्थ कतमे पञ्च पिण्डपातिका ?

मन्दत्ता मोमूहत्ता पिण्डपातिको होति, पापिच्छो इच्छापकतो पिण्डपातिको होति, उम्मादा चित्तविक्खेपा[१] पिण्डपातिको होति, "वण्णितं बुद्धेहि बुद्धसावकेही" ति पिण्डपातिको होति, अपि च अप्पिच्छतंयेव[२] निस्साय, सन्तुट्ठिंयेव निस्साय, सल्लेखंयेव निस्साय, इदमत्थितंयेव[३] निस्साय पिण्डपातिको होति ।

(4) Five (persons) who live on alms

13. There who are the five (persons) who live on alms?

One lives on alms because of his dullness and stupidity, one lives on alms because of sinful desire and moved by desire, one lives on alms because of madness and an unbalanced mind, one lives on alms because he thinks: "it is praised by the Buddhas and their disciples", and, further, there is one who just because of absence of desire, just because of contentment, just because of eradication (of sin), and because (the life is) needed, lives on alms.

१. चित्तविक्खेपो — रो० ।

२. अप्पिच्छंयेव — स्या०, रो० ।

३. इदमट्ठितंयेव — सी०; इदमट्ठिकंयेव — रो०, एवमुपरि पि ।

तत्र य्वायं पिण्डपातिको अप्पिच्छतंयेव निस्साय, सन्तुट्ठिंयेव निस्साय, सल्लेखंयेव निस्साय, इदमत्थितंयेव निस्साय पिण्डपातिको[१]; अयं इमेसं पञ्चन्नं पिण्डपातिकानं अग्गो च सेट्ठो च पामोक्खो[२] च उत्तमो च पवरो च ।

There the person who lives on alms just because of the absence of desire, just because of contentment, just because of eradication (of sin), and because (the life is) needed, lives on alms; this is the head, the chief, the foremost, the best, and the most excellent of these five persons who live on alms.

सेय्यथापि नाम गवा खीरं, खीरम्हा दधि, दधिम्हा नवनीतं[३], नवनीतम्हा सप्पि, सप्पिम्हा सप्पिमण्डो, सप्पिमण्डं तत्थ अग्गमक्खायति; एवमेवं य्वायं[४] पिण्डपातिको अप्पिच्छतंयेव निस्साय, सन्तुट्ठिंयेव निस्साय, सल्लेखंयेव निस्साय, इदमत्थितंयेव निस्साय पिण्डपातिको होति; अयं इमेसं पञ्चन्नं पिण्डपातिकानं अग्गो च सेट्ठो च पामोक्खो च उत्तमो च पवरो च । इमे पञ्च पिण्डपातिका ।

Just as the milk is from the cow, curds from milk, butter from curds, clarified butter (ghee) from butter, and the scum of clarified butter from clarified butter (ghee); so is this person who lives on alms just because of the absence of desire, because of contentment, because of eradication (of sin), and because (the life is) needed, lives on alms; this is the head, the chief, the foremost, the best, and the most excellent of five persons who live on alms. These are the five (persons) who live on alms.

(५-१३) पञ्च खलुपच्छाभत्तिका... पञ्च यथासन्थतिका

१४. [B.180; S.396] तत्थ कतमे पञ्च खलुपच्छाभत्तिका ...पे०... पञ्च एकासनिका ...पे०... पञ्च पंसुकूलिका ...पे०... पञ्च तेचीवरिका ...पे०... पञ्च आरञ्ञिका

१. पिण्डपातिको होति — सी० ।

२. मोक्खो — सी० ।

३. नोनीतं — सी० ।

४. स्वायं — रो० ।

...पे०... पञ्च रुक्खमूलिका ...पे०... पञ्च अब्भोकासिका ...पे०... पञ्च नेसज्जिका ...पे०... पञ्च यथासन्थतिका ...पे०... इमे पञ्च यथासन्थतिका ।

(5-13) Five (persons) who refuse to accept food after proper time... five (persons) who use any seats that are offered

14. Who are the five persons who refuse to accept food after proper time ...pe... five persons who use one seat ...pe... five persons who wear rags collected from refuse-heap ...pe... five persons who wear three garments (cloths) ...pe... five persons who are forest dwellers ...pe... five persons who live under a tree ...pe... five persons who live under the open sky ...pe... five persons who rest seated ...pe... five persons who use any seats that are offered ...pe... these are the five (persons) who use any seats that are offered.

(१४) पञ्च सोसानिका

१५. [N.103] तत्थ कतमे पञ्च सोसानिका ?

मन्दत्ता मोमूहत्ता सोसानिको होति, पापिच्छो इच्छापकतो सोसानिको होति, उम्मादा चित्तविक्खेपा सोसानिको होति, "वण्णितं बुद्धेहि बुद्धसावकेही"ति सोसानिको होति, अपि च अप्पिच्छतंयेव निस्साय, सन्तुट्ठियेव निस्साय, सल्लेखंयेव निस्साय, इदमत्थितंयेव निस्साय सोसानिको होति ।

(14) Five (persons) who dwell in cemeteries

15. There who are the five (persons) who dwell in cemeteries?

One dwells in cemetery because of his dullness and stupidity, one dwells in cemetery because of sinful desire and moved by desire, one dwells in cemetery because of madness and an unbalanced mind, one dwells in cemetery because he thinks: "it is praised by the Buddhas and their disciples," and, further, there is one who just because of absence of desire, just because of contentment, just because of eradiction (of sin), and because (the life is) needed, dwells in cemetery.

तत्र य्वायं सोसानिको अप्पिच्छतंयेव निस्साय, [R.70] सन्तुट्ठिंयेव निस्साय, सल्लेखंयेव निस्साय, इदमत्थितंयेव निस्साय सोसानिको; अयं इमेसं पञ्चन्नं सोसानिकानं अग्गो च सेट्ठो च पामोक्खो च उत्तमो च पवरो च।

There the person who dwells in cemetery just because of the absence of desire, just because of contentment, just becaue of eradication (of sin), and because (the life is) needed, dwells in cemetery; this is the head, the chief, the froemost, the best, and the most excellent of these five (persons) who dwells in cemeteries.

सेय्यथापि नाम गवा[१] खीरं, खीरम्हा दधि, दधिम्हा नवनीतं, नवनीतम्हा सप्पि, सप्पिम्हा सप्पिमण्डो, सप्पिमण्डं तत्थ अग्गमक्खायति; एवमेवं य्वायं सोसानिको अप्पिच्छतंयेव निस्साय, सन्तुट्ठिंयेव निस्साय, सल्लेखंयेव निस्साय, इदमत्थितंयेव निस्साय सोसानिको होति; अयं इमेसं पञ्चन्नं सोसानिकानं अग्गो च सेट्ठो च पामोक्खो च उत्तमो[२] च[३] पवरो च। इमे पञ्च सोसानिका।

पञ्चकनिद्देसो निट्ठितो।

Just as the milk is from the cow, curds from milk, butter from curds, clarified butter (ghee) from butter, and the scum of clarified butter from clarified butter (ghee); so is this person who dwells in cemetery just because of the absence of desire, because of contentment, because of eradication (of sin), and because (the life is) needed, dwells in cemetery; this is the head, the chief, the foremost, the best and the most excellent of these five (persons) who dwells in cemeteries. There are the five (persons) who dwell in cemeteries.

Here ends the specification of grouping by five.

---

१. गावा — सी०।

२. रो० पोत्थके न दिस्सति।

३. रो० पोत्थके न दिस्सति।

छट्ठो परिच्छेदो

६. छक्कपुग्गलपञ्ञत्ति[1]

(१. क) सम्मासम्बुद्धो पुग्गलो

१. [N.104; S.398] तत्र य्वायं पुग्गलो पुब्बे अननुस्सुतेसु धम्मेसु सामं सच्चानि अभिसम्बुज्झति, तत्थ च सब्बञ्ञुतं पापुणाति बलेसु[2] च वसीभावं। सम्मासम्बुद्धो तेन दट्ठब्बो।

CHAPTER SIX

6. Division of Human Types by Six

(1. A) A person who is Perfectly Enlightened One

1. There is the person who, in regard to doctrines he has not heard of before, thoroughly understands by his own effort the truths, and obtains therein omniscience as well as mastery over the powers (Balas). Such an one is to be considered a Perfectly Enlightened One. (Sammāsambuddho).

(ख) पच्चेकसम्बुद्धो पुग्गलो

२. तत्र य्वायं पुग्गलो पुब्बे अननुस्सुतेसु धम्मेसु सामं सच्चानि अभिसम्बुज्झति, न च तत्थ सब्बञ्ञुतं पापुणाति न च बलेसु[3] वसीभावं। पच्चेकसम्बुद्धो तेन दट्ठब्बो।

---

१. छक्कनिद्देसो — सी०, स्या०; छ पुग्गला — रो०।

२. फलेसु — रो०, एवमुपरि पि।

३. बलेसु च — स्या०।

(B) A person who is Enlightened for himself

2. There is the person who, in regard to doctrines he has not heard of before, thoroughly understands by his own effort the truths, but does not obtain omniscience therein as well as mastery over the powers (Balas). Such an one is to be considered Enlightened for himself (Paccekasambuddho).

(ग) महासावको पुग्गलो

३. [B.181] तत्र य्वायं पुग्गलो पुब्बे अननुस्सुतेसु धम्मेसु सामं सच्चानि अनभिसम्बुज्झति,[१] दिट्ठेव धम्मे दुक्खस्सन्तकरो[२] होति, सावकपारमिं च पापुणाति। सारिपुत्तमोग्गल्लाना[३] तेन दट्ठब्बा।

(C) A person who is great disciple

3. There is the person who, in regard to doctrines he has not heard of before, and does not thoroughly understand by his own effort the truths, but puts an end to suffering in this very existence, and attains the perfection of discipleship. Such an one is to be considered a Sāriputta and a Moggallāna.

(घ) अरहन्तो पुग्गलो

४. तत्र य्वायं पुग्गलो पुब्बे अननुस्सुतेसु धम्मेसु सामं सच्चानि अनभिसम्बुज्झति, दिट्ठेव धम्मे दुक्खस्सन्तकरो होति, न च सावकपारमिं पापुणाति। अवसेसा अरहन्ता[४] तेन दट्ठब्बा।

(D) A person who is Arahant

4. There is the person who, in regard to doctrines unheard of before, and does not thoroughly understand by his own effort the truths, but puts an end to suffering in this very existence, but does not attain the perfection of discipleship. The other Arahants are to be so considered.

---

१. अभिसम्बुज्झति — रो०, एवमुपरि पि।
२. दुक्खस्सन्तं करोति — सी०, एवमुपरि पि।
३. सारीपुत्तमोग्गल्लाना — स्या०।
४. अरहन्तो — स्या०।

(ङ) अनागामी पुग्गलो

५. तत्र य्वायं पुग्गलो पुब्बे अननुस्सुतेसु धम्मेसु सामं सच्चानि अनभिसम्बुज्झति, न च दिट्ठेव धम्मे दुक्खस्सन्तकरो होति, अनागामी होति अनागन्ता[१] इत्थत्तं । [R.71] अनागामी तेन दट्ठब्बो ।

(E) A person who is never-returner

5. There is the person who, in regard to doctrines unheard of before, and does not thoroughly understand by his own effort the truths, and (he) does not put an end to suffering in this very existence, but becomes a 'never-returner', not having to come back to these conditions. The 'never-returner' (Anāgāmī) is to be so considered.

(च) सोतापन्नो सकदागामी पुग्गलो

६. [N.105] तत्र य्वायं पुग्गलो पुब्बे अननुस्सुतेसु धम्मेसु सामं सच्चानि अनभिसम्बुज्झति, न च दिट्ठेव धम्मे दुक्खस्सन्तकरो होति, अनागामी[२] होति[२] आगन्ता[३] इत्थत्तं । सोतापन्नसकदागामिनो तेन दट्ठब्बा ।

छक्कनिद्देसो निट्ठितो ।

(F) A person who is the stream-attainer and the once-returner

6. There is the person who, in regard to doctrines unheard of before, and does not thoroughly understand by his own effort the truths, and (as he) does not put an end to suffering in this very existence, but becomes a 'once-returner', having to come back to these conditions. The 'stream-attainer' (Sotāpanna) and the 'once-returner' (Sakadāgāmī) are to be so considered.

Here ends the specification of grouping by Six.

---

१. अनागन्त्वा — स्या०, रो० ।

२-२. म० पोत्थके नत्थि; आगामी होति — सी०, ना० ।

३. आगन्त्वा — रो० ।

सत्तमो परिच्छेदो

७. सत्तकपुग्गलपञ्ञत्ति

(१. क) सकिं निमुग्गो निमुग्गो व होति

१. [N.106; S.400] कथं च पुग्गलो सकिं निमुग्गो निमुग्गो व होति ?

इधेकच्चो पुग्गलो समन्नागतो होति एकन्तकाळकेहि अकुसलेहि धम्मेहि। एवं पुग्गलो सकिं निमुग्गो[१] निमुग्गो व होति।

CHAPTER SEVEN

7. Division of Human Types by Seven

(1. A) A person who is once drowned just drowned

1. How is a person who is once drowned just drowned?

Here a certain person is possessed of absolutely black immoral qualities. Such a person being once drowned is just drowned.

(ख) उम्मुज्जित्वा निमुज्जति

२. कथं च पुग्गलो उम्मुज्जित्वा निमुज्जति ?

इधेकच्चो पुग्गलो उम्मुज्जति, साहु सद्धा कुसलेसु धम्मेसु, साधु[२] हिरी[३] कुसलेसु धम्मेसु, साधु ओत्तप्पं कुसलेसु धम्मेसु, साधु विरियं कुसलेसु धम्मेसु,

---

१. सी० पोत्थके नत्थि।

२. साहु — सी०; उम्मुज्जति साहु — स्या०, रो०, एवमुपरि पि।

३. हिरि — सी०, स्या०, रो०।

साधु पञ्ञा कुसलेसु धम्मेसू ति । तस्स सा सद्धा नेव तिट्ठति नो वड्ढति हायतियेव, तस्स सा हिरी नेव तिट्ठति नो वड्ढति हायतियेव, तस्स तं ओत्तप्पं नेव तिट्ठति नो वड्ढति हायतियेव, तस्स तं विरियं नेव तिट्ठति नो वड्ढति हायतियेव, तस्स सा पञ्ञा नेव तिट्ठति नो वड्ढति हायतियेव । एवं पुग्गलो उम्मुज्जित्वा निमुज्जति ।

(B) A person who is drowned after emergence

2. How is a person drowned after emergence?

Here a certain person emerges with faith as regards good (moral) qualities, with modesty as regards good (moral) qualities, with conscientiousness as regards good qualities, with energy as regards good qualities, with insight as regards good qualities; but his faith neither persists nor grows, but decreases, his modesty neither persists nor grows, but decreases, his conscientiousness neither persists nor grows, but decreases, his energy neither persists nor grows, but decreases, his insight neither persists nor grows, but decreases. Such a person is drowned after emergence.

(ग) उम्मुज्जित्वा ठितो होति

३. [B.182] कथं च पुग्गलो उम्मुज्जित्वा ठितो होति ?

इधेकच्चो पुग्गलो उम्मुज्जति साहु सद्धा कुसलेसु धम्मेसु, साधु हिरी कुसलेसु धम्मेसु, साधु ओत्तप्पं कुसलेसु धम्मेसु, साधु विरियं कुसलेसु धम्मेसु, साधु पञ्ञा कुसलेसु धम्मेसू ति । तस्स सा सद्धा नेव हायति नो वड्ढति ठिता होति, तस्स सा हिरी नेव हायति नो वड्ढति ठिता होति, तस्स तं ओत्तप्पं नेव हायति नो वड्ढति ठितं[१] होति, तस्स तं विरियं नेव हायति नो वड्ढति ठितं होति, तस्स सा पञ्ञा नेव हायति नो वड्ढति ठिता होति । एवं पुग्गलो उम्मुज्जित्वा ठितो होति ।

(C) A person who persists after emergence

3. How does a person persist after emergence?

Here a certain person emerges with faith as regards good (moral) qualities, with modesty as regards

---

१. ठितो — रो०, एवमुपरि पि ।

good qualities, with conscientiousness as regards good qualities, with energy as regards good qualities, with insight as regards good qualities; but his faith neither decreases nor grows, but persists, his modesty neither decreases nor grows, but persists, his conscientiousness neither decreases nor grows, but persists, his energy neither decreases nor grows, but persists, his insight neither decreases nor grows, but persists. Such a person persists after emergence.

(घ) उम्मुज्जित्वा विपस्सति

४. कथं च पुग्गलो उम्मुज्जित्वा विपस्सति विलोकेति ?

[N.107] इधेकच्चो पुग्गलो उम्मुज्जति साहु सद्धा कुसलेसु धम्मेसु, साधु हिरी कुसलेसु धम्मेसु, साधु ओत्तप्पं कुसलेसु धम्मेसु, साधु विरियं कुसलेसु धम्मेसु, साधु [R.72] पञ्ञा कुसलेसु धम्मेसू ति। सो तिण्णं संयोजनानं परिक्खया सोतापन्नो होति अविनिपातधम्मो नियतो सम्बोधिपरायनो। एवं पुग्गलो उम्मुज्जित्वा विपस्सति विलोकेति।

(D) A person who looks around after emergence

4. How does a person look about and around after emergence?

Here a certain person emerges with faith as regards good (moral) qualities, with modesty as regards good qualities, with conscientiousness as regards good qualities, with energy as regards good qualities, with insight as regards good qualities. By complete destruction of three fetters he becomes a 'stream-attainer', no more liable to fall into a woeful state, but sure to win Enlightenment (Sambodhi) as his final end and aim. Such a person looks about and around after emergence.

(ङ) उम्मुज्जित्वा पतरति

५. [S.402] कथं च पुग्गलो उम्मुज्जित्वा पतरति ?

इधेकच्चो पुग्गलो उम्मुज्जति साहु सद्धा कुसलेसु धम्मेसु, साधु हिरी कुसलेसु धम्मेसु, साधु ओत्तप्पं कुसलेसु धम्मेसु, साधु विरियं कुसलेसु धम्मेसु, साधु पञ्ञा कुसलेसु धम्मेसू ति । सो तिण्णं संयोजनानं परिक्खया रागदोसमोहानं तनुत्ता सकदागामी होति सकिदेव इमं लोकं आगन्त्वा दुक्खस्सन्तकरो होति । एवं पुग्गलो उम्मुज्जित्वा पतरति ।

(E) A person who swims up after emergence

5. How does a person swim on after (Patarati) emergence?

Here a certain person emerges with faith as regards good (moral) qualities, with modesty as regards good qualities, with conscientiousness as regards good qualities, with energy as regards good qualities, with insight as regards good qualities. By complete destruction of three fetters and by the destruction of passion, hatred, and delusion he becomes a 'once-returner', who coming back but once to this world makes an end of suffering. Such a person swims on after emergence.

(च) उम्मुज्जित्वा पटिगाधप्पत्तो होति

६. कथं च पुग्गलो उम्मुज्जित्वा पटिगाधप्पत्तो[१] होति ?

इधेकच्चो पुग्गलो उम्मुज्जति साहु सद्धा कुसलेसु धम्मेसु, साधु हिरी कुसलेसु धम्मेसु, साधु ओत्तप्पं कुसलेसु धम्मेसु, साधु विरियं कुसलेसु धम्मेसु, साधु पञ्ञा कुसलेसु धम्मेसू ति । सो पञ्चन्नं ओरम्भागियानं संयोजनानं परिक्खया ओपपातिको होति तत्थ परिनिब्बायी अनावत्तिधम्मो तस्मा लोका । एवं पुग्गलो उम्मुज्जित्वा पटिगाधप्पत्तो होति ।

(F) A person who obtains a firm footing after emergence

6. How does a person reach a fixed footing after emergence?

---

१. पतिगाधप्पत्तो — म० ,एवमुपरि पि ।

Here a certain person emerges with faith as regards good (moral) qualities, with modesty as regards good qualities, with conscientiousness as regards good qualities, with energy as regards good qualities, with insight as regards good qualities. By complete destruction of five fetters causing rebirth in the lower regions, he becomes a being of apparitional rebirth attaining the final release in that state, and is not liable to return from that world. Such a person reaches a fixed footing after emergence.

(छ) उम्मुज्जित्वा तिण्णो होति

७. कथं च पुग्गलो उम्मुज्जित्वा तिण्णो होति पारङ्गतो[१] थले[२] तिट्ठति ब्राह्मणो ?

इधेकच्चो पुग्गलो उम्मुज्जति साहु सद्धा कुसलेसु [B.183] धम्मेसु, साधु हिरी कुसलेसु धम्मेसु, साधु ओत्तप्पं कुसलेसु धम्मेसु, साधु विरियं कुसलेसु धम्मेसु, साधु पञ्ञा कुसलेसु धम्मेसू ति। सो आसवानं खया अनासवं चेतोविमुत्तिं पञ्ञाविमुत्तिं दिट्ठेव धम्मे सयं अभिञ्ञा सच्छिकत्वा उपसम्पज्ज विहरति। एवं पुग्गलो उम्मुज्जित्वा तिण्णो होति पारङ्गतो थले तिट्ठति ब्राह्मणो।

(G) A person who crosses after emergence

7. What sort of person is he who as a true brahmin after emergence crosses to the other shore and establishes himself on ground (in fruition)?

Here a certain person emerges with faith as regards good (moral) qualities, with modesty as regards good qualities, with conscientiousness as regards good qualities, with energy as regards good qualities, with insight as regards good qualities. By destruction of sinful tendencies, he lives in possession of emancipation of will, possession of emancipation of insight, free from those sinful tendencies and having come to know and

---

१. पारगतो — सी०, स्या०।

२. फले — रो०, एवमुपरि पि।

realise them by his own efforts in this very existence. Such a person is a true brahmin crossing after emergence and going to the other shore and establishing himself on ground (in fruition).

(२. क) उभतोभागविमुत्तो पुग्गलो

८. [N.108] कतमो च पुग्गलो उभतोभागविमुत्तो ?

इधेकच्चो पुग्गलो अट्ठ विमोक्खे कायेन फुसित्वा विहरति पञ्ञाय चस्स दिस्वा आसवा परिक्खीणा होन्ति । अयं वुच्चति पुग्गलो उभतोभागविमुत्तो ।

(2. A) A person who is emancipated in both ways

8. What sort of person is emancipated in both ways?

Here a certain person goes on himself experiencing the eight stages of emancipation, and dwells in touching with the body (Nāmakāya), and having seen them by insight, his sinful tendencies (Āsavas) are completely destroyed. Such a person is emancipated in both ways.

(ख-च) पञ्ञाविमुत्तो ... धम्मानुसारी पुग्गलो

९. कतमो च पुग्गलो पञ्ञाविमुत्तो ...पे०.. .कायसक्खी ... दिट्ठिप्पत्तो ... सद्धाविमुत्तो ... धम्मानुसारी ... ।

(B-F) A person who is emancipated by way of insight ... one conforming to the Law

9. What sort of person is emancipated by way of insight ....pe... an eye-witness ... who has won view ... emancipated by faith ... one conforming to the Law....

(छ) सद्धानुसारी पुग्गलो

१०. कतमो च पुग्गलो सद्धानुसारी ?

यस्स पुग्गलस्स सोतापत्तिफलसच्छिकिरियाय पटिपन्नस्स सद्धिन्द्रियं अधिमत्तं होति, सद्धावाहिं[१] सद्धापुब्बङ्गमं अरियमग्गं भावेति । अयं वुच्चति

---

१. सद्धावाही — सी० ।

पुग्गलो सद्धानुसारी । सोतापत्तिफलसच्छिकिरियाय पटिपन्नो पुग्गलो सद्धानुसारी; फले ठितो सद्धाविमुत्तो ति ।

सत्तकनिद्देसो निट्ठितो ।

(G) A person who is conforming to faith

10. What sort of person is one conforming to faith?

The faith-faculty of a person proceeding to realise the fruition stage of a 'stream-attainer' develops to a large extent. He cultivates the noble path which carries with it faith and is preceded by faith. Such a person is said to be one conforming to faith. Such a person striving after the fruition stage of a 'stream-ạttainer' is one conforming to faith; while the same person established in the fruition is emancipated by faith.

Here ends the specification of grouping by seven.

अट्ठमो परिच्छेदो

८. अट्ठकपुग्गलपञ्ञत्ति

(१. क-ज) चत्तारो मग्गसमङ्गिनो, चत्तारो फलसमङ्गिनो पुग्गला

१. [N.109; R.73; S.404] तत्थ[१] कतमे चत्तारो मग्गसमङ्गिनो, चत्तारो फलसमङ्गिनो पुग्गला ?

सोतापन्नो, सोतापत्तिफलसच्छिकिरियाय पटिपन्नो; सकदागामी, सकदागामिफलसच्छिकिरियाय पटिपन्नो; अनागामी, अनागामिफलसच्छिकिरियाय पटिपन्नो; अरहा, अरहत्तफलसच्छिकिरियाय[२] पटिपन्नो; इमे चत्तारो मग्गसमङ्गिनो, इमे[३] चत्तारो फलसमङ्गिनो पुग्गला ।

अट्ठकनिद्देसो निट्ठितो ।

CHAPTER EIGHT

8. Division of Human Types by Eight

(1. A-H) The four persons identifiable with the path and the four identifiable with the fruition

1. Who are the four persons identifiable with the path and who are the four identifiable with the fruition?

The 'stream-attainer' and one who proceeds to realise the fruition stage; the 'once-returner' and one

१. स्या० पोत्थके नत्थि ।

२. अरहत्ताय — स्या०, रो० ।

३. सी० पोत्थके नत्थि ।

who proceeds to realise the fruition stage; the 'never-returner' and one who proceeds to realise the fruition stage; and the Arahant (elect or worthy) and one who proceeds to attain Arahantship; these are the four persons who are identifiable with the path and these the four identifiable with the fruition.

Here ends the specification of grouping by eight.

नवमो परिच्छेदो

९. नवकपुग्गलपञ्ञत्ति

(१. क) सम्मासम्बुद्धो पुग्गलो

१. [N.110; B.184; S.406] कतमो च पुग्गलो सम्मासम्बुद्धो ?

इधेकच्चो पुग्गलो पुब्बे अननुस्सुतेसु धम्मेसु सामं सच्चानि अभिसम्बुज्झति, तत्थ च सब्बञ्ञुतं पापुणाति बलेसु च वसीभावं। अयं वुच्चति पुग्गलो "सम्मासम्बुद्धो"।

CHAPTER NINE

9. Division of Human Types by Nine

(1. A) A person who is a Perfectly Enlightened One

1. What sort of person is a Perfectly Enlightened One?

Here a certain person who, in regard to doctrines he has not heard of before, himself thoroughly understands the truths and attains the omniscience thereof as well as mastery over the fruition. This sort of person is said to be a Perfectly Enlightened One.

(ख) पच्चेकसम्बुद्धो पुग्गलो

२. कतमो च पुग्गलो पच्चेकसम्बुद्धो[१] ?

---

१. पच्चेकबुद्धो — सी०, एवमुपरि पि।

इधेकच्चो पुग्गलो पुब्बे अननुस्सुतेसु धम्मेसु सामं सच्चानि अभिसम्बुज्झति, न च तत्थ सब्बञ्ञुतं पापुणाति न च बलेसु वसीभावं। अयं वुच्चति पुग्गलो "पच्चेकसम्बुद्धो"।

(B) A person who is Enlightened for himself

2. What sort of person is one who is Enlightened for himself?

Here a certain person who, in regard to doctrines he has not heard of before, himself thoroughly understands the truths but attains neither the omniscience nor the mastery over the fruition thereof. This sort of person is said to be one Enlightened for himself.

(ग) उभतोभागविमुत्तो पुग्गलो

३. कतमो च पुग्गलो उभतोभागविमुत्तो?

इधेकच्चो पुग्गलो अट्ठ विमोक्खे कायेन फुसित्वा विहरति पञ्ञाय चस्स दिस्वा आसवा परिक्खीणा होन्ति। अयं वुच्चति पुग्गलो "उभतोभागविमुत्तो"।

(C) A person who is emancipated in both ways

3. What sort of person is emancipated in both ways?

Here a certain person goes on himself experiencing the eight stages of emancipation, and dwells in touching with the body (Nāmakāya), and having perceived them through insight, his sinful tendencies are completely destroyed. This sort of person is said to be one emancipated in both ways.

(घ) पञ्ञाविमुत्तो पुग्गलो

४. कतमो च पुग्गलो पञ्ञाविमुत्तो?

इधेकच्चो पुग्गलो न हेव खो अट्ठ विमोक्खे कायेन फुसित्वा विहरति पञ्ञाय चस्स दिस्वा आसवा परिक्खीणा होन्ति। अयं वुच्चति पुग्गलो "पञ्ञाविमुत्तो"।

(D) A person who is emancipated by way of insight

4. What sort of person is emancipated by way of insight?

Here a certain person without himself experiencing the eight stages of emancipation, and dwells in touching with the body (Nāmakāya), but having perceived them through insight, his sinful tendencies are completely destroyed. This sort of person is said to be one emancipated by insight.

(ङ) कायसक्खी पुग्गलो

५. कतमो च पुग्गलो कायसक्खी ?

इधेकच्चो पुग्गलो अट्ठ विमोक्खे कायेन फुसित्वा विहरति पञ्ञाय चस्स दिस्वा एकच्चे आसवा परिक्खीणा होन्ति। अयं वुच्चति पुग्गलो "कायसक्खी"।

(E) A person who is an eye-witness

5. What sort of person is an 'eye-witness'?

Here a certain person goes on himself experiencing the eight stages of emancipation, and dwells in touching with the body (Nāmakāya), and having perceived them through insight, some of his sinful tendencies are completely destroyed. This sort of person is said to be an 'eye-witness.'

(च) दिट्ठिप्पत्तो पुग्गलो

६. [N.111; R.74] कतमो च पुग्गलो दिट्ठिप्पत्तो ?

इधेकच्चो पुग्गलो "इदं दुक्खं"ति यथाभूतं पजानाति ...पे०... "अयं दुक्खनिरोधगामिनी पटिपदा"ति यथाभूतं पजानाति, तथागतप्पवेदिता चस्स धम्मा पञ्ञाय वोदिट्ठा होन्ति वोचरिता, पञ्ञाय चस्स दिस्वा एकच्चे आसवा परिक्खीणा होन्ति। अयं वुच्चति पुग्गलो "दिट्ठिप्पत्तो"।

(F) A person who has won vision

6. What sort of person is one who has won vision?

Here a certain person truly understands that "this is suffering"...pe.. truly understands that "this is the path leading to the cessation of suffering." The doctrines promulgated by the Tathāgata are perceived by him through insight as well as practised; and he having perceived them through insight, some of his sinful tendencies are completely destroyed. This sort of person is said to be one who has won vision.

(छ) सद्धाविमुत्तो पुग्गलो

७. [S.408] कतमो च पुग्गलो सद्धाविमुत्तो ?

इधेकच्चो पुग्गलो "इदं दुक्खं"ति यथाभूतं पजानाति ...पे॰... "अयं दुक्खनिरोधगामिनी पटिपदा"ति यथाभूतं पजानाति, तथागतप्पवेदिता चस्स धम्मा पञ्ञाय [B.185] वोदिट्ठा होन्ति वोचरिता, पञ्ञाय चस्स दिस्वा एकच्चे आसवा परिक्खीणा होन्ति, नो च खो यथा दिट्ठिप्पत्तस्स। अयं वुच्चति पुग्गलो "सद्धाविमुत्तो"।

(G) A person who is emancipated by faith

7. What sort of person is emancipated by faith?

Here a certain person truly understands that "this is suffering" ...pe... truly understands that "this is the path leading to the cessation of suffering." The doctrines promulgated by the Tathāgata are perceived by him through insight as well as practised; and having perceived them through insight, some of his sinful tendencies are completely destroyed, though not in the same way as in the case of one who has won vision. This sort of person is said to be one emancipated by faith.

(ज) धम्मानुसारी पुग्गलो

८. कतमो च पुग्गलो धम्मानुसारी ?

यस्स पुग्गलस्स सोतापत्तिफलसच्छिकिरियाय पटिपन्नस्स पञ्ञिन्द्रियं अधिमत्तं होति, पञ्ञावाहिं पञ्ञापुब्बङ्गमं अरियमग्गं भावेति। अयं वुच्चति पुग्गलो

"धम्मानुसारी" । सोतापत्तिफलसच्छिकिरियाय पटिपन्नो पुग्गलो धम्मानुसारी, फले ठितो दिट्ठिप्पत्तो ।

(H) A person who is one conforming to the Law

8. What sort of person is one conforming to the Law?

The faculty of insight of a person proceeding to realise the fruition stage of a 'stream-attainer' develops to a large extent; he cultivates the noble path which carries with it insight and is preceded by insight. This sort of person is said to be one conforming to the Law. Such a person striving after the fruition stage of stream-attaining is one conforming to the Law; while the same person established in the fruition is one who has won vision.

(झ) सद्धानुसारी पुग्गलो

९. कतमो च पुग्गलो सद्धानुसारी ?

यस्स पुग्गलस्स सोतापत्तिफलसच्छिकिरियाय पटिपन्नस्स सद्धिन्द्रियं अधिमत्तं होति, सद्धावाहिं सद्धापुब्बङ्गमं अरियमग्गं भावेति । अयं वुच्चति पुग्गलो "सद्धानुसारी" । सोतापत्तिफलसच्छिकिरियाय पटिपन्नो पुग्गलो सद्धानुसारी, फले ठितो सद्धाविमुत्तो ति ।

नवकनिद्देसो निट्ठितो ।

(I) A person who is one conforming to faith

9. What sort of person is one conforming to faith?

The faith-faculty of a person proceeding to realise the fruition stage of stream-attaining develops to a large extent. He cultivates the noble path which carries with it faith and is preceded by faith. This sort of person is said to be one conforming to faith. Such a person striving after the fruition stage of stream-attaining is one conforming to faith; while the same person established in the fruition is emancipated by faith.

Here ends the specification of grouping by nine.

दसमो परिच्छेदो

१०. दसकपुग्गलपञ्ञत्ति[१]

(१. क-ङ) पञ्च पुग्गला इध निट्ठा

१. [N.112; S.410] कतमेसं पञ्चन्नं इध निट्ठा ?

सत्तक्खत्तुपरमस्स[२] कोलङ्कोलस्स एकबीजिस्स सकदागामिस्स यो च दिट्ठेव धम्मे अरहा— इमेसं पञ्चन्नं इध निट्ठा ।

CHAPTER TEN

10. Division of Human Types by Ten

(1. A-E) Five persons reaching perfection here

1. By which five is consummation reached here?

The 'stream-attainer' destined not to undergo more than seven births, the 'stream-attainer' transmigrating through a few families (less than seven), the 'single-seeded' 'stream-attainer,' the 'once-returner' and one attaining Arahantship in this very existence— of these five, consummation is reached here.

(च-ञ) पञ्च पुग्गला इध विहाय निट्ठा

२. कतमेसं पञ्चन्नं इध विहाय निट्ठा ?

---

१. दसकनिद्देसो — सी०, स्या०; दस पुग्गला — रो० ।

२. सत्तक्खत्तुंपरमस्स — स्या० ।

अन्तरापरिनिब्बायिस्स उपहच्चपरिनिब्बायिस्स असङ्खारपरिनिब्बायिस्स ससङ्खारपरिनिब्बायिस्स उद्धंसोतस्स अकनिट्ठगामिनो— इमेसं पञ्चन्नं इध विहाय निट्ठा ति ।

एत्तावत्ता पुग्गलानं पुग्गलपञ्ञत्तीति ।

दसकनिद्देसो निट्ठितो ।

पुग्गलपञ्ञत्तिपकरणं निट्ठितं ।

(F-J) Five persons reaching perfection hereafter

2. By which five is consummation reached after leaving this world?

'One who dies and attains Nirvāṇa before half the age he should have lived in a Brahmanic world expires,' the 'term-curtailing passer-away,' the 'automatic passer-away,' 'one attaining Nirvāṇa through strenuous exertion,' 'one proceeding upstream to the Akaniṭṭha region'— of these five, consummation is reached after leaving this world.

In these ways are there designations of human type of the human types.

Here ends the specification of grouping by ten.

Here ends the 'Designation of Human Types'.

सद्दानुक्कमणिका

ए

ओ

क

ख

ग

फ

उपमानुक्कमणिका